Livin' The Hand I Was Dealt

God Bless!

Terri Buschmann

J Hudson

Livin' The Hand I Was Dealt

A story of love, loss and what one family would do to survive.

Terri Buschmann

St. Louis, MO

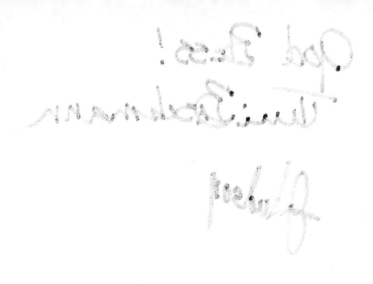

Livin' the hand I was dealt:
A Story of love, loss and what one family would do to survive.

©2020 by Terri Buschmann.

Although this story is based on an actual family, not all events and people are real. Names have been changed in respect of anonymity and some characters were created by combining two or more people into one. Not all events happened in the manner presented in this book.

It was never the intent to offend or anger anyone in the writing of this story.

Know Gene Hudson!™
www.livin-the-hand-I-was-dealt.com

Printed in the United States of America.
ISBN: 978-1-7327683-0-7

To Andrew and Marie who will live forever in the hearts of family and friends. Although your time on earth may have been short, the lessons you taught us will live forever. Knowing the two of you are together, happy, and healthy in heaven is a reason to smile.

To my mother, Joan Buschmann, the perfect example of selflessness, strength, and love. You are profoundly missed.

CONTENTS

St. Louis

San
Antonio

Mexico
City

Xcalak
(ishcalac)

Prologue

There was a time when I believed I had a blessed life. My gorgeous wife, Marie, and I had a beautiful marriage, good jobs, and a steadily growing 401(k). Our baby daughter was happy and healthy. We had an abundant supply of friends we met for happy hour once a week or a barbecue, weather permitting. I've heard it said, "We make plans and God laughs." Well, I'm not amused, and I haven't been for quite some time. Marie and I had hopes that were shattered and dreams that were obliterated by circumstances beyond our control. We suffered from medical negligence not once, but twice, which led to irreversible physical and financial damage that lasted decades. Little by little, what I saw as our perfect life was taken away. We lost jobs because of the medical complications and cashed in investments to stay afloat. Even our friends weren't around anymore. I never would have believed the life of Gene Hudson would have come to this. If there is such a thing as a quota on the pain and suffering that one family can sustain, we surpassed our limit long ago. So when push came to shove and a chance to put our financial worries to rest presented itself, how could I have said no? It's not every day one finds treasure floating in the waters of the Caribbean . . .

Wedding day

Chapter One

HUMBLE BEGINNINGS

Marie and I grew up in the same neighborhood under entirely different circumstances—she in a loving home, me in a living hell. I was twenty-two and she was seventeen when we first got together. She was my world. Our path was not an easy one, but we endured and persevered through the years.

Before Marie and marriage and another life across the border, I was just Gene Hudson, a kid that grew up in a dysfunctional household. No one knew that my alcoholic dad beat the crap out of me while my mom, a victim herself, popped her "nerve pills," as she called them, or to quote the Rolling Stones, "Mother's little helpers." My only safe haven during my childhood was the Buschmanns' house, home of my best friend, Jerry, and his family. I went over to hang out, stay for dinner, and usually spend the night. Mrs. Buschmann never seemed to mind that I was still there the next morning and perhaps the morning after that. Their yard was perfect for football, Wiffle ball, and kick-the-can, and there was never a shortage of kids on their street to play with. Jerry is the oldest of six kids, three girls and three boys, all raised by their mom, who was widowed at the age of thirty-five. Directly behind the Buschmanns' house was the St. Ann Golf Course, where we spent hours golf-ball hunting in the creeks separating the neighborhood from the golf course. After finding the balls, we would wash them with the hose in

Jerry's backyard and sell them back to the golfers for twenty-five to fifty cents. If we were lucky enough to find a perfect Titleist, we'd sell it for a dollar. Between the golf-ball sales and the money we earned at our newspaper stand, we made bank.

Years later, after working in the Oklahoma oil fields for some time, I moved back home and was living in my parents' basement, helping my old man rehab a fixer-upper. He had intentions of renting it out, and I planned to do just that. Around this time, my sister Cindy's friend Marie would come by my parents' house and hang out. I had known her and her family for years, as her older sister was our babysitter once upon a time. Marie had changed a lot during my departure. I had not given her much thought in the past, but the young woman I saw when I came home from Oklahoma had me turning my head. We would harmlessly flirt with each other, though I kept reminding myself of the five-year age difference.

I was alone at the house one fateful night when Marie stopped by. She was a 110-pound Sicilian, not quite five feet tall (though she would fight tooth and nail to assure anyone that she was), with dark curly hair—a force to be reckoned with. I had just finished making myself a frozen pizza, which I gladly shared with that foxy girl. She had on a dark blue shirt with little white flowers and a lacy collar and her Chic jeans that were filled out in all the right ways. She wore a pair of clogs, which she kicked off as we lay across my bed, listening to music and eating pizza. We talked about everything that night. She had recently learned she was the recipient of a college grant for students with juvenile diabetes that would send her through nursing school. She was smart and had focus, and I found myself severely attracted to her.

Hours later, as I was walking her up the steps to leave, she turned, fell into my arms, and kissed me. I will never forget her words: "Gene Hudson, do you know how long I've been wanting to do that?" She was my saving grace and taught me what love was all about, the only woman I had ever fallen in love with. Not long after we started dating, we moved in together and were never apart again.

Marie and I shared a rental house owned by my dad. I worked at a welding shop and she attended nursing school. The house was small by most people's standards, but we didn't need much. The pool table in the basement was the highlight of our parties, during which we shot pool, played music, drank a beer or two, and maybe passed around a joint. We enjoyed Cardinals games, concerts, and vacations with friends.

We were happy, though life was not without its challenges. I received quite an education and an up-close-and-personal view of diabetes as I watched Cathy, Marie's older sister by twenty-three years, deteriorate. For me, Cathy's struggles were a foreshadowing of what could happen to Marie, but I knew that as long as we were together, we could face anything.

Marie and I were married not long after she graduated from nursing school. I started working for Hamilton Healthcare, where I had benefits and medical insurance that covered both of us. We were happy and crazy in love with each other. We had dinner a few nights a week at Marie's parents' house, though we rarely saw my family, with the exception of my sister Cindy, who was still tight with Marie. Spending time with Marie's family and the Buschmanns showed me how dysfunctional my family was. I wanted no part and little reminder of that life anymore. It was bad enough going to my parents' house to drop off the rent.

When we found out there was to be an addition to our little family, of course we were excited, but very nervous. Marie had miscarried early in her first pregnancy and was considered high risk because of her diabetes. She had many complications during her pregnancy with Raquel and was bedridden after her fifth month. Her sugar levels were off the glucometer, putting her and the baby at great risk. The higher her sugar levels, the more insulin she took.

The more insulin she took, the more swollen she became. She was hospitalized for the last month of her pregnancy. When her blood pressure soared, her doctor decided to do a C-section before Marie stroked out.

Raquel was born at twenty-seven weeks, weighed 4 lb. 14 oz., and measured 17 in. long—a good-sized baby for being born so early. Infants born to diabetic mothers are often big babies from being exposed to higher blood sugar levels. Other than spending a couple of days in the neonatal intensive care unit (NICU) under the lights for treatment of jaundice, Raquel was healthy. She had Marie's curly hair and looked a lot like her momma. She grew rapidly and had our undivided attention.

Marie's sister Cathy and their mother, Genevieve, would babysit when we worked. Raquel was a mild-mannered child and was content with whomever she was with. I had a great life with my two perfect girls. Then we found out Marie was pregnant and our world turned upside down.

Once again Marie had complications, and she was hospitalized five weeks prior to our son's birth. Andrew was born prematurely at twenty-seven weeks and spent the first six months of his life in the hospital. Other than the couple of days a week that I could stay with Andrew and give her a reprieve, Marie practically lived at the hospital and would come home every two or three days just long enough to eat, clean up, and sleep a little before returning to his side. Each morning I would feed Raquel, bring her over to Grandma's house, and head to the hospital. I would stay until one thirty, then go to work. I'd work until ten, pick up Raquel from Grandma's, go home, and do the same thing the next day. On my days off I went to the hospital and Marie came home to spend time with our little girl. At the time of Andrew's birth, Marie worked for a nursing agency and made very good money, but when he was in the hospital, she wanted to be right by his side for every examination and blood draw. When

Andrew would turn blue and pass out, she asked, again and again, why this was happening. The doctors always said the same thing: "He's holding his breath because he's mad."

Andrew was fourteen weeks old when the NICU was visited by a new physician, Dr. Richard Bowman. He discovered that Andrew had never been given a bronchoscopy to examine the throat, larynx, trachea, and lower airways. Dr. Bowman performed the procedure, and Andrew was finally diagnosed with tracheomalacia, a condition that occurs when the trachea collapses because its cartilage isn't strong enough to support it. Andrew was given a tracheostomy, an incision in his trachea, which he had for the rest of his life.

So for the three and a half months that my son was turning blue and passing out, it was because he could not breathe, and certainly not because he was holding his breath out of anger. Being oxygen-deprived for so long caused my son to have severe cerebral palsy, and because of the oxygen that was constantly pumped down his nose and into his lungs, he also developed bronchopulmonary dysplasia, a chronic lung disease caused by scarring of the lung tissue.

Doctor after doctor and nurse after nurse told us that what happened to Andrew was the result of complete negligence, but when we asked if they would testify to that in court, each one declined for fear of being fired and not being able to find another job. The attorneys we contacted told us there was little hope of winning our case without the support of someone at the hospital to back up our claim for negligence. It would have cost us a fortune in attorneys' fees up front, and we did not have that kind of money. The total bill for Andrew's hospital stay was nearly $3 million; we were responsible for just under $300,000.

Many babies came and went while Andrew was in the NICU. Marie befriended another mother, a social worker, who asked if we were receiving social security for Andrew, and of course, Marie had no idea what she was talking about. We learned that we should have been contacted by social services, and when Marie asked the social worker at the hospital about it, her response was, "You and your husband both have jobs, and we didn't feel that you were in need of financial assistance." We were never given the option. The time to file for benefits was within days of Andrew's birth, and it had passed long ago. That social worker robbed us of what would have totaled approximately $150,000–$200,000 during Andrew's lifetime. We were never able to collect, certainly not due to lack of trying.

The hospital's staff was apprehensive about Andrew ever leaving the hospital; they suspected that if he did, he would not survive more than a couple of months. But they underestimated my wife, who was the perfect mother for a child in Andrew's condition.

Shortly after Andrew came home, we learned the spacious two-story house next door to Marie's sister, Dart and brother-in-law, Larry, had recently been foreclosed on, and we were able to buy it for about half its value. It was a true godsend. We transformed the family and dining rooms into Andrew's space and equipped them with all the comforts of a hospital and therapy room. I can still see the setup in my head: CPAP oxygen concentrator, suction machine, Pulmo-Aide, and all the tubes. Sometimes I swear I can still hear the machines running. Every day of his life, Andrew was given between six and ten breathing treatments. Whoever was giving him a treatment would cup his or her hand and pat all over his chest and back to loosen any fluids that had built up. He had to be suctioned every few minutes to clear the mucus from his trachea tube. The care he required was constant, and he could never be left alone.

We had a long counter in our kitchen where we kept all of Andrew's meds. We called it Andrew's counter. In the cabinets below we kept extra tubing, ointments, suction catheters, trachea tubes, sterile water, filters . . . it was endless. The backup supplies were kept in the basement, which we referred to as the warehouse. A chart of Andrew's daily medicines was posted above his counter; it could scare the parents of a healthy child half to death. He was given no fewer than ten different medications a day, and more if he became ill, which he often did. He could hold his own with the normal dosages of meds, but when there was an increase, you could look at him and sense his discomfort. When he was on a high dosage of prednisone, he curled his body into a tight ball, distorted his face, and ground his teeth. It was torture for everyone, but mostly for Andrew. We did not know what else to do for him. Several times through the years, Marie and I had the heavy discussion about letting him go, but there was undying hope for him to improve. There is no harder decision to make than whether to let your child die.

To say that our home life was stressful would be an understatement. It was rough. When I got home from work at night, I took care of Andrew, which meant I rarely left his side for more than a minute. Feeding him could take up to an hour and often ended with him throwing up and the inevitable cleanup of one or both of us. I slept on the couch with Andrew in my arms so I could hear and feel when his trache needed to be suctioned, which was constantly. For many years that was my nightly ritual, and it left me mentally and physically exhausted. When the doctor finally suggested a feeding tube, I was elated. Marie was apprehensive because it meant another surgery, but I begged for it—not only because I'd had my fill of being vomited on, but because in my opinion, our son was starving to death. At age seven, when he received the feeding tube, Andrew weighed twenty-eight pounds. After less than a year of grinding up his meds, mixing them with PediaSure, and letting the mixture flow through his feeding tube, his weight nearly doubled. I had a newfound appreciation for medical doctors, and we had hope for a better future for our son.

Living with the stress of Andrew's condition was ridiculously difficult and demanding. The daily tension added to the strain on

Marie's health; she started showing signs of kidney failure and her eyesight rapidly diminished. She was tired and sleeping more than usual. Her legs would swell down to her feet, often to the point that she experienced immobility. Mentally, she was a disaster; she would even hallucinate at times. She could hold Andrew, but she was too weak to pick him up or carry him. She had been on family leave for several months and was in need of a kidney transplant. I took her for dialysis three times a week, which left her so weak I had to carry her to the van after each treatment. She was deathly ill, exhausted, and beyond irritable.

After nine months of dialysis, Marie was given new life with a successful kidney transplant. Her sister Dart was the donor. Marie transformed overnight from a bedridden woman who was ready to die to feeling physically better than she had in years, with a strong will to live. She recovered quickly and within weeks was back in charge. Thank God, because I didn't know what was worse: having a wife upstairs on dialysis or a son being kept alive on meds and machines downstairs.

In the midst of the chaos in our house was Raquel. Not only did Andrew suffer, but Raquel did as well. Her upbringing was anything but traditional. She lived in a home with death on its doorstep and was given an education on medical emergencies at quite an early age. By age two, she knew to tell someone that Andrew's trache needed to be suctioned, and by age three she could handle it herself. She has a large mole in the middle of her throat and would tell everyone that it was her trache, just like her brother's. Dart, Marie, and Raquel once visited a neighbor who had just had a baby. When they were walking home from their visit, Raquel asked Marie, "Mommy, what's wrong with that baby?" When Marie asked her what she meant, Raquel just said, "He doesn't have a trache." It was her normal. She grew up with an ICU in her home. She would play on the floor next to the suction machine and kept her toys under his hospital bed.

Any nurse or therapist working with Andrew had no choice but to interact with little Raquel also. They taught her how to handle small tasks like changing his clothes, and the more challenging tasks of administering breathing treatments and changing all the tubing. When Raquel was ten, Andrew's physical therapist was unable to make an appointment because of bad weather; Raquel said she would take care of it. Her exact words were, "I ought to know how to do his therapy. I've been watching it all my life." Marie and I were not surprised. Raquel had covered for speech therapists and even a nurse a time or two. She had to know the how-to's in regard to her brother. She was continuously deprived of attention from her parents, but she never once complained or even seemed discontent with her home life.

Raquel had a special bond with her brother. Although his communication was limited, she frequently sat and talked to him. If she said something funny, he laughed. He could fully understand what was being said to him, for there was nothing wrong with his brain. She explained her brother's condition by saying, "You know how some people are mentally handicapped, but their bodies work fine? Well, Andrew is the opposite of that. His brain is fine and trapped in a handicapped body." She knew what he was feeling and thinking just by looking in his eyes. She was certain he could sense the same with her. Their relationship was special and unique, not a typical brother-and-sister relationship. Raquel and her best friend, Jana, attempted to include Andrew in their conversations, or rather, they had conversations in his presence. His only input might have been a laugh, but that was all he could offer. They would watch movies with him, letting him choose which ones to watch by blinking once for yes and twice for no. It gave the girls joy to know they could bring happiness to him, but Raquel was an easy child to be around. She was respectful, intelligent, and never one to get upset over little things. I believe that at a very early age she knew, without ever having to be told, not to sweat the small stuff.

She experienced great loss early in her life. Her aunt Cathy, whom I always considered Raquel's second mother, passed away when Raquel was nine years old; Andrew, when she was seventeen; and Jana committed suicide when Raquel was nineteen. We all learned to live life not knowing what to expect or what was around the corner.

Andrew grew bigger, which may have been more of a curse than a blessing. The longer he grew, the more his spine curved and put pressure on his organs. Cerebral palsy robbed him of strength and muscle control. He was strapped to a board every day and turned upright to stretch out and put pressure on his legs, but it felt like we were fighting a losing battle. He was weak and had no control of his body. What inevitably took his life was his ribs collapsing around his lungs, making it too hard for him to breathe. At the ripe old age of sixteen, weighing a hefty sixty-eight pounds, Andrew died in his hospital bed at home, never having been able to play with Legos or even feed himself. I never was able to teach him how to walk, ride a bike, or play catch. Not once do I ever remember saying or even thinking, "Why me?" But you can bet your ass I asked several times, "Why him?"

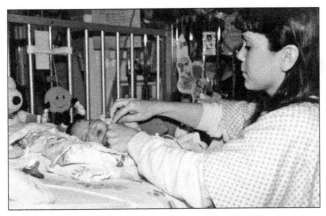

Marie and Baby Andrew in the NICU

Easter

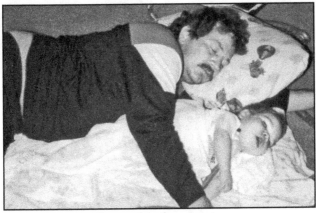

Gene and Andrew napping

Marie, Andrew and Raquel

Andrew out for a walk

*Andrew's Make-A-Wish trip
to Disney World*

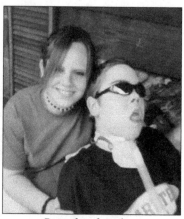

Raquel and Andrew

Chapter Two

OUR HAPPY PLACE

Regardless of what phase Marie and I were in during our lives, there was one constant: we could retreat to Mexico and find peace again. We would escape the sadness and sickness that infested our home and reconnect with each other while scuba diving or exploring ruins in the Yucatán. When the opportunity presented itself to work and live in the area we came to love, we made it happen.

Bruce, an acquaintance of ours and the owner of a small resort in Xcalak, hired me to move his mother from Wisconsin to Mexico. After the long road trip, I spent a week at Bruce's resort, diving and checking out the property. Before I left for the airport, he offered me a position. The decision wasn't hard to make.

As Marie's caretaker, I hadn't been able to work a "regular" job for the last five years, and Marie was never going to be able to work as a nurse again. Our son was gone, Raquel had graduated high school and was in classes to become a licensed massage therapist. Marie's disability check more than covered the expenses of our home in St. Louis, where Raquel would stay under the supervision of Aunt Dart next door. There was nothing keeping us at home, so Marie and I headed to Mexico, where I became a dive instructor/repairman/manager of Bruce's resort with Marie's help. A few years later we went to work for our friend Carlos, who bought the local dive shop in Xcalak, and focused on helping him grow his business.

Xcalak is a small fishing village at the end of a narrow, winding, jungle-canopy road. The area is rich in different species of tropical birds, jaguars, and other exotic wildlife. By car, it's five hours south of Cancún; by boat, it's seven kilometers north of the Belizean border. The village rests on a narrow strip of sand. To the west are mangrove forests, lagoons, and the shallow sand flats of Chetumal Bay. To the east are the turquoise waters of the Caribbean Sea with its waves breaking on the Great Mayan Reef a half kilometer offshore. Inside the reef with its coral heads, the water is clear and calm with a cool, steady breeze blowing in from the sea. Its citizens, numbering approximately three hundred, live in brightly painted wooden structures built on stilts, cement-block homes one and two stories high, and makeshift shacks built from random materials. Until recently, one had to travel one hundred and eighty kilometers for gas. Now it is only sixty kilometers away. We made sacrifices to live in a somewhat remote area, but village life was a welcome change of pace from the chaotic life we'd led back home. There was never traffic or a mad rush to get to work, and the occasional chickens and turkeys roaming through town only added to its charm.

Its open border with Belize makes Xcalak a fusion of cultures, nationalities, and gringo dreams that create a unique environment for the free-spirited. It's a destination for divers and fly fisherman seeking excitement at the edge of civilization.

Marie and I lived fifty meters north of the lighthouse and town pier. The dive shop was just outside of town, two hundred meters north on the beach road from our house. Just beyond the coconut trees in our front yard was the shimmering blue water of the tranquil Caribbean Sea. So many hours were spent on the deck looking out at the same view, but we never knew what we would see. During early morning hours, I would nurse a cup of coffee and watch pelicans freefalling for their breakfast, frigate birds soaring on the trade winds, or perhaps an eagle ray breaking the water and diving back in. Occasionally I'd see a fisherman on the shore throwing out a net to catch sardines, or on the waters heading for a favorite fishing spot. I would listen to the conversation of the chachalaca birds, the coolest-sounding birds in the world but not the brightest of God's creations. Our house in Mexico belonged to our friend Mark, who asked Marie and me to live there and just make the repairs that came along. We had hopes of buying his place and dreamed of turning the bodega on the ground floor into two separate living spaces for tourists to rent. We were thriving and embracing our life together in Xcalak. We met travelers from all over the world who came to experience the waters in our happy place. The beautiful Caribe was a part of our daily life in Mexico, and we considered ourselves exceptionally fortunate, to say the least.

Pronounced (ish-ka-lock)

Local fisherman

*Our casa in
Xcalak*

*The jungle
road to Xcalak*

*The view across
Beach Road*

*Cruising on the
Zaragosa Canal*

Chapter Three

MARIE GETS A PAPER CUT

It was mid-January, and Marie and I were working at Carlos's dive shop in Xcalak, where she ran the show. I do not know what Carlos would have done without her. She answered the emails, booked the dives, handled the advertisements, took care of payroll, ordered supplies—the list was endless, and with the assistance of the biggest computer monitor anyone has ever seen, no one was the wiser that she was legally blind. Every employee adored and respected her. The atmospheres of the dive shop and the new restaurant addition reflected Marie's personality: she was sunshine even if it was raining. When customers came in, they often asked to meet Marie, who had been so professional and friendly in their communications with her via email or Skype. Whenever there was a disagreement between Carlos and Marie, my money was on Marie. He may have towered over her by twelve inches or so, but he was mush in her hands. So was I.

At the end of a typical day at the shop, Marie would shut the computer down. I'd unplug it, pack it away in what she called a brief-case and I called a suitcase, load it in the car, and then come back for her. If she did not have something to hold on to, I was her support. I cannot recall the date, but one day she mentioned a paper cut on her finger. I was well taught about the facts of living with diabetes, and as minuscule as a paper cut sounds, it is anything but insignificant.

As the days went by, the paper cut across the middle knuckle on her right index finger would not heal. Weeks passed, and not only was the wound still there, but it was deeper. When Marie bent her finger, I swear we could see her tendon. It was Carlos who told us about Dr. Gutierrez, a doctor in Cancún who treated patients in an oxygen chamber for wound therapy. Marie and I both shrugged and decided it couldn't hurt. Raquel, now twenty-one years of age, had come down to Mexico again to spend the high season with us. She was a certified massage therapist and had developed quite a nice business for herself with the locals and tourists that stayed in the small hotels north of town. She also thought the oxygen chamber therapy sounded like a good idea and said she would take care of the three cats—Grace, Allie, and Jo—plus our two dogs, Pete and Max, that came to Mexico with us. The following day, Marie and I made the five-hour drive to see Dr. Gutierrez.

He was a tall man with long, dark hair that he kept pulled back in a ponytail. He did not wear the typical white lab coat, but a tropical shirt with blue jeans and sandals. I liked him instantly. He thought it would be beneficial for Marie if I were in the chamber with her for optimum relaxation. The chamber pressure would gradually be lowered to the equivalent of sixty feet below sea level. We would wear oxygen masks and be in the chamber for no less than ninety minutes, during which the pressure level would change, as would the percentage of oxygen we would breathe in. The purpose was to increase the oxygen level in Marie's red blood cells, encouraging circulation to her extremities. This sounded fine to us, and we said to each other, "Let's do this."

The oxygen chamber was approximately ten feet long and four feet wide. It was made of thick, white metal and had three portholes on each side. One end of the cylinder opened. We ducked our heads through the doorway and made our way inside. We were told to get comfortable, and the door was sealed closed behind us. Marie wanted to stay propped up against the wall with the security of a porthole in front of her to look out. We had brought our own pillows along with Andrew's blanket, a gift from one of his nurses who helped care for him at our home. It accompanied us on every trip we took, including Marie's occasional visits to the hospital. This trip was no exception. I propped Marie up with one pillow at her lower back as well as one behind her head, and Andrew's blanket in her hands. After I put her oxygen mask on her face, I situated myself on the wall opposite her so I could see her at all times. I put on my mask and leaned against my own pillow. I wrapped my arm around Marie's leg that was propped next to me. There was an intercom inside the chamber so we could communicate with Dr. Gutierrez and he with us.

"We're starting now," his voice echoed in the chamber. The oxygen instantly flowed from our masks, and we could feel the pressure building around us. We had been told to clear our ears as we needed to, but as experienced scuba divers and occasional flyers, neither of us were strangers to the experience. The doctor warned us of each change in pressure, after which the sound of a hiss would be heard within the chamber. I tried to relax and encouraged Marie to do the same. I rubbed her legs and gave her a hand massage. The doctor would occasionally tell us how much time had passed and ask if we were all right. Marie would answer with the "OK" sign through the porthole.

Before long, our first oxygen therapy session was over. We made an appointment for one o'clock the following day and headed to our hotel, Kin Mayab, in downtown Cancún. We decided to stay in that night and take advantage of the cable TV, which was not accessible to us in Xcalak. *Hangin' and chillin'* is what Marie called it. She had a taco in one hand and the remote control in the other, surfing from channel to channel. We were actually enjoying ourselves, and she remarked that whatever pain she'd had in her finger the day prior had diminished. It was a good sign. She became a little giddy when she found a marathon of the television show *House* on the TV. She was content, and I was a huge believer in "happy wife, happy life."

The next day, we were ready for round two. We carried in our pillows and blankets. The doctor greeted us and led us to the chamber, and we crawled inside. As we made ourselves comfortable, I noticed how much more relaxed Marie was the second time around. I resumed my position from the day before, but Marie lay down and put her feet up on my lap. Fifteen minutes into the treatment, she was sound asleep. I kept my eyes closed the entire time. I knew the reason we were there was Marie's medical treatment, but it felt like a luxurious spa treatment for the rich and famous. It was relaxing, and I enjoyed it, and I prayed it helped with the healing process of her finger. Immediately after our session, we headed back to the hotel. Marie took a proper nap and I joined her. A couple of hours later we both woke up very hungry and in the mood for Chinese. I left her channel-surfing at the hotel and walked around the corner to the Panda Express, returning thirty minutes later with vegetable lo mein, General Tso's chicken, sweet and sour pork, iced tea for me, and water for Marie. She was sitting cross-legged on the bed, taking a couple of hits from her one-hitter and examining her finger.

"Call me crazy, but I think this cut is looking better. I know it definitely feels better." It didn't look different to me, but if she was out of pain, that was definitely an improvement. I kissed her and said, "Then I'm glad we decided to do this. It's a nice little vacation." I started spreading out our Chinese buffet on a bath towel on the bed. Marie had found *NCIS* on TV for another night of hangin' and chillin'. We crashed early that night and slept soundly.

During our five-hour drive to Cancún, we'd made a list of supplies we needed at the dive shop and the house, and we reviewed the list at breakfast in the hotel restaurant. Marie wasn't up for shopping so I brought her back to our room, tucked her in with easy access to the remote control, and after a quick kiss, I was off. There was pep in my step because mega-shopping was not nearly as chaotic if I did it alone. When I went with Marie, she walked up and down every aisle and maybe meandered through the store next door. That was not my shopping philosophy at all. Get in, get what was on the list, and get out. I hit Sam's and Walmart in record time and received only one call from Marie with an addition to my list.

After my errands, I returned to the hotel with lunch, and we ate outside at a table close to where I'd parked the van. The remaining items on our list were mostly perishables, which we would gather on our way back to Xcalak the following day. Since we had another thirty minutes before we had to leave for our final treatment, I decided to straighten up the van while Marie sat in the sun. If she had a question about one of my purchases, I just brought it out and showed it to her for approval. Yes, she could be controlling, but her organizational and managerial skills had turned the dive shop around, and when it came to improvements and day-to-day operations, we were all smart enough to listen to her and do as we were told.

Once I had the van more organized, we left for our third and final session at the Wellness Center. When we arrived, Dr. Gutierrez informed us we would be sharing the chamber with another patient. She was a woman in her mid-seventies who was less than thrilled about spending ninety minutes in that metal contraption. As the doctor tried to reassure her she would be fine, Marie stepped between them, completely shunning the doctor, and not only promised the woman that she would do well, but that Marie would stay with her the entire time. A few minutes later, Marie, her new friend Juanita, and I climbed inside and started to get cozy. Marie suggested to Juanita that it might be more comforting for her to sit in front of one of the portholes, where she could see the doctor at all times, as Marie herself had done a couple of days before. Marie told her how the change of pressure in the chamber would make our ears feel like they needed to pop, like they did in an airplane, and Marie showed her how to clear her ears.

As our session began Juanita started to get nervous, but Marie just held her hand and said, "It's fine. You're OK. What is going on with you that you've decided to try this oxygen therapy?"

For the remainder of the session the women talked of Juanita's crippling arthritis and how she had been living in pain for a number of years. Her niece had heard about this form of therapy and Juanita decided to give it a try. Marie gave her a sympathetic ear and put her at ease. By the end of the session, Marie knew of Juanita's three children—the daughter in Mexico City, the son in Texas, and the other son she'd lost in a car accident three years before. Marie told her about losing Andrew. They both agreed that although others could sympathize over the loss of a child, none could fully comprehend it unless they had experienced the loss themselves. It was an exclusive club none of us were too happy to be members of.

After we exited the chamber, I made my way to the doctor and started to apologize for Marie's interruption with his patient, but Dr. Gutierrez spoke first. "I'm so glad Marie was here with Miss Juanita today. I've had many patients who are quite intimidated by the appearance of our chamber and are apprehensive about being inside for so long. I'm grateful for her help."

"That's Marie. She was always wonderful with her patients. I hope she didn't step on your toes today," I responded.

"Not at all," he said with a grin. "She can step on my toes anytime she likes if it gets a patient through treatment with less anxiety. I could use someone like her around here." I've heard those words about Marie more times than I can count, and truth be told, he was right. She was a unique woman.

I settled the bill as Juanita and Marie said their goodbyes. Juanita's words to Marie were heartfelt. "I almost canceled today because I was so afraid of being stuck in that tube and my head blowing up. God sent me an angel, and I will never forget my friend Marie. Thank you for your kindness."

Dr. Gutierrez told Marie that he was very appreciative of her help with his other patient and that he wanted updates on her progress. As we left the center, I put my arm around Marie. "I don't know how you do it, Marie. That lady was scared to death, and you just calmed her right down. You've got a special touch, girl." I squeezed her into me.

"Of course she was scared, Gene. It's a big, creepy-looking tube that she was going to sit in alone with her ears popping and feeling like her head was going to blow off her shoulders. She just needed a friend, and maybe it was God who put us here with her today to help her through it." I loved my wife.

After a nap back at the hotel, Marie suggested sushi at Yamamoto, one of our favorite restaurants in Cancún. Even though we changed up our order from time to time, one thing never changed—Marie had to have her shrimp tempura roll. The weather was perfect, and we had high hopes that the oxygen therapy would heal her finger. It felt like our weekly date night of years ago, when we did not want the night to end and reality to return by morning. We enjoyed ourselves, laughed a lot, and ended our date with coffee with Kahlua and cream, though it was a rare occasion for Marie to drink alcohol. I raised my coffee mug, nodded in her direction, and said, "To your health."

Approximately a week after our trip to Cancún, Marie woke up holding her finger and telling me it was endlessly throbbing. The once inconsequential cut had transformed into an angry ulcer. A hasty trip back home to St. Louis was inevitable. I booked a nonstop flight for Marie from Cancún to St. Louis on the next morning, Sunday, May 3. I left Raquel the task of packing for a trip back home. This trip was not the typical "It's been a while since we've been home" trip. We were in crisis, and it was quite a while after the fact that I truly understood the severity of the situation.

While I drove Marie to Cancún, Raquel packed up the house in Xcalak. This meant significantly more than just getting rid of perishable food in the fridge and locking the front door. There is no local telephone service in Xcalak, so Raquel drove around town to make Carlos and our friends aware of our departure. She also had to visit the hotels where she met with her clients to let them know of our quick return to the States. Last on her list was a stop at Leaky Palapa, a restaurant owned by our best friends in Xcalak. Linda and Marla were partners both in life and in business. Marla, a soft-spoken, attractive blonde, is a master in the kitchen; Linda, a petite brunette with a striking smile and welcoming aura, runs the business in the front of the restaurant, from reservations to bartending. Raquel filled them in on the crisis with Marie's hand and asked them to keep an eye on our house since she and I would be driving back to St. Louis.

The drive to Cancún with Marie went as well as can be expected. By the time we made it to Hotel Kin Mayab, nothing could touch her finger without causing her great pain. Instead of sitting in a hotel room feeling sorry for herself, Marie suggested we go out for sushi. She surprised me and ate quite well, even visiting my plate with her chopsticks once or twice. I wondered to myself if this was the start of Marie's slippery slope. We'd watched her sister Cathy struggle with her diabetes for years. She even underwent a kidney transplant, compliments of their brother, Carmine, the donor. Cathy's transplant lasted fifteen years before she passed away from a stroke. It had only been eight years since Marie's transplant.

We spent a sleepless night in the hotel with Marie in more pain than I'd care to see anyone in, and when she did fall asleep, I couldn't. I slipped outside and stood on the balcony, thinking about what needed to be done in the next couple of days. Get Marie on the plane, drive back to Xcalak, ask her sister Dart to have a wheelchair at the airport gate . . . and what was in store for her when she arrived back home? My mind was spinning.

I had booked a seat for Marie on the seven A.M. flight and obtained special permission to escort her all the way to the gate in a wheelchair. When it was time to board, she didn't want to go. She was scared—scared about her finger, scared about flying, scared about being alone and leaving me. She had no luggage with her. I sent her home with only the clothes on her back, carrying Andrew's blanket and the red backpack she had with her at all times. It contained an insulin pack, her wallet, her passport, a small Mayan bag containing a vial of Andrew's ashes, her rosary, and an amethyst stone that Marie believed protected her, but from what I never knew. She was begging me to let her stay, and I was pleading with her to get on the plane. I told her she would be home in three hours' time, Dart would meet her at the gate, and I would be home in a couple of days. It wasn't easy, but it was absolutely necessary she get home. An airline attendant assisted with getting Marie situated. I kissed her hard and told her I loved her. She was crying and told me she loved me too.

Holding back whatever tears I still had left in reserve, I walked out of the airport head down, climbed in the van, and let the tears roll. I cried for all the times over the years I'd held those tears back, putting on a brave face, and I cried because I felt guilty for putting that frightened woman on the plane alone. I cried tears for all the unanswered questions and for the impending answers I didn't know if I was prepared to hear. I cried until my abdomen hurt and I was finally able to pull myself together.

My drive back to Xcalak was long and uneventful. For the entire trip I listened to our iPod. Marie and I had quite a collection of albums, CDs, and mixtapes. We had been playing music since our dating years and there are hundreds of songs with special meanings for us. I tried to concentrate on each song as it played and the time and place it took me back to. I became a little teary-eyed when the song "Europa" by Santana came on. The first time we heard it together, we were on the balcony of our hotel room at Howard Johnson in Daytona

Beach, summer of 1983. She was laying out on a lounge chair wearing a black-and-white bikini, and her long, dark, curly hair framed her face. She was eighteen and I was twenty-three. We were young and in love and oblivious to what our future had in store for us.

There were many good memories I resurrected from the past during my drive. The last song I heard before pulling up to my house in Xcalak was "Against All Odds" by Phil Collins. How fitting. That song reminded me of our honeymoon in Cancún and Cozumel. Marie had recently seen the movie *Against All Odds* and chose Cancún for our honeymoon spot so we could make love in a Mayan temple like in the film, which we did. It was during that trip our love affair with Mexico and the Caribe began. It was instantaneous.

I heard from Dart that Marie made it in safely and that she wanted to stop by our house in St. Louis before heading to the hospital. Knowing Marie, she probably wanted to get high to relieve her nausea and pain and soothe her nerves. Dart persuaded Marie to leave the house and head to the hospital, where she was admitted. Marie had contacted Gloria, her transplant coordinator, the day before leaving Mexico to inform her of what was happening. Gloria had arranged for her to be admitted to the hospital upon her arrival. According to Dart, Marie was comfortable and seemed content and maybe even relieved. That was the story I was told, and I felt better knowing she was getting the medical attention she was in desperate need of.

By the time I returned to the house in Xcalak, Raquel had completed her tasks, including distributing the perishable food to friends and neighbors and making sure Marla and Linda had a key to the house. I threw a few changes of clothes and some bottled water in the van. Then it hit me: Shit! The animals' paperwork! They needed a clean bill of health with paperwork from a vet in order to cross the border into the States. The paperwork is not always checked, but without it, the animals could be confiscated and quarantined. No way was I willing to face Marie in a couple of days and tell her that her beloved pets were stuck at the border. We had to wait until morning to see the vet in Chetumal, so Raquel and I dined at the girls' restaurant that night. By the time I saw my bed, I was so mentally and physically exhausted it gave new meaning to the words "crawling to bed." I slept like a rock. Actually, more like a boulder.

After quickly repacking the van in the early morning hours, Raquel and I hit the road with the five animals for our four-day road trip back home to St. Louis. The first stop was to see Sebastian, the vet in Chetumal, where the animals received checkups and updates on their vaccinations along with letters of good health. The bill totaled 350 pesos—30 American dollars. Back in the States, that bill could have cost us upwards of $400. That was a hard lesson to learn once upon a time, but learn it, we did. Since then, Marie had taken to photocopying those $400 records and changing the date to coordinate with our trip over the Mexican border. Four hundred dollars—please. We always saw the Mexican vet for the animals' wellness visits. Price differences for the same vaccinations were quite impressive.

It took two days to get to the border and another day and a half to get home. We received occasional updates from Dart, who usually reported that Marie was on strong antibiotics to fight her infection and that she might be coming home in a day or two. The closer I was to home, the more anxious I became. I felt a pull of desperation to be there, so instead of making a typical overnight stay in Texas, I drove until we reached the driveway, shaving twelve hours from our estimated time of arrival. We arrived approximately two hours after Marie was released from the hospital.

I walked into the house and learned firsthand from Dart that Marie's finger was amputated, that she was handling it well, and she was resting upstairs in bed. She also told me Marie didn't want us to know about the amputation while we were on the road. I was grateful for being in the dark about her finger. Knowing the truth would not have gotten us home any quicker, but it definitely would have made the trip longer and more miserable.

My first reaction to Marie's hand may have been shock, but at the same time we'd both known there was a possibility of losing her finger, although those words were never spoken between us. She was lying down in bed, but when I walked into the room, she opened her eyes. She sat up at the side of her bed, cautious of her bandaged hand. I knelt in front of her and we held each other for a long while.

When I let her go, she reached for her red backpack next to the bed. She pulled out a small box and asked me to open it. I took it from her and sat back on my feet. Inside was a wedding band identical to the one I had lost a couple of years before on a dive. She pulled it out of the box and told me she'd ordered it a few months ago from the jeweler in Chicago where we bought our rings. Marie had my ring engraved with an infinity sign on the exterior and words from our wedding vows on the inside of the band. She slipped it on my finger. It was a perfect fit.

"You're always surprising me, woman!"

"Just do me one favor. Don't wear it scuba diving!" she said, punctuating her words with a kiss. "Let's sit on the deck and smoke a little weed. This hand is really starting to hurt." I could tell by the amount of support she needed and how frail she seemed that the past five days had been hell for her. I led her to the table and chairs on the deck outside our bedroom. I offered her a hit, and she told me the nausea from the antibiotics was playing combat with her body. I sat next to her listening to the events over the past five days. The wound was healing nicely. What had caused the infection was unclear, and there would be a six-week regimen of antibiotics administered at the hospital emergency room through the central line (C-line) that was inserted in Marie's neck during her surgery.

For the next forty-two days, I drove Marie to the ER for her antibiotic infusion. The treatments lasted two hours and made her violently ill. Her usual weight was approximately one hundred and ten pounds. In six weeks' time, she shrank to a tiny eighty-eight pounds.

It was during that time her mother became a supporter of Marie's pot smoking. If she smoked before and after the treatments, she was not nearly as ill. When Marie was at her worst, Genevieve was the first to reach for Marie's one-hitter or bong.

At the end of the six weeks, a trip to the infectious disease doctor, Dr. Darwin, revealed that Marie still had an unidentified infection in her body. This meant four more weeks of antibiotics and daily visits to the ER.

Marie and I were both questioning whether it was the infection that was killing her or the drugs they were giving her. I remember telling the doctor after those four weeks that I couldn't watch her go through it anymore. Marie's kidney doctor, Dr. Frank (who had performed her kidney transplant eight years prior), Dr. Darwin, and the surgeon Dr. Luden gave mixed responses. Marie could not take any more treatments or lose any more weight.

Since no one actually knew what the infection was or how best to treat it, Marie decided to quit all treatments but agreed to return in three months. Her exact words to me were "There's nothing they can do for me. Bring me back to Mexico." Marie was a nurse; she knew the health risks. If she wanted to lie in the sun and put her feet in the water, I was going to make that happen for her. We both knew her days in Mexico might be numbered, but she loved it there so much. How could I say no? I didn't.

We left two days later, leaving Raquel at home. The only ones making the trip this time were Marie, me, and the three cats. We took our time getting back—ten days in total. First stop was a visit with Marie's friend Becky in San Antonio, where we stayed for a couple of days. Becky and Marie were great friends from a lifetime ago. Their history ran deep and the stories they shared were abundant. Becky had been a great comfort for both of us when we lost Andrew. She was a sympathetic ear on the other end of the phone and someone to laugh with. Becky said Marie was her saving grace for seeing her through an abusive marriage that lasted far longer than it should have. Marie offered our home to Becky many times before she finally came to her senses and left that awful man. After violating a restraining order, getting heavy-handed with Becky and hospitalizing her, he was arrested. In his possession were heroin and a couple of guns, one of which he had stolen. Marie always said she wished she'd found him before the police did. She was not tolerant of a man laying a hand on a woman. She fantasized about loading his corpse in a big plastic bag and dropping it in a body of water that led to the ocean, where it would be gnawed on by thousands of tiny fish and never found. It was a little disturbing how she delighted in the details of his demise. I told her more than once to let it go. I wasn't driving a dead body around in the van, even though I hated the guy.

When we arrived in San Antonio, Becky was in a little bit of shock when she saw how thin and frail Marie was. Those two talked often, and Becky was fully aware of the weight Marie had lost, but seeing is believing. There wasn't any part of our lives Becky did not know about. I often wondered if Becky received more information about Marie's health than I did, but I considered her one of my best friends as well. Becky is a vivacious, very attractive, green-eyed blonde with a tattoo of a sunflower that I had seen just once. She is the kind of individual who can make anyone comfortable with a hug and a smile. Her personality is upbeat and positive. Some of the best times Marie and I have had through the years were spent with Becky, and we were both in need of a few good laughs. By the time we left San Antonio, Marie's morale seemed to be much better. She was happy and looking forward to laying out in the sun. We both wanted to take our time and enjoy the music. We stopped for our favorite ribs at Heifetz's BBQ and at Rosario's, her yogurt place, before crossing the border. In a travel book about Mexico, I had highlighted a couple of places to see, knowing how Marie loved to check out churches and missions. We meandered our way through the country, visiting three missions built in the 1700s. Very cool stuff. Marie wanted to spend the night by the ocean and since our conversion van was equipped with electricity, we could watch movies downloaded on our computer. I had removed the middle seat before leaving home and the back bench was reclined into a bed. The cooler was full of drinks and snacks. With the windows open, we fell asleep listening to the waves hitting the shore. We were quite cozy.

Marie in Mexico

Andrew's blanket

Good day diving for lobsters in Xcalak

Gene's Island Girl

Chapter Four

FINDING OUR TREASURE

I swear the closer we were to Xcalak, the better Marie felt. She loved the water and the tranquility of our lives in that remote little village. We made a stop in Chetumal and loaded up on food and supplies for the next two months. Two hours later, we pulled up to the house and I carried Marie up the steps. After unloading the van and opening the house, I collapsed in bed next to her, where we stayed for the next two days, getting up only to nourish ourselves or use the restroom.

Marie started laying out on the deck again to replenish her lost tan. I knew she was feeling better if she wanted to resume her tanning routine. It was her thing. She could lay out for several hours a day. I think it made her feel better psychologically, and who cared what it was that made her better. Hour after hour, she lay there listening to music. Day after day, I watched my wife grow stronger, feel better, and get darker. Maybe it was the sun that gave her strength. One particularly memorable day, I was looking at her through our living room window, her tiny body sweaty from the sun, when the song "Aqua Marine," another gem by Santana, started playing in the background. It was one of her favorite songs. When we played the album in our little rental house, she would turn the music up and dance for her audience of one. I loved it. I still looked at her like I had when we were first dating nearly thirty years ago. I never lost my attraction for Marie. She was always very cautious with her weight and fitness, but I was just as attracted to her in her worst days as I was the day we were married. It was a tossup to me what her most attractive aspect was—brains or beauty. She was everything in one hot, tiny package.

The next three days were nothing but storms and rain, giving me ample time to catch up on all my new duties. Getting back in routine was nothing routine for me. Marie's weakened condition left her unable to help with cooking, dishes, laundry, or even showering herself. I was accustomed to doing most of the work anyway, but this was 100 percent the Gene Show. I was fulltime caretaker, housekeeper, cook, nursemaid, and chauffeur. It was my new norm. So while I kept house, Marie watched her favorite movies. I knew, without being in the room with her, what scene was playing from which movie. Her top five favorites were *An Officer and a Gentleman, Pretty Woman, Against All Odds* (which brought us to Mexico in the first place), and her latest favorites, *Sahara* and *Fool's Gold.*

Moi stopped by on the first clear morning to see how we'd weathered the storms and to ask us if we were up for a boat ride. We were happy to accept. Moi worked up the coast as a boat captain for the small hotel Marie and I ran for a while. He was such a great captain that we brought him on board at the dive shop. He was a dark-skinned, stocky, blue-eyed Mexican man, no more than five and a half feet tall. His hair was always disheveled and his beard unkempt, but those white teeth would flash a killer smile and the single women would practically throw their panties at him. But he was a happily married man who loved and respected his wife. Moi was very pleasant to be around and a handy guy to know. He was not just a boat captain, but a great mechanic and carpenter as well. The balcony he built for us was Marie's favorite spot to lay out. It is nice to have talented friends.

At that moment the skies were not the most pleasant, but according to our boat captain, who was an expert at reading the skies, the clouds would be dissipating and the sun would be peeking out in

a couple of hours. We agreed to meet at Moi's boat around two-ish.
In Mexico, we always added the "ish" in reference to time. We called
it Mexico time. Marie was usually on Mexico time no matter what
country we were in. When we arrived at 2:45, I could tell by the look
on Moi's face he was a little annoyed. I shrugged at him as I walked
to the passenger side of the van to help Marie. It was the first time
Moi noticed the changes in her. She was twenty-five pounds lighter
and needed my assistance to walk. His look of irritation quickly
turned to one of compassion. When he saw her that morning at our
house, she was tucked in the corner of the couch under a blanket,
sipping on a hot vanilla chai tea. She was often cold and under layers
of blankets or clothing unless she was sun worshipping. He did not
get the full impression of the changes in her until he saw her walking
toward him with me holding her steady.

"Lo siento," Marie told him, which translated to "Sorry." She
knew he would not be mad, at least not for long.

"No hay problema," he said, approaching us. He gave me a
wink, scooped up Marie, carried her to the panga (his modest-sized
fishing boat), and set her on the back bench. I helped him push the
panga into the water and jumped in next to Marie. Moi started the
60-horsepower Yamaha, and off we went.

The water was tranquil, the sky was clear, and for a short while
it was easy to forget the past few months. Typically, the surface was
a smooth greenish blue. If you were to look down into the water,
you could see the bottom. Today that was not the case. Remnants
from the storms left the water a little murky and the waves hitting the reef were bigger and louder than usual, but we were safely
inside the reef, so no worries. We stayed closer to the shoreline,
which was rich with mangroves and the occasional coconut tree
towering above. We headed toward the Zaragoza Canal, approximately six kilometers south of town. Moi never said exactly where
we were going, but I had a fairly good idea we were heading to

Chetumal Bay and down to the Río Bacalar Chico, the border of Mexico and Belize and the best place to find manatees. Given their vast size, manatees were about the only animal Marie could see in the water anymore.

Approximately forty-five minutes after leaving town, Moi was trolling through a narrow part of the river—maybe all of ten feet wide and a meter deep, the bottom covered in turtle grass. As I looked down, I saw a couple of stingrays resting on sandy patches. On either side, the mangroves had grown so tall they had collapsed together, creating a tunnel. As we exited the tunnel and entered a cove, Moi killed the engine and we drifted a bit with the mild current. The three of us sat quietly. We turned our heads from side to side, looking for shadows in the water while listening to the water hit the side of the boat. I think it was Marie who heard the first manatee as it snorted when it surfaced. It came from behind and slowly rolled past on the left side of the boat. It actually did a complete roll, as if performing for us. The manatee looked every bit of ten feet long, about half the length of the boat. The gentle giants of the water, manatees are known for their grace and playfulness. They are curious animals, and they seem very slow, but if they sense danger they whisk away quite quickly. This guy was in no rush.

Within a few minutes, Moi pointed out a second manatee heading in the same direction as the first, hugging the mangrove abundant in turtle grass, their favorite food. We coasted into a shady area for a bit. We could hear the chatter of parrots in the trees, and as we floated closer, we disturbed a flock of roughly forty, and they took flight. It was late afternoon and the skies were getting cloudy. I could tell Marie was getting tired and had had enough excitement for one day. Or so I thought.

We started to head back, following the river toward the Caribbean Sea. Moi exited the mouth of the river and veered to the right to enter the sea, then changed direction quite abruptly. I steadied Marie in the panga and she held on to me as we unexpectedly made that sharp turn. Finally, Moi raised his engine and coasted into the shallows.

Marie called behind her, "¿Qué pasa?"

Moi answered in perfect English, "I see something over here. Just want to check it out." I was certain of what Moi had seen. I had never come across one before, but I'd heard many stories of those who have. And then I saw it. Tucked in the mangroves along the shallows was a package. It was dark and a couple of feet long, but I could not tell how wide; it was camouflaged by seaweed and bobbing slightly in the water. I did not say anything; neither did Moi. Marie finally asked me what was going on. She could not see the package with her diminished eyesight. I lowered my voice, though there was no one within kilometers of us, and explained that there was a dark package stuck in the mangroves.

We all knew that package was either marijuana or cocaine. Moi and I jumped out of the panga and pushed it across the shallows through the turtle grass. I steadied the boat while Moi retrieved the package. As he untangled it from the roots of a mangrove, it floated freely. "Jesus Christ!" What I thought was a small package now looked to be every bit of three feet long. Moi pushed the package through the water until he reached us. He pinned it between himself and the panga, settled his hands on the side of the boat, and with a smile said, "Square fish! ¡Coca!"

"No fuckin' way!" was all I could think to say.

Moi told me to lift the floorboards in front of Marie. She moved quickly to the side as I jumped back into the panga. I lifted the boards from one side, leaving the other end in place. Moi lifted the package into the boat and dropped it into the hull. I lowered the boards back in place and jumped back out. We pushed ourselves through the turtle grass, out of the shallows. When we were in deeper waters, Moi and I climbed back into the panga. He lowered the motor and fired it up. It did not take long to get into the channel heading north.

I steadied Marie, and she said to me, "I can't believe this is happening! Moi, you know the right guy to get rid of this?"

"I know a guy in Majahual," he replied. His eyes never moved from the view in front of him. He looked very stern. We were all probably going down the same mental path, asking ourselves the same questions: Where were we going to store this stuff? Would anyone find out?

We were fast approaching the Zaragoza Canal Naval Base, whose function was to stop drug trafficking, human trafficking, illegal immigration . . . Anything that happened on the water, they watched, and they had complete authority to board and search boats if they so desired. I had not given them any notice on our way to Chetumal Bay. Funny how they had my full and undivided attention as we passed by a second time. I sat casually with my arm around Marie, thinking to myself, "Nothing to see here, boys." I turned around to face Moi.

"Did you notice the naval base on our way earlier?"

He laughed and shook his head. "No, Genie. I did not." I pulled Marie close to me and squeezed the side of her arm and just beamed a stupid grin at her.

"This is really happening," she said with excitement in her voice. She loved a good adventure. I was excited myself, but I had some concerns, like getting caught and going to jail in Mexico. It was all happening quickly and unexpectedly, and I did not know what to think.

"How many times over the years did we say, 'What would we do if we ever found coke floating in the water?' Looks like we're gonna find out, baby!" I said.

"Where there's one, there's more," said Moi in a serious tone. "It's more than likely part of a bigger cargo that had to be dumped. Someone was probably being chased by the marinos, and it all went overboard. Who knows where it came from since the weather's been so terrible."

"Who knows and who cares?" I thought. Finders keepers.

"Where are we keeping this treasure and how are we getting it there?" asked Marie. "Gene, just drive down by the boat to get me and block the view with the van." Marie was in the habit of asking questions, then answering them herself. I just nodded in agreement, something I was in the habit of doing. We could see the rain rapidly approaching as we coasted in to the beach just south of the old town pier. There was nobody around. I relayed that to Marie, knowing she could not see very well.

We jumped out of the panga and pushed it ashore. Outwardly, I may have seemed calm, but I felt anxious. I knew Moi would split the findings with us, but would anyone find out? Could this be our chance to gain some financial footing? I hurried to the van, apprehensively turning my head from side to side. I parked the van perpendicular to the boat and with Moi's help put Marie inside the vehicle just as the rain came pouring down. In the tropics, the weather can be unpredictable and spontaneous. Moi was already back at the boat, lifting the boards out and putting them aside. I looked from side to side again . . . no one coming. To my surprise, Moi opened the package. He emptied a cooler of a few bottled waters, then filled it with nine packages, each one grayish in color and about the size of an encyclopedia. I grabbed a couple of towels from the van, and we used them to bundle the remaining kilos, which we then loaded in the side door of the van along with the cooler. The rain was a blessing because when it rains, the beach is empty of people. I waited in the van with Marie while Moi finished securing his boat. He gestured for me to leave as he ran up the beach to his car.

"You are planning to park the van in the bodega tonight . . behind locked doors, preferably?"

Yes, I knew Marie's question was rhetorical, but sometimes I responded just to let her know I was listening. "Yes, Marie. I was planning to park in the bodega." A great hiding spot popped into my head. "The cistern on the left is empty."

"Oh God! That's right. That would be perfect!" Marie said. Score one for Gene. "On top of the cistern right now is Linda and Marla's stuff. I think we should leave the van undercover tonight in the bodega. Tomorrow, I'll move all their stuff out of the way, put the treasure in the cistern, then put all their stuff back on top. No one will ever know it's down there." I was feeling rather proud of my idea.

"No one can know about this, Gene. Not Linda and Marla, not Carlos, no one. Agreed?"

"No shit!"

When we arrived back at the house, I jumped out of the van and unlocked the door to the bodega. I took a hammer to the pins at the bottom of each side and freed the garage door. Moi arrived as I started to lift the door. I looked at the pile of the girls' belongings. It looked no different than the day we moved it there earlier in the year. Linda had a key to the bodega and could come and retrieve whatever she wanted, whenever she wanted. I was glad they had not removed anything yet. I moved the van inside and helped Marie out of the vehicle while Moi helped himself to one of the twenty-five packages. I locked up the van and asked Moi to reinstall the pins and lock the door behind him. He had stored his boating materials in our bodega for years and, like Linda, had his own key.

Marie and I walked out to the steps leading up to the house. I locked my arms under her butt and hiked her up over my shoulder . . . seven steps to the landing, turn right, then seven more. I set Marie down, unlocked the door as Moi joined us, and Marie led the way inside. I grabbed a Coke for myself, a beer for Moi, and made hot tea for Marie. I was not a beer drinker, but we kept it around for guests. In fact, there were a couple of cases in the bodega for that reason. When we ran out in the fridge, I would grab a half a dozen to chill. With no local phone service available, it was protocol for guests to drop by unannounced.

"Well that was an exciting day," I said as I passed out the drinks and sat down at the table next to them.

Moi had the package in front of him on the table. He had already cut a slit across the top with his knife. First, he licked the top of his index finger and tapped it in the stiff powder. He licked it off his finger and rubbed some on his gums. He wasted no time in dipping his pinky nail into the package and snorting it. My apprehension had begun to fade once we were safely inside the house, but suddenly I felt downright jovial. Moi burst out laughing. He was literally laughing loudly for joy. I believe that was the happiest I had ever seen him. He grabbed a big pinch of the compressed powder and made a small pile in front of himself on our glass tabletop. He stood up, still laughing a little, and gestured for me to try it.

It had been over twenty-five years since Marie and I had done coke. It was something we never really got into. Weed, yes. Cocaine, no. However, this day was different. It was one of those moments that, no matter what you believed in or approved of, you had to throw yourself into in order to fully absorb the situation at hand. I grabbed a 500-peso note, rolled it tightly, and snorted some coke. Marie reached for the peso note and tried some herself.

I do not know if it was the adrenaline, the coke, or the excitement of the past few hours, but I felt euphoric. This kind of thing did not happen to us. It was what movies were made of. There was no guilt, no worrying, and no sadness. There was just laughter and mutual giddy disbelief as we exclaimed, over and over, that we could not believe this, and wondered aloud how much it was all worth. But mostly I remember the laughter. Marie and I hadn't had much to laugh about as of late, and whether it was wrong or right, the coke gave us pleasure that night. It felt a little like having a winning lottery ticket, just an illegal one. Moi kept drinking beer, I switched my drink to rum and Coke, and Marie requested I put on some tunes and turn it up. The party was on. I may not have done coke for many years, but I remembered the feeling well. It felt like all my senses were heightened. Music sounded better, rum tasted better, and the energy in the room was abundant.

Marie felt it, too. She even started dancing in the living room and was joined by Moi. He clumsily attempted to twirl her, then scooped her up in his arms and dipped her forward and backward to the music. After their dance, he placed her in my lap, and I squeezed her into me. I wasn't just happy, I was exhilarated. When I felt myself coming down from my high, I did another line to bump myself back up.

Moi told a story of finding a square fish ten years ago and another of finding a sizable amount of playata (weed) a few years back. The stories were more than likely embellished upon, but he had a captive audience, and all the stories seemed to end with big paydays and happy endings. Who doesn't want that? We were dreaming of financial security and easier times. It was like playing the "If I Won the Lottery" game, but with a twist. Moi suggested that he take thirteen kilos and Marie and I keep twelve. We were more than satisfied with that. He explained that it was customary to split your findings with anyone who assisted in securing the coca. Since then, I have often wondered if that was true, or if he had put together that Marie and I were in somewhat of a financial pinch. Moi agreed with us about keeping our findings very quiet. By the time he left, the cold beer was gone. I located an empty container for the open kilo of coke and Moi left with it tucked under his arm. I stood outside the door, small-talking with my new partner in crime as he walked down the steps to his car. I wasn't too concerned about his ability to drive under the influence since his home was all of two hundred meters away. He started his car and said he would be back in the morning.

"OK. Mañana."

I locked the door behind me and looked across the room at Marie, who was cozy in the corner of the couch. I went to the kitchen to tidy up a bit before bed.

"Can you believe this day?" I called into the living room. All I heard her say was "Come here, Genie Boy!" When Marie called me Genie Boy, it meant she was feeling amorous. I got the nickname from the movie *Dirty Dancing*, another favorite of Marie's. She had changed the song lyrics "Come here, lover boy" to include my name. The nickname also meant Genie was about to get lucky. I flipped the light switch in the kitchen. Screw the dishes. I walked toward Marie and bent down to carry her to bed. She wrapped her legs around my waist and her arms around my neck. I carried her like that to the bed, and for the first time in more months than I like to admit, we made love like we were honeymooners. We were stupid buzzed, happy, and care-free—literally free of any care in the world. What had happened that day was such a welcome distraction. We did not think at all about the medical issues or the financial woes this last emergency had caused.

Marie had lost so much weight I could manipulate that little body so easily. After some time in the bedroom, I moved Marie's thin sunbathing mattress outside. I brought a few blankets with us since she was easily chilled. We made love again and slept outside, naked under the stars. Why waste a good buzz, especially one that makes you horny?

I knew it would take Marie a couple of days to recover from our big adventure the day before. She slept for hours, woke up to eat something, then drifted back to sleep. We had a couple of short conversations between naps about what to do with our half of the cocaine. Our credit card had taken a beating lately. I had not been able to work as a dive instructor since Marie was so reliant on me for everything. We decided to give Moi two of our twelve kilos to sell immediately and to save the other ten for a later date, insurance for a rainy day. We were hoping for a payday of around 150,000 pesos, about 12,000 American dollars. Moi arrived at our door around ten A.M. I left Marie sleeping while Moi and I went down to the bodega. We stood by the van, discussing the possibilities of what to do with the treasure.

"We're in no rush to move with our share, but if you have a buyer in mind, would you consider selling two kilos for us?" I asked him.

"Absolutely, mi amigo. Whatever you want."

Moi was a good friend of mine, no question, but he had a soft spot in his heart for Marie. Miss Marie, he called her. He knew about the loss of our Andrew, her kidney transplant, and her declining health. She had been his boss the last three years at the dive shop, and if I wasn't around to assist her, he was. Moi would do anything for Miss Marie.

"Hey, Moi, if anything was to go wrong, I do not want Marie's name mentioned."

Moi half grinned and interrupted me. "I'd never let anything happen to Miss Marie. Or you either. No worries."

Moi decided to take his entire share with him, which was fine with me. He took his twelve kilos and two of ours. I promised to pay him a percentage of our profit, depending on the payoff, and waved as he pulled out of our driveway with two backpacks containing fourteen kilos of cocaine. I went upstairs to check on Marie, then immediately returned to the bodega to start unburying the cistern cover. I have no clue why this house had two cisterns, but it did. One collected rain water that ran through the pipes in the house. The other was an empty, bone-dry ten-by-ten concrete box, about six feet deep, with a square lid that had to weigh a minimum of seventy-five pounds, if I had to guess.

I found a duffle bag and emptied it of toys we kept for families with little kids that would come by to visit. I filled the bag with the ten kilos, zipped it up, and after making sure the concrete box was indeed bone dry, dropped the bag in the hole followed by my eight-foot ladder. I climbed in the hole, tied a piece of rope to the bag, and hung it on a piece of rebar jutting out of the top far corner. The bag was suspended, and I felt better knowing it was not sitting on the concrete floor. I climbed back out of the cistern and removed the ladder. Before replacing the lid, I made sure the duffle bag was not visible. I moved Linda and Marla's crap back on top of the cistern and locked up the bodega, then replenished the beer in the fridge. I found Marie in the bathroom.

I asked her, "How about pancakes and sausage for breakfast?"

"Oh yeah. I'm starving."

I filled her in on my discussion with Moi while I made breakfast. "Moi took his share, plus two of ours to sell, and the other ten are safely hidden in the cistern." I pointed the metal spatula at her and said, "And I did not tell him where we are hiding our share. No one other than you and me will know."

"Agreed. I wonder how much Moi will get. Can you imagine being able to put some money away, Gene?"

"That would be nice."

"This is a blessing for us," she said as she snatched a piece of sausage. "I still can't believe it happened."

"I know," I said with a laugh. "I bet I've said that to myself a dozen times this morning."

After breakfast, we took a shower together. Marie could wash her face, but I took care of everything else. I would wash her hair and her body, shave her underarms and legs, even pluck her eyebrows when need be. Spa Gene was full service. Our shower in Mexico was very roomy. We kept a small stool in it for Marie to sit on if she needed to, and it was easier for me to shave her legs if she was sitting. I loved that shower. I miss that shower. After we cleaned up, we took a nap. I always held Marie very close to me because it was difficult for her to get warm after a shower. Her tiny body would be curled up with me spooning her from behind, my arm around her little waist. She would sleep with at least one big blanket on top of her, sometimes two. I'd have a thin sheet.

When we woke from our nap, we lay side by side discussing the events of the past twenty-four hours. Both of us could hear the helicopters in the distance. It was common for a helicopter to fly over the coast, checking the shoreline after a storm, but there was more than one flying around on that day.

"Hey, Gene, you think they're looking for the coke that we found?"

"Maybe. Perhaps there was another package found somewhere, but we're safe. There was no one around where we found it, and the beach was empty when we unloaded it. No worries, babe."

The truth was, it gave me a lump in my throat knowing that what they might be searching for was hidden in the cistern below with my fingerprints all over it, but I had no intention of admitting that to her. We would possibly hear something in a day or two from the coconut telegraph, our town gossip line.

It was two days before we heard anything from Moi. He stopped by in the early evening hours and told us he had gone to Majahual the day before. He has family members that work in restaurants near the cruise ship pier. They also have certain connections. He emptied the contents of a grocery bag—a stack of money totaling 150,000 pesos (equivalent to $12,000 dollars) and a half ounce of pot. He told us to expect a kilo of pot to arrive in a day or so. The pot was part of the payment. He knew Marie smoked every day to keep up an appetite and to control pain from her neuropathy. I gave Moi 30,000 pesos, his cut for selling our two kilos. It was all about knowing the right guy, and we felt better about Moi selling it for us for a variety of reasons. First of all, he had connections. Second, it was little risky for me. Lastly, a gringo would not be able to sell coke in Mexico for a decent price.

Moi seemed pretty pleased with his cut, and although we were playing it very cool at the moment, I knew Marie was ecstatic about our profit as well. I knew I was. Moi had a celebratory beer, smoked a joint, and left shortly after.

"Holy shit, Gene!" said Marie once he had gone. "A hundred twenty thousand pesos! Let's count it."

So we did. We went to the bedroom and started counting. One hundred 1,000-peso notes and forty 500-peso notes, totaling 120,000 pesos. I had never seen that many pesos before. It was an easy decision to keep it in the safe at the bottom of our bathroom closet.

"You know how long it would have taken us to make twelve thousand dollars back home?" said Marie as I closed the safe door.

"Or a hundred twenty thousand pesos at the dive shop?" I said.

"And there's five times that in the cistern. You just might get lucky tonight, Genie Boy."

I laughed, secretly hoping there was some truth to that statement.

That night we lay around listening to music and talking about the money and what we should do with it, if anything. Marie's disability checks more than covered our bills, and even though our credit card had a few thousand on it from our last hasty trip home, we didn't have huge amounts of debt hanging over our heads. However, there were no savings to speak of. We potentially had $55,000 to $60,000 hidden below if we chose to go through Moi again. If we went to the States, we would probably get three times the amount, and that might be lowballing. We were in no rush to make any decisions. It's quite true when there are no immediate financial woes, one sleeps much better.

In two days' time Moi returned, carrying a black backpack containing one kilo of weed. Then he lifted a piece of the tape covering a hole cut into the kilo. Moi explained that he had opened and sampled it when he made the transaction. I gestured to him that it was OK. I walked to the fridge and grabbed him a beer, myself a coke. I asked Marie if she wanted anything, to which she responded no, but I put a glass of water in front of her anyway. By the time I sat down, Moi had rolled a sizable joint for us to share. The weed was purple—a vivid purple, with red and green mixed throughout. I had never seen anything like it. I was expecting the pot to be in a brick-sized block, greenish brown in color. It weighed the same as a kilo of cocaine, of course, but its size was nearly double. I was getting quite an education these past few days. There's probably a new kind or strain of pot created daily, so I don't know why I was so surprised by the purple color, but I was. "My first hit of purple pot," I said. We passed the joint around a few times. It was potent weed. I am no expert, but I was sure this pot was pretty good stuff. I was buzzed. I had not partied in years like I had these past few days. When I'm high, I think very out of the box. I'm in my most relaxed state of mind. Any feelings of inhibition simply dissipate. I couldn't have cared less about how much my wife smoked that night. She'd had to endure more than any one person should in their lifetime, and she was all of forty-six years old. What did I care if she smoked pot to feel good? I would rather she do what she needed to stay out of pain.

Chapter Five

MARIE GOES TO THE PODIATRIST

Weeks passed, and Marie and I made little mention of the treasure hidden below. It was there for a rainy day, and recently the weather had been fairly clear. Marie continued to tan and grow stronger. Her hand was healing well, and the residual effects of the antibiotics seemed to be wearing off. She had put on a few more pounds, and according to her blood work her creatinine levels were good, which meant her kidneys were still functioning. Life was good. We were looking forward to a trip back home to visit family and celebrate the holidays.

We asked Xesus, an instructor from the dive shop, and his girlfriend to stay at our house and watch the cats while we were gone. Our house sitters were usually instructors from the shop, who were all too happy to house-sit for us. They came from all over the world and worked at the shop until they fulfilled their contractual agreements, and then they moved on to work and dive somewhere else on the planet. While they were in Xcalak, they shared a very small residence, the Pink Palace, with several others. So when our house became available, we had no trouble finding someone to stay, unless they had pet allergies.

It was November 28 and we were flying home to St. Louis. For many years, our tradition was to celebrate Christmas with Marie's family during the second weekend of December. The busy tourist season for the dive shop began in late December, so celebrating the holidays early back home gave us plenty of time to get back to Xcalak for the rush. This particular year we traveled to Cancún and stayed in town for a few days before flying home. We did a little Christmas shopping at Mercado Veintiocho, Market 28, an outdoor market with vendors selling everything from tattoos to jewelry. Everywhere I looked there were brightly colored shirts, shorts, dresses, cover-ups, swimming suits, and hats in every shape and size. There was pottery in every other stand, and Marie loved to look at pottery. I felt like we were on a little mini vacation. I didn't have to cook, which was a real treat for me. I perused a menu, selected my daily food choices, and waited for someone to refill my glass. We even laid out by the hotel pool a couple of days. It was a great escape from reality.

When we flew home, Raquel picked us up at the airport. Nine weeks had passed since we had seen her, although we talked a few times each week. She thought her mom looked great, and I had to agree. We were looking forward to being at home with family around, but first we had to make the rounds on the doctor circuit. There were visits to the kidney doctor, Dr. Frank; the infectious disease specialist, Dr. Darwin; the orthopedic surgeon, Dr. Luden; and Dr. Kent, the OB/GYN. Every appointment went well and there was nothing but positive feedback. It was the best Christmas gift we could have received.

And then there was the visit to the podiatrist, Dr. Cole. Due to her neuropathy, Marie's insurance covered a biannual visit for a foot exam and a nail trim. The tool he used to buff her nails smooth was a Dremel with a cylindrical buffing bit. On this memorable visit, as the doctor was smoothing the rough edges on Marie's toenails, he looked up as the bit's abrasive surface shaved off the skin on the top of her left big toe.

I couldn't say who was more horrified, Marie or me. We stared at each other in disbelief with mouths gaping open. I knew in a second what her eyes were saying, and I'm sure she saw the same in mine. We knew this had the potential to be very bad. The look of surprise on Dr. Cole's face as he saw his handiwork spoke a thousand words, none of them spelling a positive outcome for Marie. His initial reaction may have been of surprise and guilt. However, his instant change of demeanor by making light of his potentially dangerous mistake was nothing short of an Academy Award–winning performance. He said, "I sure am sorry about that, but I don't think there's anything here to be concerned about."

A little paper cut had led to an amputation. Who knew what this could lead to? Time would tell, but we didn't want to dwell on it and spoil our visit home. We made little mention of it, and as always, kept our eyes wide open.

———•••••———

A week after the visit to the podiatrist, we found ourselves celebrating Christmas as usual at our house in true Italian fashion. Food came from several directions, and as always, it was abundant and delicious. Homemade spiedini, ravioli, escargot, asparagus, hash brown potato casserole, numerous salads—and it wouldn't be Christmas without my mother-in-law Genevieve's cannoli and Italian cookies. I looked forward to this meal for months and always consumed a week's worth of food on that one day. We could graze on leftovers for days. We had great memories of Christmas parties at our house, sharing stories and laughing with family and friends. Our door was open to whoever wanted to stop by.

Raquel had yet to book her ticket to Mexico, but she had plans to return to Xcalak to work. It was not as hard leaving home knowing she would be visiting us in a couple of weeks. The day prior to leaving, we said our goodbyes to everyone except Dart, who gave us a ride to the airport. Dart was the only one who knew about the shaved toe and asked us to keep her informed of any developments that occurred.

Traveling back to Xcalak was quieter than usual. The last three weeks had taken their toll and Marie was exhausted. She slept through much of the five-hour drive back to Xcalak, which was fine with me. I've always enjoyed road trips even if I was making them alone. We stopped in Tulum to do some mega grocery shopping, grabbed some cheap Chinese food, then drove the remaining two hours back to Xcalak. Xesus had taken very good care of the cats and the house. Nothing to report; muy bien. It may not make for good storytelling, but that was the way I preferred it. I had to check out the bodega even though I knew the treasure was undisturbed. But seeing is believing, and it made me feel better just to see that pile of stuff on top of the cistern. We looked forward to the tranquility of our little village and no doctor appointments. We lay low and Marie laid out.

We spent Christmas Eve at Moi's for his annual Christmas party, seeing friends and catching up on the town gossip and news at the dive shop. Some of Moi's relatives worked for the small hotels on the beach road. We made sure to tell them Raquel was coming in three days' time and would be available to give massages for the guests. She had come up with the name "La Mesa Azul"—The Blue Table—for her business. Marie had made flyers and business cards and Moi's family was happy to hand them out as they had done in the past.

Moi was keeping himself rather busy these days with the new boat he had recently purchased. He had arrangements with dive shops in Tulum and Majahual to charter his boat. The dive shops supplied the divers with tanks and equipment, and Moi captained the boat and provided a divemaster to lead the dives. He had also started on an addition to his house. As he was walking us through the unfinished construction, he gave me a wink. I smiled back and lifted my rum and Coke to him, knowing full well how the addition was being funded.

Carlos dropped by our house a couple of days later. He had been contacted by regular customers of the dive shop, Pancho and

Adriana, whom I had taken on private dive trips for the past few years. They were also massage clients of Raquel's. Carlos thought I might be interested in getting back in the water. He could not have been more right. Raquel was due in the following day, and Adriana and Pancho were coming the day after that. ¡Perfecto! Marie was excited to hear they were coming. They were more like friends than clients, and while they were in town we would join them for dinner at their rented beach house or at Leaky Palapa, an absolute treasure in our little village. Adriana, a professional food critic and chef, was particularly impressed with the restaurant, and agreed with the description offered by a popular tourist magazine: "A five-star restaurant providing gourmet cuisine in a tropical setting that serves fine foods like grilled octopus, wild mushroom–stuffed ravioli, fresh lobster, grouper, and a steak I could have become addicted to." At the end of their stay, Pancho and Adriana always insisted on giving us any supplies they had brought and didn't want to waste. That was where my Weber grill came from. They were also very generous tippers. I was excited for the opportunity to get my feet wet again.

Raquel flew into Cancún the following day and caught the bus to Carrillo Puerto. Marie and I made the two-hour drive northwest of Xcalak and met her in the plaza next to the bus station. The three of us found a bench in the shade after buying lunch from a lady selling her homemade dishes. We enjoyed our reunion in the heart of the plaza, with its towering royal palms. Across from us was a beautiful old mission church, Parroquia de la Santa Cruz, built in the 1700s. It was made of stone, stood no less than thirty-five feet tall, and was designed to protect the citizens of the town if under attack. The sides of the church were lined with tiny windows from which to shoot guns. I called it a fortress church. The front of the church that faced the plaza had been restored, and the old stone was covered with pretty stucco, dark tan in color, with double-arched wooden doors. The rest of the building remained true to its original build, and the stone had weathered to several shades of gray, which we thought was more beautiful than the stucco front facade. As we walked around the plaza, I couldn't help but think how good it felt for the three of us to be together in Mexico once again. I walked beside my girls, feeling very proud to be the husband and father of two incredibly resilient women. We all had suffered great loss in our family, and I was proud of how we persevered. I wrapped my arms around their shoulders and pulled them in to me for a big squeeze and a kiss on the head. It was going to be a great season.

Following a celebratory dinner at Leaky Palapa, we visited with Linda and Marla. Marie decided to make a standing reservation for 6 P.M. every Saturday. At first the girls and Raquel thought she was kidding, but she wasn't. Marie reasoned that all we seemed to do was work at the dive shop while in Mexico, so this year she was just going to lay out, visit friends, relax, appreciate life, and enjoy herself. Besides, she could never get enough of Marla's grilled scallops in cream sauce. The reservation was set.

The next morning, I met up with Adriana and Pancho at the dive shop. Adriana is a beautiful woman who looks like a Mexican Barbie doll with flowing, coal-black hair, wide hips, and tiny waist. A local celebrity with a cooking show in Guadalajara, she is very successful in her own right. She is married to Pancho, a television producer. The two are as nice as any couple we had ever met. They were both certified divers, so I was more of a guide for them than an instructor. We made two dives a day for five consecutive days, one midmorning and another in the early afternoon. Pancho was an avid photographer, always taking pictures above and below the water. Adriana also enjoyed photography. The dive I remember most was at Poza Rica. Adriana and I were pivoting on the sand bottom about fifty feet down. She was trying to capture a picture of a sailfin blenny as it popped in and out of its home, an old wormhole in a dead piece of coral nestled in the sand. She wanted to catch the blenny right at the moment its dorsal fin was extended. One advantage of a private dive is there's no rush—you can take your time and get your shot. When I looked up to check on Pancho, he was waving and pointing in the direction of a huge loggerhead turtle slowly making its way toward us. The visibility was picture perfect, a hundred feet plus. I touched Adriana's arm to get her attention. When she spotted the turtle, she headed straight for it with her camera aiming forward at it. As she approached him, he casually circled around her and swam in my direction. Within moments I found myself, quite literally, eye to eye, nose to beak with the very inquisitive reptile. We just stared at each other, hovering in the water. I had seen many loggerheads but had never encountered one so up close and personal like that guy. I am certain there was an uncontrollable smile on my face. After a few seconds and with one thrust of his flippers, he rocketed past my head and into the deep blue waters away from the reef. The encounter may have lasted only seconds, but the memory would last forever, especially since Pancho filmed the entire event.

I learned a few things about myself during the time I spent with Adriana and Pancho. I had no idea how much I had missed diving until I was in deep waters again. For the past several years in Xcalak, I had been in the water all the time, almost daily if I chose to be. Now it was more of a luxury. It wasn't just being able to dive again. It was "me time." It had been so long since I did not have to put some-one else's needs before my own. It was a great relief to have the time away, if only for a few hours each day, and knowing that Marie was being taken care of by Raquel allowed me to fully enjoy myself. I was in my element in the waters. The feeling of being submerged and surrounded by God's handiwork cannot truly be explained by words or captured by photography. It is indescribable to be in the presence of unique creatures and coral of every size, shape, and shade of color. I loved my wife more than I could ever put into words, but I needed a little time to nurture Gene and take care of myself. Time to myself made me a happier person and a better husband and dad.

Marie was hearing from people in town that the dive shop didn't have the same ambiance without her. It tore at her. She struggled with the fact that she might never run the shop again. "That shop was my baby," she would tell me, distraught, with tears falling down her face. I tried to console her and told her to let it go for now and to concentrate on regaining her strength. Carlos did want her back at the shop, but there was no way she could have physically handled it. But I didn't say those words to her. I just told her that next season Carlos would be begging for her to come back. I was hoping she had more faith in my words than I did.

Marie also told me that although Raquel did a fine job helping her out during my five days with Adriana and Pancho, she just wasn't me. No one knew Marie like I did. I knew what she needed and had it ready before she thought about it, whether it was her meds, finger sticks to check her sugar levels, food, or hot tea. I spoiled her that way. Truthfully, Raquel had done an excellent job caring for her mom, and she was already seeing some massage clients. She had done very well for herself with her little business the previous year before making our hasty trip back home to St. Louis. There was at least one hotel that promoted Raquel's massage service as one of the amenities they offered to their guests. As the weeks passed, she saw clients on a regular basis. She came home and had dinner with us, then we all sat around talking, or playing Farkle (the best dice game ever), or watching a movie. We had at least a thousand movies burned on DVDs. The TV was in our bedroom, so when we watched a movie, we all just piled on the bed. Marie was in the middle and was usually the first to nod off. These nights reminded me of when Raquel was younger and always in our bed. I usually slept on the couch downstairs with Andrew while Raquel slept with Marie. Even if I did get to sleep in my own bed, Raquel still slept with us.

A daily event for Marie and me was planning a family dinner. Of course, I would cook and Marie would instruct me, except on Saturday nights when we made our weekly trip to Leaky Palapa per Marie's standing reservation. The Palapa was no cheap place to dine and was typically for special occasions. It was nice having a cushion in the safe on the floor of the bathroom closet, where I could lay my head down and sleep better, figuratively speaking. I was a little surprised when Marie made the weekly reservation, but I supposed she too felt the comfort of our stash in the safe.

Raquel asked once when we were dining at the girls' restaurant, "How can we afford to eat at the Palapa every week? Did we win the lottery and my cruel parents aren't telling me to teach me some life lesson about hard work and character building?"

Her mother's response was priceless. "First of all, my child, if I bought the ticket, there would be no 'we' won the lottery, and your father and I have decided that since you're earning decent money this winter, you're gonna start buying." No such conversation had ever taken place between Marie and me, but the statement was priceless because Raquel shut up and dropped the subject. It was not very often one could shut Raquel up so quickly.

The wound across Marie's big toe had more or less healed. The skin was tough and leathery where the abrasion had occurred, but the surrounding area was the problem. It was very hard, dark, and thick like a callus. In my opinion, it was dying skin. People with neuropathy suffer from poor blood flow in their farthest extremities, which is why diabetics often lose toes and fingers. It is also the reason why I massaged Marie's hands and feet daily. Marie and I were afraid of infection and the end of the toe rotting off, so she started taking an antibiotic, which she always had available for us in Mexico if we became ill. She had me cut the hard surface of her toe away with a razor blade until it began to dribble blood. The premise was to get rid of the dying tissue and hope the blood flow would stimulate circulation. It made sense at the time. Marie was trying to come to terms with losing the toe. She knew the moment the doctor made that horrid mistake that the probability of losing it was real. We both did. Losing the toe was not what was worrying her so much. It was the drugs from the treatments that were the hardest to take. She told me that if there was no pain or infection, we were staying in Mexico until our planned trip back to St. Louis the first of May. I agreed to shave away the top of the toe for her and watch closely for any expansion of the site. It was a weekly procedure and one I never enjoyed.

I was checking the fluids and preparing the van for the trip home and slowly cleaning and closing the house for the summer. The mood was positive. The past few months were about healing, both physically and mentally, and I think we accomplished that. We spent much-needed quality time together as a family. I was really going to miss those weekly dinners at Leaky Palapa and was sad to see the visit to our cherished Xcalak come to an end. Of course, the unspoken question we both had in our minds was, What would the doctors have to say about the toe?

Chapter Six

ROAD TRIP NORTH

In the early morning hours of May 1, I was loading the van with the last of the supplies we needed for our trip back to St. Louis. We had our milk crate filled with toiletries, the cooler packed with snacks and drinks, duffle bags stuffed with clothes, the litter box and cat food piled in back. I had a couple ounces of pot in an airtight container behind some books in the overhead cabinet above the driver's seat. I kept a one-hitter in my pocket. Between the front seats was Marie's red backpack. We also had several pillows and blankets and the iPod. We were set. After loading the cats, I helped Marie into the van. We had decided to keep her legs elevated for the majority of the trip, so I supported her legs with extra pillows and covered her with a blanket. Her captain's chair was slightly reclined, and I must say, she did look comfortable.

Raquel had no desire to be on the road with her mom and dad and three cats for a week, which really did not hurt my feelings. When Raquel and her mom would have a mother-daughter "moment," it was usually easy for me to walk away and stay out of it. However, if it happened during a long road trip, well, that could stink up the environment quite quickly, and no way out for me. We dropped Raquel off at Carrillo Puerto to catch the bus to the airport in Cancún for a five P.M. flight home to St. Louis, where Aunt Dart would pick her up. We said our goodbyes to Raquel and were off to Chetumal to see Sebastian the vet for the cats' requisite wellness papers.

It was early evening by the time we made our way across the dense jungle of the southern Yucatán to the waves breaking on the Bay of Campeche. We stopped in Sabancuy, a popular spot for food sold by street vendors. We loved that place. The only problem we faced was trying to make up our minds as to what to get. The smells hit us long before I had the van in park. It wasn't just the smells that intrigued us; the food was beautiful, so bright in color and unique in shape. Marie called it "sexy food." After visiting quite a few vendors, we would leave with entirely too much food and nibble on it for the next few hours. It was hard for me to resist the sugar cinnamon churros at times, but I usually did for Marie's sake. She loved them, but her diabetes forbade them.

We traveled south, hugging the coastline until we found a deserted stretch of beach. I pulled over, spread out a blanket, and laid out our smörgåsbord. We ate lazily in the sun, watching and listening to the waves beating the shore over and over again. We strolled the seashell-laden beach, picking up a few beauties to add to Marie's collection. We held each other and watched the glow of the sun descend toward the sea. Before making our way back to the van, we posed for a selfie with the waters as our backdrop. With the exception of our wedding photo, that is my favorite picture of Marie and me.

As we traveled, the scenery changed from an ocean view to that of tropical lowlands with fields of pineapple plants and banana trees. We spent the night in Córdoba at an auto hotel, where each room has its own garage and you pull your vehicle in, closing the garage door behind you. Inside the next door is your hotel room. Auto hotels are convenient places to stay when you travel with pets. I just opened the doors to the van and hotel room and let the cats stretch for a while. We ordered room service while Marie took advantage of the cable TV and watched a couple episodes of *House*. We were early to rise and on the road with granola bars and yogurt drinks from the cooler. From Córdoba, we drove up pine-covered mountains toward the city of Puebla. We stopped halfway for a proper morning meal at Buena Vista, a restaurant that's built off the side of the mountain, with tall pillars coming out of the mountainside supporting the structure. We stood on the deck of the restaurant that morning, looking down at the clouds below.

"That's a view one doesn't see very often," she said, and I agreed.

After breakfast, we continued our journey up the mountains to the city of Puebla. Until now we had reached several checkpoints and were waved through. I had to exit the van at the military checkpoint past Puebla and was asked our destination. The soldier seemed satisfied when I told him we were headed to Santa Maria del Rio, and I rejoined Marie, who was allowed to remain in the van. Just beyond the military stop we jumped onto the Arco Norte Highway that led us around Mexico City. We stopped in Santa Maria del Rio and shopped for pottery. Marie found a statue she fell in love with that was soon to adorn Andrew's grave. We made our way to Saltillo and checked into an auto hotel called The Oasis. The cats were enjoyable to watch as they explored the hotel rooms. At least they were entertaining to me. Marie seemed quiet and aloof. I assumed she was just a little tired from traveling, but I was wrong.

Marie had a rough time sleeping that night and no appetite in the morning. We were a couple of hours outside of Saltillo and a short distance from the border when she mentioned her toe was hurting. The pain was controlled with a pain pill, but after a couple of hours on the other side of the border, it began to throb. She told me not to make a big deal about it since we were heading home. If the pain became too much, she would let me know. I tried to tell myself that maybe it was just the neuropathy and not actually her big toe. She sometimes experienced reflective pain, where discomfort is felt in a location other than the actual source of the pain. I was hoping this was the case. I had her lift her leg in my direction and rest it across the middle console between the seats. I rubbed up and down her lower leg and massaged her foot while I drove. I made a mental note to give her a nice rubdown that night.

We had planned to stop and visit Becky in San Antonio for a couple of days, and we made it to her house by six. Marie gave Becky a call when we were a few blocks away. As we turned down her street, Becky opened the garage door, and we pulled straight in. She closed the door behind us and greeted us at the van.

"Well, look at you!" Becky said, gesturing to Marie's pyramid of pillows. "You look like a queen on her throne." Becky opened the van door and put her arms around Marie's neck.

"Hey, I've earned this throne," Marie said. "It is quite cozy."

Becky helped Marie into the house. I carried our duffle bag and Marie's red backpack upstairs to the spare bedroom. Marie was hungry, which I was happy to hear, so we took Becky out to her favorite place, House of Sushi.

"I cannot believe how much better you look than you did a few months ago. You look great, and I'm not just talking about that killer tan, you bitch!" Becky gave her a wink and a smile and continued. "I'm very serious, my friend. You look so much healthier."

"Thank you. I rested up, totally relaxed and recouped, thanks to this guy," said Marie, gesturing to me. "However—"

"However, what? What happened now?" Becky asked while helping herself to another piece of sushi.

"At my last podiatrist appointment in December, the doctor accidentally shaved off the top of my big toe, and we've been dealing with that all winter long," Marie started to explain. I was surprised that this was the first time she had mentioned it to Becky, but knowing Becky, she would have objected to Marie going down to Xcalak, given her recent history with infections.

Becky put her hand over her mouth in disbelief while trying to choke down that last bite of tuna roll. Shaking her head, Becky asked, "What do you mean 'dealing with it'?"

Marie explained how we were treating the toe through the winter, which got a little graphic for Becky.

"Stop!" she said with her eyes closed and the palm of her hand toward Marie. "What did the podiatrist say after he shaved your toe?"

"He said he was sorry."

"What do you think is going to happen?"

"I think they're gonna cut my toe off," said Marie, which was rather blunt, but she was speaking truthfully.

I offered my two cents. "Her toe hasn't gotten any worse, although it hasn't gotten any better either. It truly has not bothered her the past few months until now. She has doctor appointments scheduled in a couple of weeks, so we'll see what they have to say then. In the meantime, there's other news we have, but let's get out of here and we'll fill you in at your house."

"You guys are killing me," she said.

It wasn't until we made it back to Becky's house that Marie started telling her about the treasure we were sitting on. It was the first time in seven months we had discussed it with someone other than Moi. Once Marie started talking, there was no holding her back. She was busting at the seams to finally tell someone, namely Becky, about the coke.

"Holy shit! Are you guys serious? You found coke floating in the water seven months ago?" Looking directly at Marie, Becky leaned across the kitchen table and said to her, "How were you able to keep that to yourself?" I often wondered that myself. She stood up and exclaimed, "I need a glass of wine. Any takers?"

"I'll join you." I didn't want to be rude. I made a hot tea for Marie, then ran up the steps for the one-hitter at her request. For the next hour, we sat in the living room and sipped at our drinks, telling Becky how Moi sold a couple of kilos for us. For the next hour, it was Q and A time, though we never disclosed how much coke we actually had. Jokingly, Becky said we should bring some to Texas because Laura, her business partner, and Laura's boyfriend belonged to a swingers club, and there was always coke available at their parties. As soon as I heard it come out of Becky's mouth, I looked at Marie just in time to watch her eyebrows raise with intrigue.

I wanted to say, "Do we possibly have a connection to sell the coke?" Instead, I asked, "How many are usually at these parties?"

"From what I've heard, it's a very exclusive club, anywhere from twenty-five to a hundred people—the majority of them very wealthy," she answered. I didn't understand the choice of lifestyle, but hey, whatever makes them happy. I was liking these people the more she talked: rich and cokeheads. I stored the info in my long-term memory, knowing if we could sell the coke in the States, we could possibly triple or quadruple our profit. Becky knew of our desire to buy Mark's house. If we could sell the treasure, we would use the money to do just that.

Before we turned in that night, and while Marie was in the bathroom, Becky asked me how serious the toe was. All I said to her was, "It doesn't look bad, but it could get bad very quickly."

"Is there a real possibility she may lose it?"

I nodded, lowered my head, and said, "Absolutely."

She just winced a little and shook her head from side to side. "God, Gene. How much more can she take?" That was getting to be a very popular question. There was nothing like having a front row seat to such a horrible show.

As Marie took another pill before climbing into bed, I asked how bad the pain was. She replied with her typical answer: "It's not that bad." Hmm. I was at 70 percent disbelief, but 100 percent wanted it to be true. I knew the truth when she woke up in the middle of the night needing another pill.

Our plan for the following day was to check out Becky's new antique store. The store had been her dream for years. I'd often teased her that what some people considered antiques, others called junk. After cleaning the litter box and reloading the van, we went out for breakfast, then followed Becky to her store. The outside of the store was stylishly trimmed in reclaimed barn wood. Half the store was set up with individual booths that were rented out, the other half with antiques Becky and Laura had purchased at estate sales or online. I walked to the middle of the store and held out my right arm.

"So, Becky, on this side you sell your junk, and on this side"—I raised my other arm—"you sell someone else's junk?"

"Gene! You're gonna get such a punch in the gut," she teased back, lowering her voice as she walked past me and said, "Asshole." She turned to Marie and asked, "Tell me again why you married this guy?"

We made our way outside and we told Becky how nice the store was and how happy we were for her. She turned around and looked at the storefront and replied, "Yeah. It's been a long time coming. It's exactly what I want to be doing." She hugged Marie for quite a while and told her to phone when we made it home. I helped Marie into the van and gave Becky a big hug. She knew why we had cut our visit short and made me promise to call if anything happened. I gave her a kiss and pulled out of the parking lot. In my side mirror, I watched her stand in front of her shop, one hand in her front pocket and one in the air still waving goodbye.

Chapter Seven

MARIE'S SECOND AMPUTATION

I had been looking forward to taking our time getting home, but now I wanted to get back ASAP. We drove sixteen hours straight through to St. Louis. We had Marie's standard doctor appointments in a couple of weeks, but we decided to move up the appointment for the orthopedic surgeon, Dr. Luden. Marie started making calls from the road. The soonest they could see us was in four days. Not good enough. She called the infectious disease doctor. Same response. So Marie called Gloria, her kidney transplant liaison, and explained how her pain was worsening with every mile marker. Gloria had to speak with a doctor, and when she called back in ten minutes' time, she told Marie to head straight to University Hospital first thing in the morning and be prepared to be admitted. Marie repeated Gloria's words as she spoke them. I felt the blood run out of my face. When Marie hung up the phone, she started to cry. I grabbed her hand and kissed it. I tried to find something comforting to say. I was at a loss for words.

"This should never have happened, Gene." Still crying, she gestured to her foot up on the dash. "It was a doctor that did this to me! What did he say that day, Gene? Oh yeah. I remember—he was SORRY! Sorry, my ass. You know they're gonna cut off my toe. You know that's what's gonna happen. But as long as he's sorry!" She closed her eyes and laid her head against the headrest. "I'm just tired of being sick. I'm sick of being tired. I don't wanna go to the hospital. I just wanna go home, get the cats out of this van, and sleep in my own bed. Just take me home, Gene."

"We're on our way, baby. I'm not taking you anywhere else." I kissed her hand again.

"Fuckin' doctors," she said as she popped a couple of pills and tried to close her eyes for a while.

Neither one of us wanted to talk about the impending trip to the hospital. I do not know when she took it out of her backpack, maybe when I was pumping gas, but I noticed Marie was holding her Mayan bag with the rosary, Andrew's ashes, and her special stone. I was curious what was going through her head, but at the same time, maybe I didn't want to know. There were no words I could have said to ease her discomfort, and I was beyond sick and tired of seeing a family member suffer. I rubbed her shoulder a little and massaged down her arm and of course her hand and fingers. As I drove we listened to the songs on our iPod, and we pulled in the driveway a little before three in the morning. I helped Marie upstairs, trying to keep the dogs from jumping on her. I returned to the van to set the cats free and grab a few perishables and left the rest of the supplies in the van until morning. I found Marie in bed with both dogs, and I fell in beside her. She woke up around seven in a lot of pain and in need of a pain pill. She also requested cornflakes with fresh blueberries and one Sweet'N Low. If she didn't eat when taking strong pain meds, she would be sick for certain.

Raquel and her mother had made a grocery list over the phone the day before, and the fridge was well stocked. I made myself a cup of coffee and Marie's bowl of cereal as well as hot tea with milk, put everything on a bed tray, and carried it into our bedroom. The house looked good and smelled of lemon-scented Lysol, compliments of Aunt Dart, I was willing to bet. I was about to put the tray across

Marie's lap when she said, "Let's eat outside." We've always kept a table and chairs on the upper deck off our bedroom, and it was a nice morning. We sat side by side overlooking our backyard. I nursed my coffee and watched what I guessed was a groundhog making its way through a hole in our fence into the woods. Note to self: repair hole in fence.

"When are we going to the hospital, Marie?"

"When we make it there," she said, which translated to I'm not in a hurry. I'm getting cleaned up and taking my time.

"That works. That'll give me time to unload the van." I stood up at the railing to better inspect the yard. Everything looked pretty decent. Depending on the outcome of the hospital visit, I could possibly get some yard work done, but if Marie had to be admitted, it meant I would be bringing her dinner every night at the hospital. She never ate hospital food. I asked her if she needed anything from the kitchen and started to head down the steps off the deck for another coffee. When my eyes were level with the deck, I glanced over and noticed our dogs, Pete and Max, under the table smelling Marie's foot. I didn't take that as a good sign at all.

It was about four in the afternoon when she finally conceded to going to the hospital. She was, indeed, admitted. The following day she would be visited by the kidney doctor, orthopedic surgeon, and infectious disease doctor. I referred to them as her Dream Team. Each doctor asked the same questions: How did the original abrasion happen? When did it happen? How have you been treating it? What have you been taking for pain? Each one of them said they would be in touch with each other, but what would probably happen was a toe amputation. There just was not enough circulation for it to heal properly. The only chance to stop any infection from occurring and for proper healing was to remove the toe.

The first phone call was to Dart to fill her in, and the second was to Raquel's cell phone. I left a message for her to call. Marie was started on antibiotics with an IV. Those antibiotics always made her so sick. She begged me to take her to the van in the parking garage so she could get high. It was the only thing that helped her nausea and anxiety. So I did. We found a wheelchair, and I pushed her and the IV to the van and let her do a couple of hits. I received a call from Raquel when we were outside. I told her about the surgery, but since there was not a time scheduled yet, to stay put and I would be in touch.

On our way back to the room Marie said to me, "How did we get through all of this, Gene? We've been dealing with this shit for how many years? I don't know how much more I wanna take. We've spent four months trying to save my toe and my first day home, they wanna cut it off. I know it was an accident, but it should never have happened. Andrew should never have had to die. I feel like a piñata sometimes. Every once in a while, life takes a whack at me. Ya know what I mean?"

"Hell yeah, I know what you mean. I can't stand this feeling of helplessness, knowing I can't do anything to take away your pain. If I could, I would. Actually, no—I'd take away this problem, give it to the doctor that caused it, and take you to Cozumel." She laughed a bit.

We were revisited that evening by the surgeon, Dr. Luden. He told us surgery was scheduled for eight the next morning. If all went well, Marie would be discharged in one to two days. Well, swell. That sounded like great fun! Sign us up. Dart and Genevieve stayed at the hospital that night. I didn't want to leave Marie, but since we had just returned from Mexico early that morning, I had to get things ready for her recovery at home. I had unloaded the van, but I had not un-packed or put anything away. I started going through some piled-up mail, threw in a load of laundry, and decided to just go to bed. I was exhausted, and tomorrow would be a long, long day. My phone was pretty busy that night with calls about Marie. My last conversation was with Becky before passing out.

When the alarm went off, I jumped up, took a five-minute shower, and told Raquel not to come down to the hospital until later that afternoon. There wouldn't be anything to do but wait around anyway. Surgery was anticipated to take about an hour, a couple of hours in recovery, then the inevitable waiting hour after endless hour for the next couple of days until we could get her back home. I hated hospitals. I felt the same about doctors. I didn't trust them. They didn't seem to care that the transfusions she had to endure made her deathly ill. The first thing they stuck in her arm was that same poison. At ninety-five pounds, she had never gained back all the weight she had lost last year from having that crap pumped into her. I was extremely concerned with how she would handle it this time. Why couldn't a doctor just say, "Those treatments seem to be a little too strong for you. Maybe give this one a try"? She was only forty-seven years old. I wanted to scream at any doctor who would listen, "Help her! Fix this! I'm begging you! These drugs are killing her! Don't you care?" I thought doctors were supposed to help us. I had deep-rooted mistrust in them, and my wife's life was in their hands . . . again. It was so hard for me to let them make life-altering decisions.

It was 7 A.M. when I walked into Marie's room. "Hi, baby," I said, and I hugged and kissed her. Dart updated me on Marie's condition while Genevieve worked on a crossword puzzle. I told Marie that Raquel wanted to come down, but I suggested she wait until this afternoon. Marie said, "Tell her to stay put and I'll see her tomorrow when I get home." She was determined. It wasn't long until a porter came to bring Marie to surgery. I left Dart and Genevieve in the room, and I went with Marie. I stayed by her side until she was taken to the operating room, and the doctor reassured me she would be fine, like that made me feel better. I caught up with Dart and her mom in the surgery waiting room on a different floor. I spotted a coffee machine on a table, poured myself a cup. I sank into a chair with a long exhale and sipped on my coffee. Genevieve and Dart sat on either side of me. Genevieve grabbed my free hand and Dart rubbed my shoulder. I didn't want pity or anybody to feel sorry for me. They were hurting just as much as I was. This was their daughter and sister. I felt badly for both of them as well. I think the worst thing anyone could experience in their lifetime is losing a child. I knew this firsthand. Marie might have been my wife, but she was Genevieve's child and she had already lost one child to complications from diabetes. Cathy had died fourteen years prior, at the age of fifty-four.

After surgery Marie was moved to the recovery room, and we were told we could see her within the hour. "Well, that's that," I said. We waited until the coast was clear for Marie to have visitors. The first thing I noticed when I saw her was the port back in her neck. Awake but groggy, she was in good spirits. I told her that Dr. Luden said everything had gone very well and she would possibly be leaving tomorrow.

"Did he cut the right toe off?" She was joking, of course. "And yes, I am leaving tomorrow." Genevieve and Dart left after they saw her. I stayed with her all day and into the evening. Raquel showed up around eight, to my surprise, and told me to go home. She said she would stay the night with her mom. I gave them both hugs and kisses before leaving. I had made all the customary phone calls earlier in the day from the hospital, and now I was alone with my thoughts, which were not always the best company. Being at the hospital often brought back a flood of memories of Andrew's stay. Not good memories at all. I couldn't stop those thoughts from flooding in. More than a couple of times, I wished I could just flip a switch in my brain and shut it all out. I never could find that switch.

I called Marie's room around seven the following morning to make sure all was OK. Raquel answered the phone and said her mom had a decent night. I asked to talk with her mom, who simply said, "Come and get me, baby." I smiled to myself a little, delighting in the way she called me baby. I was back in her room a little after eight. She was being discharged, just waiting for prescriptions, paperwork, and all the routine visits from her Dream Team of doctors. Marie wanted to leave so she could get high. She was still on the meds that made her so sick. We were instructed to make follow-up appointments for the following week. The nurse finally came in with the discharge papers and instructed me on how to change the bandage on Marie's toe. She told me to get Glad Press'n Seal plastic food wrap for when Marie wanted to take a shower. That was truly good information. I wish we would have known about that stuff when her finger was amputated. The daily antibiotic infusions were to start the following day. No rest for the weary. I pulled the van around to the front, and Marie was brought out in a wheelchair. After loading her in the van and before we were out of the parking lot, I gave her a couple of one-hits.

I had Marie home within forty minutes. Genevieve had spent the day before cooking all of Marie's favorites. She was a typical Sicilian woman and a great cook. She liked to start cooking dinner at eight in the morning. We could smell the food before we even made it to the door. I was starving; Marie was sick to her stomach. I carried her straight up to bed then returned downstairs to make her some tea. I told Genevieve that Marie was pretty sick from the antibiotics, the same crap she was on before.

"Don't tell me she has to go to the emergency room every day again." Genevieve sounded irritated.

I just nodded and said, "Starting tomorrow."

"That stuff is gonna kill her!" She snatched a plastic bowl and headed to the backyard. She was going to make Cicoria. It was an old family recipe. She would cook the greens of the dandelions and make a broth, add a little salt and pepper, a little garlic, and a drizzle of olive oil. It was not long before she showed up in our bedroom with a bowl of Cicoria for Marie. I couldn't stomach it, but Marie always said it truly did help with the nausea. About an hour later, Genevieve came up with a cup of adad-do water, boiled water with bay leaf and sugar. Now, I have had adad-do water, and that works for an upset stomach. It gave Genevieve great joy to help care for Marie and cook for us, which was a real treat for me.

The following day we headed to the emergency room for the first of forty-two daily infusions. Marie took several hits before we arrived. It just seemed so many different kinds of wrong to be bringing her through an emergency room full of sick people, especially since she'd had her toe removed two days ago. Marie felt the same way, and on our way home she made a call to our primary doctor to see what he could suggest. Within hours he arranged for Marie to receive her infusions at St. Louis Cancer Care center. What an improvement! At the cancer center, she sat in a recliner and either gazed at the traffic on the highway below, watched TV, or listened to music with headphones. Each chair had its own television attached with a movable arm. We tried to make the appointment for the same time every day. We arrived around eight in the morning, and her meds would be waiting for her to receive them. She would sit in her chair, and a nurse would hook up the IV to the port in her neck while I sat in the waiting area reading *Missouri Conservation* and drinking coffee. The emphasis was not only on the patients being treated but also on their family members. These patients were battling life-threatening diseases, which absolutely do affect the entire family. The compassion we were given at the center made the situation much more tolerable.

<hr />

One afternoon when Marie was lying in bed back home, she couldn't seem to get her feet warm. I knew I had a couple pairs of thick wool socks somewhere in one of my drawers, so I started to dig. I came upon a clay pot I had made in junior high art class. It was about four inches tall and six inches in diameter, blue and yellow in color, with a matching lid. I had not seen it in years, and for some reason I pulled it out and opened it. Inside was a folded piece of paper, and it had my name doodled all over it: in cursive, in all caps, printed, and even written diagonally. I brought it over to the bed and showed Marie.

"Do you remember this?"

As soon as she saw it, she gasped a little and took it from my hand as if she had found a lost treasure. "Oh my God! Where did you get this!"

"Do you know when this was from?"

"I was hanging out at your parents' house writing on a piece of paper at the kitchen table while you were cooking," she said, enthused. "I even remember what you made—potatoes and onions with a fried egg on top. I was pretending to be there to meet your sister Cindy, but was really hoping to run into you."

"You're kiddin' me! Did you really?"

"Hell yeah! I knew Cindy was hanging out with her boyfriend. I cannot believe you kept this paper!" She held it directly in front of her face to see it. "I never knew you kept this."

"What can I say? I'm a romantic guy." I took it back from her and put it back where I found it. "I'm just a sentimental fool for you. I can't believe you remembered it."

"Gene, my eyes and my body may be breaking down, but my mind is as sharp as can be."

Marie had been home for a week and it was time to visit the Dream Team. Dr. Luden said that the toe looked great. It was healing well, and that we should keep doing what we were doing. Dr. Darwin was still not certain what the infection was, but was adamant about treating it with the antibiotics for an entire six-week cycle. He wrote a prescription for some pills that were useless for easing nausea.

The last couple weeks were the worst for Marie. Her weight had plummeted to an all-time low of eighty pounds. After each treatment, we would arrive home around ten o'clock, I'd carry her upstairs straight to the bathroom, and she would throw up. She wanted to quit the treatments. She thought they were killing her anyway. She begged me not to let her die that way. All I could say was that she was almost done. She used to say, "Let's get this over with," and out the door we would go. Now it was, "No more. I'm not going. I'm done." I would beg her to continue, pleading my case that I needed her to be with me and wanted the infection dead and gone. She would eventually give in.

As treatments progressed, the sicker Marie became, and the more Genevieve cooked. More times than not, the smells of food made Marie even queasier. But who was going to tell her elderly mother that? Not me. I was grateful for the help.

Marie's morale improved greatly after the treatments were over. Truth be told, so did mine. Typically, we would be in Mexico during the summer months, but since we were home, we decided to go to the Buschmanns' annual Fourth of July party. Although Marie was still weak, no one could be in a bad mood at that party. Mrs. Buschmann had hosted it for the past twenty-plus years, and although it almost happened once, it had never been rained out.

The Buschmann house holds many good memories for me of growing up. There's the hole in the fence that leads to the creek and the golf course. I remember when the city put up that eight-foot fence to stop people from getting on the course and playing golf for free; Jerry and I cut a hole in the fence. We needed access to go golf-ball hunting in the creek. I'm not sure how many times the city came back to repair that hole, but they finally gave up and left it alone.

The number of people in attendance at the party was somewhere between sixty and eighty, and many were old acquaintances we had not seen in years. They had badminton, washers, a piñata for the kids, a swimming pool, and the inevitable game of volleyball to the death—adults only. But the volleyball game did not start until all had gorged themselves on the obscene spread of food put out at this party. Barbecued pork steaks, burgers, grilled chicken, bratwursts, chicken and beef kabobs, and all the sides. It was the best time we'd had in many months, and even though I love my mother-in-law and appreciate her cooking, the food at this gathering was the best. After stuffing ourselves, we let the food settle for just a bit, then the volleyball commenced. Selection for teams was random; the only goal was to have an equal number of tall players on each team. Kids swam in the pool while the adults who did not play either sat back at the tables in the shade or pulled up lawn chairs by the "court," defined by lines painted on the grass. Marie had a cozy seat under a tent close by and was planted next to Mrs. Buschmann, deep in conversation. We played for a couple of hours. There was lot of razzing and teasing involved in the game.

"Jerry, I remember you being able to actually get up off the ground when you would jump. What happened?"

And maybe he would follow up with "Hey, that's funny, Gene. I can still kick your ass on the golf course!"

"Well if you did, that would be a first." Back and forth. During a short break in the volleyball game, the desserts were put out. There's always a choice of about eight to ten different desserts, but Terri, Jerry's sister, would insist it's all about her Peanut Butter Pie. I would not argue about the pie. After dessert, more volleyball, until someone decided the next game would be the last. I'm proud to say I was part of the winning team that year. Being at the party was uplifting for both Marie and me. Most of the guests did not know about Marie's recent surgery, and we didn't bring it up.

Chapter Eight

DÉJÀ FUCKING VU

Two days after the Fourth of July party, Marie and I were lying in bed, watching TV. I was massaging her hands and fingers with cocoa butter when I felt a little rough spot around the cuticle of the pinky on her left hand. I took a closer look, and there was a little leathery spot starting to form. Who knew what caused it. We would never know. I cleaned it with peroxide and colloidal silver in the bathroom sink. She made an appointment for the following week to see the surgeon.

"Let me just make a little prediction of what is going to happen. There will be another surgery, of course. But how much of the finger will be removed? Just the tip, the whole finger, maybe two. It's like déjà fucking vu."

"I know, baby. We'll get through it." I tried to be positive, but I was scared to death!

We met with Dr. Luden two days later and he confirmed what we already knew. There was to be another surgery, but before he could suggest a call to the infectious disease doctor, Marie made it abundantly clear that since she had just finished a six-week treatment and had a follow-up appointment three weeks out, she had no intention of speaking to him before then. The doctor seemed satisfied, and the following day the top of her pinky was removed to the first joint. She did great. She had no pain to speak of, it healed up very nicely, and she felt fine. We were truly optimistic, but also very cautious.

Marie continued to regain her strength and even gained a little bit of weight back. Her appetite was starting to return. She was maybe ninety pounds, but she was getting stronger. That was until we met with the infectious disease doctor. He was very perturbed that he was not contacted about the partial amputation of the finger and insisted she go back on the drugs to stop any other infection. He was arrogant and ignorant and irritated that the "Almighty Doctor" wasn't notified about the surgery. I wanted to knock him on his conceited ass, but Marie did it instead, figuratively speaking.

"Now look! This is my body that's being carved up, not yours! I can deal with losing a toe or a finger, but those drugs are killing me! I puke my guts up all day long for weeks on end on that shit! I'm skin and bones. Not you or anyone else will tell me what I *have* to do anymore! If this infection kills me, then it kills me. But I'd rather die from that than the shit you've been pumping into me! Unless you yourself have experienced the effects of that shit day after day and week after week, don't you dare stand there with your pompous attitude in judgment of me because you don't have clue fucking one!" I wanted to applaud. It was a beautiful thing to witness, and I wish I could have recorded it.

After a moment, the doctor leaned up against the counter. He actually sighed a little as if to collect his thoughts before speaking. "No. I have never experienced what you have, and I am deeply sorry if I upset you. What you and your husband have had to endure is unfair, and I will never fully understand what you're going through. But it is my job to get you healthy. To help you battle whatever this is. And unfortunately, the best drug to give you has some very harsh side effects. I'm at a loss for what else to do. What do you want to do?"

"Nothing. I'm done!"

"Marie. I can't let you do that. We've come this far together. I know you think the side effects are harming you, but in reality, the antibiotics could very well be keeping this infection from spreading more rapidly. It possibly would have traveled to your heart already and killed you if not for the antibiotics."

"If it's quick and painless, I'm for it. This is not the life I want to live anymore. Do you understand that?"

"I understand. Do you understand that as your doctor it is my job to help in whatever way I can?" He held his hand to his chest as he said it. Maybe he actually did care.

Marie the nurse easily agreed. "I understand that."

"Let's compromise here. How about a five-week series of treatments?"

Marie the patient strongly disagreed. "No. No fucking way!"

"OK. OK. Four weeks. Work with me here."

"Two weeks tops."

"Marie, there wouldn't be any point in doing the treatment for only two weeks."

Marie responded, "Three weeks. That is all I'm doing. Regardless of what happens from this point on, no more. You either find me another drug, or I find another doctor. Deal?"

"It's a deal." He smiled the first smile I had ever witnessed on his face, and they actually shook hands.

As we were walking out of his office, Marie said, "What did I say! Déjà fucking vu!" Treatment started the following day.

As soon as Genevieve found out about the recent "treaty agreement" between Marie and the doctor, she started her grocery list and began planning our weekly meals. We had our standard eight A.M. appointment at the center for treatment, then we headed home for the vomiting to commence by ten A.M. Our house smelled of marinara sauce and other tasty dishes, which was good for me, yet bad for Marie. Who was going tell Genevieve the smell of food made it worse, not better? This lady was doing all she could think of to help keep her child alive. No way was it going to be me who told her she could not cook anymore. No way.

After I carried Marie up to the bathroom, Genevieve was certain to follow with a cup of adad-do water, asking the same question: "How did it go?" I'm not sure why she asked me that every time, as if she expected a different answer. I usually responded, "The meds are just too strong." She would put her arm around my waist, and I'd put mine around her shoulder. We would stand outside the bathroom, offering each other support, feeling helpless.

The next morning, we were back at the center for more torture, but this day was different. On this day, we would meet a woman who would change our lives for the better. While Marie was receiving her infusion, the social worker with the St. Louis Cancer Care center noticed Marie and inquired about her condition. The nurse told her about the recent amputations and these daily treatments. The social worker, Barb, pulled up a seat next to Marie. Marie explained that this was her fourth round of antibiotics in a sixteen-month period and that the drugs made her sick for weeks. Barb asked why there wasn't an arrangement for her to receive the treatments at home since they were so difficult on her. We told her that the social worker at the hospital, whom I'd lovingly nicknamed the Amazon Woman, said treatments at home would not be covered with insurance, and it would cost us $3,000 a week. Barb was also informed and was shocked that the treatments at the hospital were through the ER.

"That's what we thought," Marie said, "so I contacted my primary doctor, and he made arrangements for me to come here." Barb told her to hang in there, she was going to make some inquiries; she asked Marie and me to meet her in her office after the treatment. So we did.

Barb told us that since Marie had both Medicare and Medicaid coverage, there would be no extra cost for her to have treatments at home. We were happy and pissed off at the same time. All along, we could have had the treatments at home. No surprise that once again we'd been given faulty information. Barb gave us the contact name and number for the nurse who would come to the house initially to get us set up. A carrier would arrive sometime that day with enough meds to last a week. Every week a carrier would come with more meds.

Marie was elated. She would not have to be dragged out of the house against her will anymore. She would say how much she would take, if any at all. What a blessing meeting Barb was to our lives.

That evening the carrier came to the door with a big box and a small cooler. I opened the cooler and found seven frozen packages. The poison came frozen and had to be thawed daily. Six went in the freezer; one went in the fridge. The big box contained an IV pole that snapped together, individual packages of tubing, and a log book. I knew all about the IV pole assembly and the tubing from the years of caring for Andrew. I had flashbacks of Andrew as I put the excess supplies in the cabinet below his counter in the kitchen. It was uncomfortably familiar.

Marie was still very nauseous, but there was a kind of happiness about her. She had already planned on weaning herself down and off the drugs long before the agreed-upon three weeks were up. I didn't blame her. The following morning a nurse came to the house to go over the supplies and tell us what we should write down in the log. We just let her talk and do her explanation like we hadn't heard it all before. She did not know we had treated our son for years with various treatments and, truth be told, probably had more knowledge than she did about some of the equipment we had to keep on hand. She flushed out the lines in Marie's port in her neck. There was no IV pump. That was new to me. The meds were designed to flow when a clip was released on the bag. The nurse stayed for the entire duration of the first at-home treatment. I was a little disappointed. It would have given me great satisfaction to have clipped that bag closed long before it was emptied.

The next day we started the infusions on our own with no supervision. It was empowering for Marie to be in control. Dart and I were the ones to set Marie up with her infusions. She opted to be in bed with one of her favorite movies playing for distraction and Andrew's blanket in her arms. For the first week, she received only 90 percent of the full treatment. She was still getting sick, but we often slowed down the flow, even stopped it, and then reconnected it later. It was all up to her and what she could tolerate. We started the following week with only three-fourths of a treatment, and we declined from there. By the end of week two, we gave her only half. By week three she did not want any more at all, so we just threw it away. Of course, the daily logs we kept always indicated that the complete infusion was given. There was another visit to Dr. Darwin, who told us again that he did not know what the infection was, and he was hoping for the best results. He made Marie promise to have him on the list to call if anything at all happened.

"Oh, you're on my list all right!" she told him. "Rest assured. You'll be on my list for a long, long time."

"Hey. I thought we were friends again! You just take good care of yourself and call me for anything."

I believe he had a newfound respect for Marie after she'd ripped his head off and handed it back to him on that glorious day. I was certain he wouldn't forget it. I knew I never would.

It was the beginning of October, and Marie was too weak to travel. We were alone at home, which was a rarity. We were sitting on our lower deck, smoking a little weed. What a nightmare this trip had been. We had decided to just stay in St. Louis until after our family Christmas party and then make our way back to Mexico. We had not discussed the treasure since we'd left Becky's. Now that we were forming a plan to make our escape again, we started to talk about what to do with the remaining ten kilos. Should we go through Moi again? We didn't want any more pesos. We guesstimated we could live off of what was in the safe for a couple of years in Mexico and were toying with the idea of bringing the coke across the border and selling it ourselves. Then one of us brought up the conversation we'd had with Becky regarding her partner and friend, Laura. Laura the swinger.

"I think I'll call Becky tonight," Marie said matter-of-factly. "I wonder how much Laura reveals to her about those parties. Becky said Laura claims there's always a pile of coke for anyone who wants it. You think that's true? Remember she said those people are fairly wealthy? If that's true, Gene, we may have a legitimate connection." There was a little burst of exuberance in her voice. "What time is it? Can you bring my phone out here?" I came back with her phone and a glass of water.

I dialed Becky for her and handed Marie the phone. "Hey, Becky. No, all is well." Small talk for ten minutes that I could not have cared less about. "Hey, you remember the treasure we're keeping down south? We were thinking about bringing it back home. To Texas." Marie was trying to communicate in code because someone could intercept the conversation. Very *Charlie's Angels* of her. I was amused.

"We're planning on leaving mid-December and hoping to stay with you for a few?" A pause, laughing, and something about being happy for Becky, store doing well, she's selling a lot of junk and other people's junk, blah, blah, blah . . . I tuned out and honestly don't remember Marie getting off the phone.

"Well, Gene," she said, sounding very pleased with herself. She said Laura's favorite hookup guy is the one who brings the coke to the party. "He's a real estate developer, but Laura's pretty certain he dabbles in coke sales, and he's loaded."

Wow. I thought they were just girl gabbing. They were actually communicating in code. "You exchanged all that information in that one phone call?"

"Yes." She rolled her eyes.

"Well. That impresses me, babe." I took a hit. "I've never been more attracted to you." We busted out laughing. Maybe we just needed a good laugh. It had been so long since we both felt the smallest sense of joy. We stopped, then started laughing again. It was infectious and spontaneous. She was so happy for a few minutes. Her eyes squinted shut as she belly-rolled forward, laughing. "So, we're leaving right after the second weekend in December?" I asked. Leaving right after the family holiday celebration was OK with me. We were in need of an escape. I wanted very much to mark the past five months as done and over. And I knew it always made Marie feel better when she had a tan. She said it made her look healthy even if she felt like shit. And we both hate being cold. So, like always, I waited.

Chapter Nine

WE VISIT MY PARENTS

Midway between Thanksgiving and Christmas, we visited my mom and dad in Steelville, Missouri, approximately ninety miles from our home in St. Louis. My parents had bought the property twenty-five years ago, and my dad built a house on it. At one time, he owned a few rental properties, and we rented one for several years. All was well with the living arrangements until I asked him to come by and ground the outlet in the living room. I had arrived at the hospital to see Andrew in the NICU and was told he was being released the following day. We had to have a grounded outlet for his equipment, and I called Dad to ask him to take care of it. He reluctantly agreed. I ran into him at the rental house late that evening after picking up Raquel from Genevieve's house. Raquel had fallen asleep in the car, and I carried her in and laid her in her crib. I walked past my dad, who was finishing up in the living room.

"You know, you coulda done this yourself, or at least gave me more notice. This is bullshit."

I remember the time of day, what I was wearing, and the look on his face, but mostly I remember the feeling that my ole man was an insensitive, incomprehensibly uncompassionate asshole of a human being.

"Are you being serious with me right now?" I was six feet away and could smell the beer on him.

"Yeah, I'm fuckin' serious. Who are you to tell me I gotta get this done in a day?"

I couldn't believe my fucking ears. "We were told today my six-month-old baby, who has lived at the hospital since birth, is being released tomorrow. His equipment will be delivered in the morning, and if there isn't a grounded outlet, he won't be released!" With every word, my voice grew in volume. "I called you within minutes of finding out myself!"

"You still could have taken care of this yourself."

I started counting off on my fingers. "Number one, I left here this morning at seven to drop Raquel off at Genevieve's. Number two, I went straight to the hospital for a few hours so Marie could get some sleep. Number three, I went to work. Number four, I picked up Raquel, and now it's almost eleven and I'm just getting home. You were just sittin' at your house when I called. You live a few miles away, and this is your house."

"Yeah. It is my house, and you didn't pay rent last month."

"What is wrong with you? My son, your grandson, is coming home tomorrow! Marie has been at the hospital since he was born. Down to one paycheck here, Dad! I've lived here for six years, and I've never missed a payment. You'll get your fuckin' money." As I turned to go check on Raquel, I said, "There's something seriously wrong with you. You're such an ass." And I left him standing at the door holding his tool box. When I came back, he was gone.

The ole man made one attempt to see my son, but didn't stay long. Andrew was in the NICU, and Dad walked in and said, "I can't stand to look at him with all those tubes comin' out of him," and walked out. These were the memories that came to mind while driving out to visit them on that day. I rarely saw my folks, which was fine with me.

It was midafternoon when Marie, Raquel, and I arrived in Steelville. As soon as I pulled in front of their house, I felt that familiar uneasy vibe. It was an anxiousness I felt when I was young, too scared to walk past him for fear of getting smacked. It had been years since my dad tried to lay a hand on me, but I would never turn my back toward him, literally speaking. I knew that was a feeling that would never leave me, even though he was dying from a lung disease, and I don't know what it was because I never asked. I could not have cared less.

So there we were having our annual awkward Christmas dinner with my parents. Two to three hours was about all I felt obligated to stay. Our conversations were forced and awkward. My dad had been sober for several years, but he would still say the most insensitive things. We made it through dinner, and before dessert he told a story about having worked for McDonnell Douglas and how there was a huge layoff of white people in 1968 just so the company could hire a "bunch of niggers." How he loved that word. He said it with such discontent and disgust. He went on to say how we could never understand how hard it was on him and the sacrifices that were made for us kids when he was laid off. How so many lives were ruined just for a bunch of niggers. I had my arms folded and resting on the table in front of me. I could not even look at his face. I couldn't believe he was telling me about responsibilities, hard times, and sacrifices. I could feel my face flush and my leg bouncing uncontrollably out of frustration. I would never understand how hard it is making sacrifices? Was he kidding me? There was no way this asshole was going to give me a lecture on what he had to give up for me.

Marie slipped her hand under the table and squeezed my leg to stop the bouncing. She lowered her head to mine for a second. I said to her in a hushed voice, "We're leaving." What I wanted to do was get up, knock him to the ground, stand over him, and scream at him like he did to me when I was small. I wanted to tell him that he knew nothing about sacrifice and to stop the bullshit about being a supportive dad when he would spend his unemployment checks at the bar. I could search the archives of my memories and not come up with one good one with that man. I wanted him to start to stand up so I could lay him out with one punch he would never see coming. But I just stood up and said that we had to get home. Sometimes I would lie about Marie having to take meds at a certain time of night as an excuse to leave. This time I made no excuse. We left before dessert.

When we got in the van, I turned to Marie and said, "This was the last time. That man is not my family, and to sit with him, listening to how hard he had it, is like drinking arsenic. I don't care if that was the last time I lay my eyes on him."

It may have sounded harsh, but it was certainly how I felt. We hid nothing from Raquel and she knew what an abusive man he was. As we drove, I shared a story with her that happened when I was in high school.

"I was on the track team and I qualified for regionals. My event was the mile race." I turned to look at Raquel in the backseat to see if she was listening. She was. "I was one of twenty runners on the track from all different high schools around the St. Louis area. The race was at Ritenour High, my school. It seemed like thousands of people were there. I had never seen the stands that packed before."

Marie chimed in, "I remember your sister telling me about it."

"It was my junior year, and the top three runners would qualify for state. I didn't know if I had it in me to win, but I thought I had a pretty good shot at qualifying." I gave another quick look to Raquel, who was still listening. "From the start of the race I just poured it on, pumping my arms and legs as hard and as fast as I could go. The race was four laps, and right from the start a guy had taken the lead, and I was about a stride behind and tied with another guy. The last two hundred yards, I swear my arms and legs were numb. The first runner, the state champion from the previous year, crossed the finish line about two full strides in front of me. The second-place runner beat me by one tenth of a second. I ran that mile in four minutes, twenty-three seconds—the fastest mile I ever ran."

"I didn't know you went to state, Dad!"

"Well, I did. All kinds of people started rushing onto the track. One of the first ones was my coach, congratulating me on my time. I was breathing hard and just trying to catch my breath when from behind my coach I heard my dad making his way toward me. He pushed his way through the people and stood in my face and yelled, 'Do you have any idea what you just did? You just embarrassed me in front of my friends! You just lost to a nigger!' He was loaded drunk. I looked around at the people watching him make a complete fool of himself and me as well, and I just walked away from him and headed to the locker room."

I'm sure there were many people that congratulated me on my race, but that's not what I remember about that day. The first eighteen years of my life are littered with stories like that.

"I'm sorry, Dad. But don't feel like you have to explain yourself to me. I understand. There's no way I could ever relate. I don't recall ever getting a spanking from you guys."

"Raquel, your father wouldn't allow it. Not even a tap on your diapered behind."

"Is that true? Dang! I wish I would have known that growing up . . ."

To which her mother joked, "It's never too late to start, little girl."

It was true, though. When Raquel was three, her mother was disciplining her for something so insignificant that I cannot recall anymore, but Marie gave her a little slap on her hand. I just reacted. I overreacted. I scooped up Raquel as if to protect her from a vicious attack and told Marie that we would never hit our children, a tap on the hand or otherwise, and we never did. I was typically the one to follow Marie's lead in many aspects of our lives, but this was the one thing I was adamant about, and she knew it.

"How did you do at State, Dad?"

"I blew it. I was near the back of the pack."

"Still really cool that you qualified, though."

"It was cool. Thanks, little girl."

After my dad made that horrendous scene on the track, my spirit was crushed. When I ran for state, I did not have the focus, and I knew it. To run well, I had to be mentally and physically connected. A writer won't write well, a painter can't paint, and an athlete will have an off day if his or her mind is not in the game. Running was something I was good at, and it was mine, and he ruined it for me.

My mother was at the regional race where my ole man made such an ass of himself, and she was also at state. She said to me, "I don't understand how you could do so well one week and lose so badly the next."

"Might have something to do with your piece-of-shit husband ruining my life. Thanks for the pep talk, Mom."

I would have liked to have told her to take another "nerve pill," but I didn't. It amazed me how my family would overlook my ole man's behavior like it never happened. I could not have anything in my life that he didn't destroy. My senior year, I just shut down. I started partying and smoking weed and selling joints at school on the days I didn't skip. One afternoon, Dad came home drunk and picked a fight with me, and I fought back. I fought back hard. The fight started in the kitchen, but we tumbled through the living room and wound up in a bedroom. I had him pinned on the floor and I told him I'd let him up if he would stop. When he agreed I released him. I was walking out of the bedroom when he got up and tried to kick me, so I grabbed his leg and flipped him over the bed. I heard the pop and knew I broke his leg. I went out the front door with no regrets. I spent that night at the Buschmanns', and the next day with Mom and Dad still at the hospital, I went home and gathered some clothes and moved in with a friend from school and his mother. My dad never touched me again.

Getting together with members of my family might be unpleasant, but we enjoyed our holiday celebration with Marie's side of the family immensely. When this family got together, it was an actual party, a real celebration and not a group of people that felt obligated to get together because they are related. We ate all day, had the best wines, mixed drinks, and alcoholic or nonalcoholic slushes. As always, a steady flow of guests gathered throughout the day and into the night. I had such a feeling of thankfulness that holiday season. I hugged every person at the party and let them know how grateful I was to have them in our lives. This was my family. They were the ones I loved and who loved me in return. That year we had almost lost Marie, and we all knew it, whether it was said aloud or not. I was so thankful for her and to anyone who'd helped us through her medical emergencies. She was still here with us, visiting and embracing our family and friends who came through our door that day. She boasted about her spa appointment scheduled for the following Monday, the annual Christmas gift from Raquel to her mother, and teased everyone, saying, "I'll be thinking of all of you when I'm laying out in Mexico next week while you're all freezing your asses off." She left them with an open invitation to visit us.

Chapter Ten

ROAD TRIP SOUTH

Three days had passed since the Christmas party, and we were ready for the road trip back to Xcalak. Marie enjoyed her day at the spa just prior to our departure and said she felt like a new woman. She read off her list of what to bring for the trip, and I retrieved the items and packed the van. I made sandwiches with the spiral ham left over from the party and put them in the cooler. I also picked out my favorite Italian cookies Genevieve made for the party, but left some at the house for Raquel. Marie had her travel log notebook, her red backpack, the iPod, extra blankets (including Andrew's blanket), and easy access to the cooler. She was reclined in her seat with pillows propping up her legs and her feet on the dash. She could easily sleep if she wanted to, and as long as she was comfortable, I could drive forever.

If Marie was awake, we were talking about the possibility of a buyer for the treasure. Marie was a cautious person and she was very intelligent. We thought of several situations that could occur if we made the decision to bring the drugs across the border, and we played through many scenarios. Every emergency with Marie was very costly for us. There was no savings to speak of. We had Marie's disability check. That money would stop coming in the event of Marie's death. We weren't thinking of huge riches; we were thinking of a cushion. It would be great to be able to pay off our house. Could we also buy Mark's house in Xcalak, build the rental units below, live in Mexico, and work for ourselves? Raquel could live in the house in St. Louis. We would have a home in both places and visit back and forth. It was a nice dream, and we were thinking that the contents of the cistern could very possibly make that dream a reality.

It had crossed my mind hundreds of times what I was going to do for money if and when Marie passed. I used to deliver medical supplies to people at their homes in Missouri and southern Illinois. I worked for the company for fifteen years and had to stop driving when Andrew was born to stay close to home. I moved to the ware-house and unloaded trucks and put away inventory. What skills did I have to get a decent job, and how could a fifty-three-year-old man unload trucks for a living? I've always been a fairly fit guy, and all those years of diving helped keep me in pretty good shape, but un-loading trucks again was not gonna happen. Let's be real.

The first night on the road, we slept in a Walmart parking lot in Texarkana, Arkansas. From there we drove another six hours to visit Mark, our friend and the owner of our house in Xcalak. He and his wife, Stacy, had a beautiful home. It was about three times the size of our 2,300-square-foot house in St. Louis. He'd bought the house in Xcalak as a second home to have in a tropical area. His wife disliked our little village, but Mark had been building a huge casa on the waters of the Caribe that were much more suited to Stacy's style of living. It was a magnificent three-story stucco home—three bedrooms on the second floor and one huge master bedroom on the top floor that opened up to the Caribbean.

Mark had had a heart condition for as long as I had known him. While working on the house in Mexico, he became very run down and quite sick. He took a six-month hiatus from construc-tion and went home to recuperate. When he returned, he learned that the Mexican government had built the Zaragoza Canal from the sea to Chetumal Bay, supposedly to assist with border patrol. I don't know how that turned out, but the peninsula Mark had built this dream house on had become an island. Living in Mexico or any foreign land can be quite different from living in the United States. If it is to benefit the government, there is no need to contact homeowners to let them know they may want to trade their car in for a boat because that would soon be the only way to get to their home. He was screwed. Legally there was nothing he could do. Quite a distance offshore the house appears very beautiful and grand. Up close, it's a hot unfinished mess.

Mark knew as long as Marie and I were in his house in Xcalak it would be well taken care of. He was hoping to sell it, and we were hoping to buy it. He knew the situation we were constantly battling with Marie's health, and he was more than sympathetic. We always made improvements to the house, too. If something needed to be fixed, I would fix it. It was clean, painted in vibrant Caribbean colors Marie and I picked out. The sand in the yard was always free of weeds. We had built a deck overlooking the property. It was and still is a nice place. When we were kids and played kick-the-can or some other game, as long as you were on, in, or touching base, you were safe. To me and Marie, that house was our base. It was the place to go to let the stresses fade away. Both of us were in need of a good, long, stress-free stay.

We went out to dinner that night with Mark and Stacy and caught up on everyone's lives. Of course, the majority of the discussions were about the recent surgeries. Like a pro, Marie downgraded their severity; talking about the amputations often made others uncomfortable. She was thoughtful that way, and she was sick of talking about it as well as thinking about it. After breakfast the following morning, we said our goodbyes and told them we were planning to stay in Mexico until May. Unless they happened to come down to Xcalak, which we knew was highly unlikely, we would hopefully see them on our return trip back home. I put Marie in the van and piled the pillows under her legs while Mark looked on. He told her that her travel setup was pretty sweet. It truly was. He walked me to my side of the van, patting me on the back, and told me to hang in there and also to let him know of anything newsworthy in Mexico. I just responded with a "Will do," knowing full well there was no way in hell he would ever be told of the coke we were hiding in the bodega. Next stop, Becky's.

It was an eight-hour drive to Becky's house. During Marie's last conversation with her, they discussed a possible plan to have dinner with Laura. I had never known anybody who was a swinger before. Well, I take that back. Maybe I did know someone who was a swinger, and I just did not know that part of his or her life. I myself could never embrace the idea of my wife being sexually active with another man, let alone me having sex with another woman. But whatever makes people happy, and whatever makes it work. We had a contact for a possible buyer and could not have cared less who was doing whom. It seemed like a lifetime had passed since we initially found the coke. We never spoke of it while Marie was recouping from her finger surgery, and now that we had, it was almost all I could think about. But how did one actually find out the value of a kilo of coke? Google it? I wasn't sure. In my mind I had an idea of maybe $200,000 for all ten kilos. But it was a ballpark number. Bigger payoff, bigger risks for selling it in the States. I asked myself, "¿Tienes los huevos? Do you have the balls?" We were about to find out.

"Marie. We haven't done anything to get busted for any reason as of yet. We have to think one thousand percent seriously about this."

"Yeah. If we get caught, what are they gonna do to me?" she joked. I looked over at her just to make sure she had a smirk on her face. She did.

"OK. You'll be fine. But what happens to Gene?" I asked.

"I don't know. Sucks to be you."

"That's funny. Not hilarious, but funny."

"In all seriousness, Gene, we have brought weed across the border every time we crossed. We've smuggled plants back home, medication, solar panels, guns—" As soon as I heard the word gun, I shot a look at her. Ten years ago, when Bruce hired me to drive his mother from Wisconsin to Xcalak, hidden amongst her belongings and unbeknownst to me were four guns, a very serious offense in Mexico. Before I could say anything, Marie continued. "I know, I know! You didn't know it was packed in the trailer, but here's my point, because I have one: we have carried something across illegally every single time whether we knew it or not. So let's do it!"

"Marie, they're not gonna throw my ass in jail for a little weed for personal use. I mean, this is a lifetime in big-boy prison if I get caught . . . we're months from having to make any decision yet. I'm not saying yes, but I'm not saying no either."

"Just think about what I said."

"I'm not an idiot. I know what we've traveled with and what we got away with—a little weed, tile for the backsplash in our kitchen. Do you think they'll want it back?" I know I was being sarcastic. Even if the tile had been found in our vehicle, it would not have been confiscated. We both stopped talking for a while. I was thinking about what she said, and I knew it would make her happy if I just went along with her, at least right now. I was truly on the fence about the idea. I could only imagine what it must be like to not have financial worries, but I could not shake the possibility of prison from my mind. A few days ago, I'd been almost completely convinced. Just grow a pair, Gene, and "be all that you can be." But I already had a pair, and this was no commercial for the army. I went back and forth constantly. I was annoying myself, but Marie was irritating me, too. I always had to go along with her just to keep the peace no matter how whackass crazy her ideas were. I swear nothing would piss her off more than if I was to just say no to one of her suggestions without ever considering it.

We arrived at Becky's around six P.M. without any incidents. The cats camped out in the garage again, and we went out for sushi shortly after arriving. Most of the conversation was about Marie's health and her treatments and how the toe incident should never have happened. We relived the past seven months with her. Not that they hadn't talked on the phone with each other, but I noticed this about women a while back. Women like to repeat their stories to each other and get a little more animated the second time around. We're all a little bit guilty of exaggerating the truth, but she didn't do it this time. Marie told her the facts again as they happened. There was no need for stretching the truth. It was awful already and Marie never liked being pitied. She was oh-you-poor-thinged to death. She hated when people would say that, not that Becky would ever say that to Marie. She just sat across the table and shook her head and grimaced every once in a while. Marie didn't like that, either.

"You look good to me, girl! I'm so sorry I wasn't able to get up there and see you. I wanted to, but the store has been crazy busy . . . it's a blessing and a curse. I love it, but I feel like I'm married to it. But I don't mind too much. I prefer being busy over the other extreme. I just feel like I wasn't there at all for you."

"Becky. Knock it off. No worries. It's usually not so comforting for people to be standing around while I'm puking all the time. I preferred you didn't come. Seriously."

I paid the bill, and we were back at Becky's house in fifteen minutes passing around a joint. Marie asked Becky about Laura and if she thought Laura was trustworthy.

Becky was taking a hit and raised her eyebrows at Marie. She exhaled and said, "Marie, I wouldn't be entrusting my entire future in just anyone's hands. She's my business partner. I've known her for a while. There's no one I trust more, present company excluded."

"What does she know already about the coke?" Marie asked.

"She knows my two friends have some coke in Mexico and want to move it this way, but need to be as anonymous as possible. I told her vaguely how you found it, that it's pure and uncut. She asked me the amount you have, and I told her I had no clue."

Marie filled her in. "There's a couple of kilos. It's very good, I swear. We tried it the night we found it."

"Want me to invite her over for dinner tomorrow? I'm opening and she's closing. We close at five on Saturdays. I'll make dinner."

I spoke. "I want to meet her. I'm just not real comfortable with her meeting us. Do you know what I mean? The less people that can connect us with this, the better. I go back and forth about this all the time. It's really my ass on the line here. If I have one twinge of discomfort about any step we take, I'm not doing it." I got up, grabbed a can of Lime-A-Rita from the fridge, and walked outside to the back porch for a few. I took a minute to breathe, alone. I have let Marie make decisions regarding so many aspects of our lives. There have been very few times when I stood my ground, and I was not going to back down now. It was my life at risk here, no fucking way to think otherwise. I had never been in trouble for more than a traffic ticket. This was serious shit.

When I went back inside, I found Becky sitting alone. Marie was in the restroom. I motioned to the bathroom. "Is she OK?"

"Yeah. I think so. Are you?"

I sat down. "I'm OK. I'm sorry. She's getting set on the idea about bringing the coke this way. Becky, you and I and Marie know that it is my ass on the line. I didn't spend the last twenty years of my life as a nursemaid just to spend the next twenty as a jailbird."

I sighed and leaned my head back as if to look at the ceiling. "If this is gonna happen, I wish it was now rather than later. So I don't have to keep thinking about it."

Marie came out of the bathroom and sat with us.

"Are you sure that you want to do this, girl?" Becky asked her.

Marie looked across to me and said, "We don't have to make a decision for five months. That's when we'll be heading back this way from Mexico. But if we're both comfortable with everything, then I don't see any reason not to. Yes, Gene, you will have the final say."

Holy shit! In the last thirty years, I had never once heard those words come out of her mouth. The best part about it—there was a witness.

"However," she continued (I knew that victory was short-lived), "I see no reason not to meet with Laura and continue as if we were going to sell the coke, even if we pull out later. We should at least talk with her. Don't you agree with that, Gene?"

"I agree."

So that was how we ended it. Marie lectured Becky on how she couldn't stay married to the store, and how would she ever meet anybody if she was cuffed to a building. Becky told us business was better than they had anticipated, and if it stayed that way, they were going to hire some extra help by summer.

"I know it seems like all I do is work, which is true," Becky said. "But at the same time, it's like being at school. Every day there's something I'm learning about. Whether it's accounting, the value of antiques that come in and what they are, monthly expenses, decorating, which I love doing . . . every day is something new. On some days, time flies by. I trust Laura totally as my partner, as my friend, and I would never have agreed to talk with her about the 'treasure,'"—she made quotation marks in the air with her fingers—"unless I was completely OK with it. I promise you that."

"So, you're happy with the store?" Marie asked, but she was smiling at Becky because she knew the answer already.

"I'm in love with the store."

"Well, I am very happy for you and the store. You make a lovely couple," Marie said with a wink.

"Thank you. And besides, there's a guy that's come in a few times, and yesterday he brought me an iced coffee and he hung around for about an hour. All I know is he's a retired pilot, divorced only once, ten years ago. He's very witty, a vegetarian, which I can deal with . . . we'll see what happens."

"What's his name?"

"Gary. Any more info and you're gonna have to pay me for it. Let's go to bed."

A couple of hours into sleep, I woke up. Marie was sleeping very well that night. She usually did on the road as long as she was healthy. I thought about how Becky said she would never have agreed to put Laura together with us unless she was completely comfortable. She had no skin in the game. Becky didn't know Marie and I had agreed that if we were successful in the coke transaction with Laura, we wanted to give her a percentage of whatever we made. There was no reason for us not to meet with Laura. If we were OK with her, and she was cool with us, then this might very well be an easy transaction. The only questionable part was getting across the border. And when. And now I may have changed my mind again. I was leaning toward the yes and not the no.

Marie woke up and whispered, "Your brain gettin' busy over there, babe?"

"I was just trying to remember your exact words when you said, 'And yes, Gene has the last word,' or something like that. What were those exact words when you said that I got to be the boss? What did you say?" I teased.

"Ha ha. You're real funny in the middle of the night."

"Yes. Yes, I am," I said, and I pulled her into me. "I was thinking about what Becky was saying about Laura. You know there is no way she would ever involve us with anyone shady. This could actually be very easy, Marie."

"Oh—my—God, Gene! Pick a side at least for a solid twelve hours. You're so back and forth that I'm seasick!"

"Hey, it's a big decision," I said in my defense.

"Gene. We've got five months."

I knew she meant we had five months until we came back over the border, but I was thinking five months to live. It was chilling. All I wanted to do was trudge on and go forward as long as she wanted to, for better or worse, for the good and the bad. I scooted up to lean against the headboard and pulled Marie on top of me. I gave her a few long kisses and pulled her T-shirt up so I could feel her bare back with my hands. She had her head on my chest and her legs draped over mine. We always had a very healthy sex life with great imagination and energy. However, when her kidneys were not functioning at their best, it would cause all kinds of issues, and sex became very painful for her. So I opted for intimacy. Marie loved to be touched with my fingertips. I would start with her hair, which was one of her favorite things to have done to her. I would rub my fingers all over her scalp and up and down her back. I touched her from her head to her toes that night, front and back.

I woke up early in the morning, and after slipping on some lounging pants and a T-shirt, I eased out the bedroom door and found Becky in the kitchen. Marie was still sleeping, and I expected she would sleep late.

"What should we have for dinner tonight? I'll stop at the store when I leave the shop," Becky offered.

"Becky. I'll go to the store and get dinner."

She put her hand up to me. "No, Gene. You said she'd sleep for hours, and I don't want you to leave her alone in my house. Do you know how freaky it is to see you carrying her up the steps? It's messed up. I mean, how much more can she take? Both of you?"

"You know, I heard that question every day around our house when she was going through those treatments. Becky, that shit was killing her. But it's over now, and she wants to be in Mexico, so I'm gonna bring her. If something happens before May . . ." I had an instant lump in my throat and I felt tears welling up in my eyes.

I didn't make eye contact with Becky and just said, "Let's just see what happens tonight with Laura."

Becky saved me. "Nothing's etched in stone. The month of May just might come earlier this year, or later. If you want to do this with Laura and her swinger friend, I'll keep my ears open for you." She hugged me. "I love you guys."

"We love you, too. Go sell some more of that shit out of your store," I teased.

She smacked me in the back as she walked past. "Be nice! Besides, I make good money selling that junk," she said over her shoulder, smiling as she walked out the back door.

I checked on Marie, making sure she had her cell phone next to the bed, and went into the garage to play with the cats for a while. The cats seemed to enjoy the road trips, taking turns sleeping on Marie's lap in the van. Jo Cat would jump up on the dash and lie between Marie's feet and the windshield. Marie's feet were always cold, so she would rub them against Jo and thank her for keeping them warm.

I cleaned the litter box and straightened up the van for a bit.

I hadn't cleaned the box since before we left Mark's. Not a good idea with all three cats using one box. Maybe I should just put the coke in a flat Ziploc buried in the stinky litter. On second thought, that would be an obvious hiding spot. I picked up Jo, who was demanding some attention. I sat in a lawn chair with her on my lap, thinking about where I would hide a kilo of coke in the van. I stayed in the garage until my cell started to ring. It was Marie. "Be there in a minute. I'm in the garage with the cats." I left the cats and made my way up the steps. I flopped on the bed next to her. "How are you, babe?"

"Pretty good. What's the plan today?" She requested that we take a shower.

"Becky is working until noon. She wants to cook dinner and Laura is coming over after she closes the shop. Should be here around six-ish."

I helped Marie get undressed, and we took a shower together. We were still very cautious with her finger. If it was bumped, it would send electric shocks through her arm. It was just easier for me to wash her. I would start with her hair, which I always thought was a super sexy thing to do. She would be facing me with her arms around my waist, her head tilted back. Our bodies would be wet and pressed together while I soaped up her hair. What's not to like about that? She asked how the cats were. I told her they were fine and they said hi. After I washed her hair, I soaped up her body. Lord have mercy. I had amazing willpower, but I didn't want to.

After we took a shower, I helped her get dressed. Her hair dried quickly by itself. She had lost quite a bit of it and was still losing more, but her hair was very curly, which helped hide the balding areas. She was still a beauty to me. I made her some tea and myself some juice and we sat on Becky's back porch. "This morning you were fairly keen on the idea of bringing our treasure this way. What about now?" she questioned.

"I think you're right and we need to just talk with Laura. There is no harm in that."

"That's what I've been saying all along, you ass," she teased.

"Hey! Be nice and I'll rub your feet." And she pretended to lock her lips with an invisible key. We sat in a couple of chairs on the back porch, her feet in my lap, and I massaged them for about an hour. Then I moved to her hands and fingers. It made me nervous when I examined her fingers and toes. I would look and feel for hangnails, little abrasions, and small leathery spots. It was a little nerve-racking and always a relief not to find anything.

Becky made it home a little after one in the afternoon. She came through the back door, balancing a couple of grocery bags in front of her. "We're having grilled salmon, risotto, spinach salad, and asparagus for dinner and grilled peaches and vanilla ice cream for dessert. Am I a good friend or what! I haven't cooked for anyone in so long, I'm all giddy. What did you two do today?"

"We took a shower together. Gene washed my body, then he gave me a foot and hand massage."

"What a bitch." Becky pointed in my direction and said, "You spoil her."

"Eat your heart out. No Gary today?" Marie and her inquiring mind wanted to know.

"No, and don't make me regret telling you about that. I don't even know what's going on there yet. But I did have an interesting conversation with Laura."

"How interesting?" I asked.

"She saw her friend last night and told him about you, and he wants to try some of your coke," she said while unpacking her groceries. She popped open a wine cooler for herself and gestured to Marie if she wanted a drink. Marie accepted, and Becky handed her the bottle and continued. "What I know about this guy is that he has a lot of money. He's a bigtime real estate developer in Austin and San Antonio."

"He's that loaded?!" I asked enthusiastically.

"He is that loaded! Gene, this guy has more to lose than you and I could ever imagine. He flies around on his private plane. He has huge money." She took a drink from her wine cooler, then handed it back to Marie. "I was thinking it's gotta be a fairly good sign if this guy wants to try the coke. Don't you think—"

"I'm not a drug dealer, Becky. I'm not certain what the protocol is here. We're kinda flyin' by the seat of our pants."

"Just talk with her tonight and see what you think, and in the meantime, wash that spinach for me."

"Another bossy woman. I can never have too many in my life." I asked for a colander, and Becky pointed to a bottom cabinet.

"Gene and I have decided that if and when this happens, we want to give you a percentage of whatever we make," Marie told her.

"That's not necessary. It would be great to be able to help you guys out," Becky said with all sincerity.

"Becky, we wouldn't have a contact if it wasn't for you," Marie pointed out.

"I tell you what, let's talk about it in a few months. How much is a kilo of coke, anyway?"

"I think we're gonna ask around twenty thousand," I answered.

"Sweet," Becky said with a little squeal.

I carried Marie upstairs for a nap and told her if she wasn't up by five thirty, I would come and wake her up. I showed her the cell phone next to her on the nightstand and I returned downstairs to the kitchen. Becky was making a marinade for the salmon with a teriyaki glaze, garlic, and green onions.

"How are you feeling about this? Are you still OK to meet with Laura?"

I just nodded.

"Nothing's passing hands today, Gene. I know you'll be comfortable with her. Besides, she's an important person in my life and I want you two to get to know her," she said very convincingly.

I told her I was fine with the idea of Laura coming over, and I was actually looking forward to it. She was unwrapping the salmon, putting it in a casserole dish, and making sure it was well coated with the marinade. "I haven't made this in a couple of years. I don't know why. I love it." She snapped the ends off the asparagus, tossed them with a little olive oil, freshly minced garlic, and salt and pepper, and left them to sit in a skillet for now.

I washed Becky's dishes as she dirtied them. I sliced French bread, and she made a Parmesan cheese with artichoke spread and instructed me to smear a generous amount on each slice of bread and lay them out on a baking pan. Becky excused herself and ran upstairs to change her clothes. By the time I had finished, Becky had returned with her hair pulled back in a ponytail, wearing a pair of jeans, sandals, and a short-sleeved denim shirt. At five thirty I went upstairs and woke Marie. When we returned to the kitchen, Becky was on the back patio grilling the salmon. The spinach was in a bowl with chopped pecans, Craisins, and cubed smoked Gouda and was ready to be tossed with a basil dressing Becky promised was so good that I would want to drink it. I was hungry and a little nervous, but not about the food.

It was a few minutes after six when Laura arrived with a couple bottles of pinot grigio under her arm. She was an attractive woman, with blue eyes and shoulder-length blond hair. She was a well-spoken, very friendly, tiny woman who I never would have suspected of being a swinger or coke user. She extended her hand to both of us. "It's so good to meet you both. I feel like I know you already. Becky has told me so much about you."

"I agree, and I'm glad we are finally getting together," Marie said.

Becky came through the back door carrying a platter of salmon that smelled amazing. "Hey. Right on time," she said to Laura. "Oooh . . . pinot grigio. Yes, please!" She retrieved a bottle opener and four wineglasses, although Marie passed on the wine.

Becky put the French bread in the oven under the broiler and heated the asparagus on the stovetop. The risotto, prepared earlier, was warmed in the microwave, and the salad was tossed. We had the food set out buffet-style across the counter. Everything was incredibly delicious, and we were all very complimentary to Becky. I couldn't stop eating the bread. We made small talk through dinner. Laura told us about some of the strange items they had found for sale in the booths. On one particular day, a renter asked for the phone number of another renter. When Becky asked if there was a problem, the woman said there was a painting of considerable value with a small price on it and that the renter clearly did not know what he/she had. Laura was all too happy to hand over the number while Becky retrieved the painting and kept it in their office for safekeeping. The painting was valued at approximately $15,000. Becky had already told Marie the story when the painting had been discovered, but it was a cool story and worth hearing again. Both the girls were looking forward to hiring some extra help soon. Their enthusiasm for the store was infectious. I was very happy for both of them, especially for Becky.

It was Marie who finally started the conversation about the real reason we had all gathered that night. "Becky may have told you a little bit about us, but to fill in any blanks, this is not something that we're in the habit of doing. We've carried our own personal pot across the border, but nothing like a kilo of coke. We have tried it. There is nothing mixed in it. It's completely pure."

Laura was nodding through Marie's speech. Then she spoke. "Yeah, Becky told me of your findings. That's just crazy. How much did you find?"

I told her that we split it with a friend we were out boating with, we had a couple of kilos left, and we were wanting to possibly bring it back to the States. I had no intention to let her know we had ten kilos to move. I didn't even want Becky to know that.

Laura spoke again after sipping on her wine. "I have a friend who is very interested. I guess the big questions are obvious, like when will you have it here, how much are you asking for it, how you want to make the transaction . . ."

It was Marie who filled in those blanks. "We're planning to come through here in May—twenty thousand cash for the entire kilo. Will it be you we make the transaction with, or will it be someone else?"

The conversation was easy and very relaxed, but I could feel a little increase in my heart rate. I looked at Becky a few times. She had her wineglass in her hand and her eyes followed whoever was speaking at the time. She stayed quiet, but was very present.

"No, no one else. I'm fairly certain it will just be me. And if it's OK with Becky, we can just do it right here." She looked at Becky. "Is that OK with you?"

"As long as it just involves the four of us, I have no problem with that," Becky responded.

Laura continued, "So twenty thousand for the entire kilo, and do you have a specific date you're thinking?"

"Nothing specific at this time. I have doctor appointments we have to get back for, so as long as all goes well we should be back here mid-May. Do you know how much your friend actually wants? Does he want the entire kilo?"

"He would want the entire amount, yes. He would want to try it first, and if it's all you say it is, it could be as early as the next day that I can bring you the cash. And just to let you know, I have never done this before myself, but I don't mind being the go-between as long as it's . . ." She paused for a moment then said, "Uncomplicated. I'm feeling fairly at ease. How about you?"

"Yeah. We're good," said Marie while I nodded. "We like uncomplicated. The simpler, the better."

"Agreed," Laura said, then raised her glass to Becky, Marie, and me as if to make a toast.

Becky jumped up and started pulling plates. "Gene, do you mind clearing the table? I'll start on the peaches." We had halved the peaches earlier and had them in a bowl in the fridge with a little balsamic vinegar splashed on them. Becky relit her gas grill on the back patio. I cleared the table and started loading the dishwasher, leaving Marie and Laura to converse at the table. Laura told Marie how sorry she was regarding the recent surgery and that Becky was keeping her up to date on her progress. There was conversation about Andrew and Raquel as well, and I could tell Marie was very relaxed with Laura. It was a good meeting. I didn't think there was any way for it to get better, that is until Becky came back in carrying those grilled peaches. She put a couple of grilled halves in each bowl and topped them with vanilla-bean ice cream and a little of the balsamic syrup over the top. The evening just kept getting better.

By the time Laura left, I felt relieved. So did Marie, and she thanked Becky for turning us on to Laura. I finished loading the dishwasher and cleaning the kitchen while the girls sat at the table a little longer. Becky was examining both of Marie's hands and said she hoped and prayed we had seen the last of the surgeries. We all did.

We decided to leave the following morning, so I loaded the cats and all of our belongings, and we said our goodbyes. We promised to keep her posted when we were back in Xcalak. Becky assured Marie that she would be the first to know of any developments with Gary, the vegetarian retired pilot. We had barely made it out of the driveway when Marie said, "We have a buyer, Gene. I can't believe it."

"I'm trying not to get my hopes up just yet," I told her. "I will admit it's hard not to."

Next stop was Laredo, Texas, specifically the Walmart in Laredo, to pick up whatever we forgot from home as well as last-minute supplies for the road and for the winter in Mexico. After our shopping trip, we grabbed a quick lunch and headed to the border crossing in Columbia, twenty miles west of Laredo. When we arrived at the crossing, there was a line of about twenty cars ahead of us. Any other time we would be the only car. What would usually be a ten-minute stop took forty minutes; not too long, but Marie bitched about it anyway. The cars in front of us had packages loaded down on top of their vehicles. There is a two-week waiver period before the holidays for the Mexicans to come into the States, Christmas shop, and bring their purchases back across the border tax-free. I inched the van up with every vehicle checked, but I was mesmerized by the hundreds of cars coming into the States. The vehicles traveling northbound that were stopped and checked over belonged to Mexicans, and I thought this may be a perfect time in the future to bring the treasure back to the States with us. It was something to chew on.

The procedure going through the border is as follows: the cars proceed over a bridge into Mexico in single file. As you drive through, you are given either a red light or a green light. If you receive a green light, you simply keep driving, pull into a designated parking lot, and head to the immigration building to get your tourist card for twenty dollars, plus a permit for your vehicle, another thirty-five dollars, that is good for as long as your tourist visa. If, on the other hand, you receive a red light, you stop your car and open your doors so customs can take a look in your vehicle. Today was a green-light day.

From there we drove to Saltillo, Coahuila, and dinner at Sushi Ito. Every city in Mexico has a Sushi Ito, and I would know. It was Marie's favorite food. I knew the best sushi places in Saltillo, Querétaro, Puebla, Villahermosa, and any town we frequented. After dinner, we checked into one of our favorite auto hotels, The Oasis. I asked Marie if she happened to notice all the cars heading north at the border.

"No. I couldn't see, but I saw all the cars loaded down with shit piled on top of them going southbound. I was wondering how they get so much on top of those cars and it doesn't fall off. It kind of reminded me of the Flintstones car that fell over with the brontosaurus ribs. Remember that?"

"Yeah." I smiled. "I remember that. You know that's probably a good time to cross with our treasure, because of all of the Mexicans heading north to go Christmas shopping. There are probably a thousand Mexicans to every gringo. We don't fit the profile. They'll just check our passports and send us through. They won't even have second thoughts about us or any 'cargo' we may have. I was just thinking . . ."

"I think you're right."

"If we bring a couple of kilos back with us next May, then maybe the remainder in December . . . two gringos going home for the holidays."

"So now you're all onboard with the plan? Quit thinkin' about it and just do it!" She was very convincing.

"Yeah. Maybe?" I responded, but I was thinking to myself, "This just might be easy."

Chapter Eleven

MARIE STARTS SNEEZING

We just stayed in bed and around the house for the first couple of days back in Xcalak. On Christmas Eve we went to Moi's family get-together as usual. We heard the latest on the coconut telegraph—who split up, who bought a new boat, and whose babies had just been born. Moi was working at the dive shop during the holiday season, the busiest season of the year. He had made several improvements to his family's compound. He pulled me aside and privately asked how Marie was.

"We made it back," I told him, but I confessed that she'd had a rough time, and filled him in on the highlights of her medical journey. Marie had now lost her toe and one and a half fingers. Miss Marie was a special member of the town of Xcalak. Maybe someday she would have her own holiday here.

We stayed at the party a few hours and went home where we had our own Christmas celebration. We had a small tree we would put up every year, and there was always a present or two Marie and I managed to smuggle for each other that would find their way under the tree.

We Skyped back home to St. Louis on Christmas Day and talked with Raquel, Dart's family, and whoever was gathered together. Marie boasted about the weather—eighty-two degrees, nice breeze, blue water, blue skies, and sunshine—while Raquel complained about freezing her ass off. Marie talked to everyone while moving the ornaments around on our tree, probably the ones I hung, while I finished making a couple of lasagnas, one for us and the second for a gift. She was largely in charge of helping with the lasagna. I was allowed to cook the noodles alone, but Marie was underfoot during the entire process of making the sauce, tasting the sauce, adding ingredients, and assembling the dish.

The following day Marie resumed her sun-worshipping regimen. I helped her into her black bikini, and she lay back on her lounge chair listening to music. She was a happy girl. Linda and Marla called out to the sun goddess as they climbed the steps to the deck. "I want a six o'clock reservation for New Year's Eve" was how Marie greeted them.

Marla responded, "Scallops for you, steak for Gene. You're already in the book." I brought them each a Dos Equis beer and told them we had a lasagna with their name on it, our Christmas gift to them. They'd recently learned they were required by law to spend at least six months back home in Canada or risk losing their insurance. They would be leaving in a few months. That would take some getting used to, being in Xcalak without Linda and Marla. "I'm sure gonna miss that steak when you're gone," I teased.

Linda put her arm around me. "Don't be so broken up about missing us. We still have a few months together."

I felt my face flush as soon as I heard her words. Marie had just said the same thing a few nights ago, and I didn't like it much then. We sat out on the deck catching up on each other's lives, smoking a little weed, and taking turns looking out on the blue water of the Caribbean.

Marla mentioned that if their stuff in the bodega was ever in my way to just let them know and they would take care of it. "No problem, honestly. Take your time" is what I said, but inside I felt a little skip in my heart. I knew I had no reason to worry. For anyone to find the coke, they would have to obtain a key to the bodega, move all the girls' stuff, then muscle the heavy-ass lid off the cistern and stick their head down inside with a flashlight. No one knew the cistern was empty of water with the exception of Marie, Mark, and myself. It was essentially a buried treasure. If something happened to me and Marie, no one might ever find that bag of coke.

After the girls left Marie had a craving for guacamole, so under her close supervision, I made it for her. Smashed avocados, freshly squeezed lime juice, Worcester sauce, salt and pepper. If it was in my power, and especially if it sounded good to me, my baby got what she wanted. After dining on guac and totopos, (guacamole and chips), Marie returned to her lounge chair outside, tanning topless, for my eyes only. She woke from a nap in the sun asking me to help her get cleaned up. She wanted the entire makeover treatment and for me to take pictures of her. So that is what we did. We showered and I blow-dried her hair. I applied her makeup and helped her pick out a couple of outfits. I knew she was feeling vulnerable. Her hair was thin, the surgeries had left her scarred and disfigured, her future was uncertain, and she wanted to feel beautiful. We took photos against a wall, posing on the couch, out on the deck, hair up, hair down, in different clothes. She was having fun with it, and truthfully, so was I. Following the photo shoot, Marie and I made love. I wanted to savor that time we shared on that special day, for it was a rare event that Marie had desire and stamina for sex. I didn't want it to end. In a way, it never did end because I still look at those pictures I took of her and relive that day each time I look at them. To me she was, is, and always will be beautiful.

From time to time I took short walks to Moi's or to the girls' restaurant for a quick visit, leaving Marie alone, but for no longer than an hour. I just needed to regroup, maybe think about something else besides Marie, though she was the topic of conversation if and when I did break away. She was getting her tan back, which made her feel better, or so I thought.

Marie started sneezing one night while we were watching a movie. She blew it off as a stupid cold and told me not to worry about it. It was quite normal for her to have an off day every once in a while. It was also normal for her not to be truthful about how she felt. I was used to it, but I hated it.

The following morning, Marie woke up with no desire to eat or shower or even get out of bed. Her energy level had plummeted to a new low. I knew it could pass, or she could be on a real slippery slope, and I prayed it wasn't the latter. Either I didn't pray hard enough or early enough, because it didn't help. When Marie told me to cancel our 6:00 P.M. reservation for scallops and steak, I knew she really wasn't well, so I started putting in some overtime worrying. Marie spent most of her time in bed that day. When I walked over to Leaky Palapa and told Linda to cancel the reservation, Marla poked her head out from the kitchen and asked why.

"I'm not sure what's going on yet," I said with my head lowered. I could have cried on command, and I was holding back the tears. "She hasn't felt good for a few days, she's not tanning, she's barely eating, and she has no energy."

"Oh, Gene!"

"Yeah, it's not good. I'm checking her fingers and toes a few times a day. I don't know what to think yet. I'll let you know if I need you." I had a feeling I would. Sometimes it doesn't pay to be right.

Later that evening, Marie and I were cozied up in bed when we heard Marla calling to us as she was walking up the steps. I opened the door, and there she was with two dinners for us—steak for me and scallops for Marie. When I saw what she had for us, I called to Marie. She came out of the bedroom and just started crying. We were both just shocked. She walked up to Marla and hugged her, and thanked her. At that moment, Marie felt such gratitude and joy to have such good friends. She told me later that night we were lucky to have some good friends in Mexico, to which I added, "And your awesome family back home in St. Louis."

The next two days Marie lay low. She watched TV and slept. She had little appetite and didn't want to drink or even get up. The afternoon of January 3, Marie woke up from a nap and the remainder of her left pinky was swollen and the swelling was moving down into her hand. I freaked out.

"It's fine. It'll be back down by morning," she responded, but she was in denial, and I knew it.

"If it's swollen tomorrow, we're going home," I told her.

By morning it was worse, and the swelling was spreading to the next finger. She didn't want to go back. She was scared, and she wasn't the only one. We hadn't seen anything like this before. I was able to book two one-way tickets on American Airlines leaving Cancún at seven the following morning, flying through Chicago to St. Louis. We would be home the following afternoon. I told her we were leaving in about an hour or so. I ran over to the girls and told them what was happening. They would watch the house and the cats. They both hugged me. I was trying to not show fear, but I was terrified. I shut down the pump to the house. I put three fresh litter boxes in the living room and put a bigger bowl of food out. Marie was crying. She didn't want to leave the cats, but we had no choice.

On the road when she asked me to give her a pain pill, I knew the pain had been going on longer than she'd told me. I asked her, "How long?" and she knew what I meant. She didn't answer me.

"We should have made this trip back home a couple of days ago. Am I right?"

She ignored me.

"Marie, I'm not yelling here. I just want to know what's going on. Do you have any idea how this feels for me? Do you know if I could have taken any of this away from you I would have? The pain I've had these last several years, I can't take a pain pill for!" I picked up the pain pills and tossed them. "We have been in this together! Have you seen me move from your side even once? We are partners, and how am I supposed to know what to do if my partner shuts me out? Do you understand me at all?"

She was looking out the side window during my whole speech. "Do you understand how it feels to be whittled on like a Thanksgiving bird? Or how guilty I feel for not being able to give you a normal life with a healthy spouse instead of an invalid who's being picked apart? I don't want to be sick again, Gene. It feels like torture, and I don't know what I did to deserve it. I'm not trying to have a pity party, I'm just over it. I've just come to my fill. I probably have taken you for granted for years and I'm sorry. And I'm sorry for what I may tell the doctor back in St. Louis."

"What are you planning to tell the doctor?"

"I'm done. I want to make this decision for the both of us. This is what I am going to die from. I don't want any more surgeries or treatments, or puking, or anything. Bring me home, Gene, and let me die there."

"Marie, I do not think we need to have this conversation, not yet. Let's just get back and get to the hospital. We'll talk about this when we need to. Not now. Come on . . ."

"You finish the deal with Laura and her friend. I know you can do it, Gene. Come back across next Christmas. Bring one kilo back, then see how easy it is. You're right. You don't fit the profile. They won't look twice at you. I believe in you to do this. I'll be with you, no matter what."

"Marie . . . I'm right here. Do not shut me out! Talk to me about how you're feeling! Maybe we should have stayed home instead of come back down here—"

She interrupted me. "Listen to me. I don't like being cold, I love the ocean. If I didn't have the ocean in my life I would have died years ago. And don't think for one minute I don't know how many times I used the word 'I,' and that I don't know how generous you are to let me have my way, no matter how crazy my ideas. You always give in. I know you pretty well, Gene Hudson. I know you miss making love all the time. I miss it, too. You deserve to be with someone who can give all of herself to you. This is punishment for both of us. So let me just end it. You won't hurt for not knowing what to do anymore. I'm not very nice to you when I'm sick because physically this"—gesturing to her hand—"can be so painful that I can truly only think of myself." She had started to cry. "I can go to Andrew, and you stay close to Raquel. Don't lose her, Gene."

The tears were flowing down both my cheeks. "I would never let that happen, Marie. And let me thank you for setting such a gloomy tone on our trip here. We've been on adventures for years, baby. They're not over yet. This isn't the last one. We'll be at the hospital tomorrow. We will get through it again, and then we'll have another adventure." I dried my face on my sleeve.

"Hey—"

"Don't 'hey' me, Marie! Stop. No more talking about dying. I'm driving here, and tomorrow is quite a ways away. Don't make this trip feel any longer than it has to be. Please!"

"Well, then let's talk about you writing a book about our adventures."

"Oh my God!" This woman could not stop telling me what to do.

"No, no. Just listen to me," she began. "You are a great writer. You write me beautiful poems. Write our story."

"OK, Marie. I get to be a coke smuggler and now I'm gonna be a writer. Thank you for telling me what to do with my life. You've saved me so much time by doing all my thinking for me. Thank you! In any time in my future do I get to wear the big-boy pants and make my own life choices?"

"Kahlua and cream, oh what a dream." She started to recite the last poem I had written to her.

"That is a good poem," I had to agree.

She continued, "When my baby has her Kahlua and cream."

"Stop! You're mutilating my work of art."

"That's how the poem goes, you asshole."

"Those are, indeed, the words. But it's all about the tone and the delivery. And personally, I don't think you sincerely mean it."

"What are you talking about? I said that with great feeling."

"No. I did not feel it." I was teasing her.

"A sister shares, life blooms new," she quoted from a poem I had written years prior when her sister donated a kidney to her.

"Oh. That is another masterpiece. Please don't go there, Marie. You're gonna make my ears bleed."

I was trying to lighten the air a little. I didn't know how she could make me want to run the van off the bridge and into the ocean and then pull me right back off the ledge. She made me crazy, and I knew that trip was getting shorter every day. I had no clue what was waiting on the other side of that flight tomorrow. I knew she wanted to quit, and how would I know when it was the right time to support that decision? I wouldn't want to feel tortured every day. I wouldn't want to rely on someone to bathe me, clean up my puke, and wipe my ass because I had no hands to do it myself. I wouldn't want someone to carry me because I didn't have toes or feet to walk. Her sister Cathy's last amputation was at her midcalf, left leg. Five weeks later, she had a massive stroke when a blood clot went to her brainstem. She was never conscious again. She died with tubes coming out of her in the hospital. Marie made me promise many times not to let her die like that. I would not allow that to happen. I just wished it was tomorrow already. Time flies, but not when you want it to.

We checked into the Kin Mayab hotel. Marie's hand was definitely getting worse. The second finger was completely swollen, and the swelling was spreading through her hand. When we got to our room, I handed her an open bottle of ice-cold water for her to take more pain pills followed by a couple of hits.

"Gene, I think we need to go out for sushi," she said. Her arm might be amputated tomorrow, but she wanted sushi.

"Of course we do. Just tell me when you wanna go."

"I wanna go now." The woman definitely knew what she wanted.

"OK. Let's go."

We took a cab to the restaurant. They knew us there. We had been going to that place for about ten years. They knew her favorite roll was the shrimp tempura roll and that she liked a little bowl of tobiko (fish eggs) on the side.

Back at the hotel, she consumed pain pills at an even pace. She wanted to "stay in front of the pain," as she described it to me. She said it was easier to keep in front of the pain than get behind it.

We made it to the airport by 5:30 the next morning, and I asked her if she wanted a wheelchair. She shot me a look that said, "No, damn it, and I dare you to say that again!" She didn't want people to think of her as handicapped. She was very vain at times. With the aid of my arm, she walked herself to the gate. Good thing. I didn't want to carry her, the overnight bag, and the red backpack. She might not have wanted to be thought of as handicapped, but she was perfectly OK with being first in line when they asked anyone needing extra assistance to board first. She was all over that.

On the flight, Marie did well. We asked for an extra blanket to wrap her arm. We could literally smell her hand. If someone was to ask me what it smelled like, I would tell them to imagine the smell of rotting flesh. It was unpleasant to say the least. I asked Marie midway through our flight if she was sure she didn't want a wheelchair available at the airport when we landed. The airline attendant could make arrangements for us to have one. She just shook her head no. We both closed our eyes for a while. I was fortunate Marie never had to use the restroom on a flight with my assistance. Not long before, security was called when I was in a stall with her in Walmart. Looking back, it's a funny story, but at the time, not so much.

When the flight landed and we were exiting the plane, she spotted a wheelchair with a porter. She just said, "I'm taking it." We were sent through immigration, customs, and then security, no waiting. When we boarded the next flight, Marie told me that she should be smuggling a kilo on her body since she was not searched. I lowered my head and my voice and muttered, "Now you tell me."

When we arrived in St. Louis and exited the plane, there was a wheelchair available; we'd arranged it before our flight. While waiting to board in Chicago, Marie had called Gloria, the transplant liaison, to tell her the latest situation. We were to head straight to the hospital, and Marie would be checked in through admitting instead of the emergency room. It sounded like a plan.

Marie had another plan. She had Dart drive us home. She wanted to get high and pack a bag for the hospital. While she putzed around at home, Dart asked me what I thought about the hand. I shook my head and responded, "I'm not sure what to expect. We asked for an extra blanket on the plane to wrap around it to try to mask the smell."

"Is that what I smelled in the car? Oh my God!" Dart was floored.

I told Marie we had to go. Admitting closed at five and I did not want to go through the emergency room. We were there by four in the afternoon. She was checked in and hooked up to an IV for fluids. She was on a morphine drip and had a button that she could push to administer more morphine as she felt she needed. It never seemed to help much. I think the button was like a placebo. As long as you pushed the button, it made you feel better. Dart volunteered to stay the night with her. I accepted the offer and slept in my own bed.

I woke early, showered, and was back in Marie's room by seven A.M. Marie was asleep when I arrived, so Dart brought me out into the hall and told me how she was during the night.

"She is twelve different ways of mad that she's getting that antibiotic again. She told me about the conversation she had with you about wanting to just tell the doctors she's done. We talked about that for quite a while and about Cathy. I think she's going to go have the finger removed for sure. She also wants to make sure we can get drugs administered at home again. So I leave you with that. I'm going home to get some sleep."

"Her hand looks horrible," I said. I could see from the hall how much it had swollen during the night.

"I know it does. I swear I could practically watch it grow overnight. It blew up so quickly. It's just terrible. I'll call you later." And Dart was gone.

Marie was beyond pissed when she woke up and had that rat shit being streamlined into her. Her left hand was elevated and huge. What remained of her pinky was completely black and the rest of her hand was bright red with infection. Her skin looked like it could tear from the swelling. It was nasty. After the doctors' initial examinations, it was unanimous that surgery happen immediately.

Dr. Luden, the surgeon, explained that when Marie had her cold, the bacteria attacked the weakest part in Marie's body, which was the hand, and her compromised immune system was unable to fight infection. It made complete sense. So she was about to lose at least one finger because she had been sneezing and had a little bit of a runny nose. It was all wrong.

Surgery began at ten A.M. and was over by eleven. The remainder of her pinky was removed. That was no surprise. The surgeon also cut about an inch below the pinky into her hand. A few days later, the finger next to the pinky was removed at the middle knuckle, leaving only half the finger. In two days, the rest of that finger was removed and so on. During her twenty-day stay in the hospital, Marie had a total of ten surgeries. By the time the surgeon was done whittling away at her hand, she was left with half her hand and her thumb, all because of a cold. It looked like her hand had been cut off by a chop saw with her skin stretched over the top. We never knew if or when the infection would spread. It was like fighting an invisible force. It was exactly what Marie did not want to do. She wasn't doing it for herself. She was doing it because she knew we wanted her to. She was still alive, but at what expense?

I did my due diligence of contacting friends I promised to keep updated. I emailed Xcalak and received emails in return saying everyone was praying for Miss Marie. And of course I called Becky daily. She was in complete disbelief. Her typical response was, "Oh my God. Oh my God, Gene." I heard it from everyone. I had my share of "Oh my God" moments.

Marie was to be moved to a rehab facility where she was to stay for three weeks. As soon as we saw her room, I said to her, "There is no way you're staying here!" We'd been told she would have her own room. She didn't. The beds were about a foot apart from each other with a curtain pulled between and the smell in that room was overwhelming. I do not know what was happening with the lady in the other bed, but she needed to be bathed. The restroom was located down the hall and Marie was expected to share it with at least six other rooms of patients. No fucking way did I want to leave her, but she insisted on giving it one night. I was reluctant to leave her, but I did.

I was back to the shithole the following morning. Dart and Genevieve were already there. I bent down to kiss Marie and she pulled me close to her. Her exact words to me were, "Gene, get me out of here! They're gonna kill me!"

There was no registered nurse on staff, and they had not gotten hold of anyone to come in and give her painkillers other than Tylenol. All Dart and I wanted to do was take her home, where she would be most comfortable, eat the foods she wanted, have her own bathroom, drink her adad-do water, and most important, have her pot. I told her I was getting her out of there. I talked with the administrator about the dissatisfaction we had with the facility. Marie, a recent amputee patient, could not be expected to share a bathroom facility with numerous other patients. We had been told she would have a private room. There wasn't even an RN on staff to administer her painkillers. I told the administrator we were out of there, but she said if we left the facility, unless we went back to the hospital, insurance would not cover the one-night stay, which probably cost thousands.

"Just so I'm clear," I responded, "if I take my wife out that door and bring her home, her insurance won't cover the night she spent here, the night she shared a room with a patient that reeks to high heaven, where she had to go down the hall to go potty, where there is no registered nurse to give her drugs?"

I knew I was getting loud. I was so far beyond pissed off, I'm surprised I didn't come over the desk.

"Do you know that my wife asked for some water in the middle of the night and finally got it three hours later? Did you know that? It'll be a cold day in hell when I agree to pay for this shithole!" I walked away, saying out loud, "This is the most fucked-up excuse for a health facility I've ever seen. Pay out of pocket! Fuck you!"

I discussed it with Marie and Dart, and we decided to go back to the hospital. We made calls before leaving the rehab facility and were informed we had to be admitted through the emergency room because supposedly there were no empty beds available on the kidney floor we had left approximately twenty hours ago. Marie had been on that floor at University many times over the years. Never once had I witnessed an overflow of patients.

I had borrowed Dart and Larry's pickup since our van was in Cancún. I pulled around to the front of the shithole facility and helped Marie inside. As I was buckling her in, she told me if she wasn't high by the time she got to University, she wasn't getting out of the truck. I knew that was coming and had already filled her one-hitter. She said, "I'm so sorry this is all happening. We should be in Mexico. That was our plan. I liked that plan."

"Yeah, I liked that plan, too. We've been postponed a few weeks. That's all. We'll be back soon." I was trying to be positive.

"Postponed, my ass. I'm so mad I could just spit nails! Do you remember the conversation we had the last time we were in the van? Because I remember verbatim! This is the exact shit I was afraid of. I knew this would happen! Gene, this is beyond stupid! Look at this. I lost my fucking hand! Do you remember I said to let me put us out of our misery? Do you remember I said to just bring me home and let me die with dignity and not vomiting multiple times a day? Do you know I'm gonna die anyway? It's soon, Gene. It's sooner than anyone wants to say. Do you honestly think it's wise to let Raquel remember me with my parts being cut off, half out of my mind from pain? Look at me! No more. Please! You've got to get on my side. It can't get any worse."

When she finished that speech, she was drying her tear-soaked face with her shirtsleeve. I was crying myself. My God. What had I done to her?

What I told her was "I love you. Baby, you tell me what to do, and we'll do it. Are you telling me you don't want any more treatment? If that is what you're truly telling me, then I will turn around and we'll go home! Right now. If that is what you're telling me. But if you can continue to fight with me, I'll try to be braver on the day that I let you go. Because right now, Marie Hudson, I'm not ready for that day. But if you can convince me that you seriously want to go home, then I will take the next exit, and you will never see that hospital again. So tell me what to do." I was way beyond tears.

Her reply was, "Just take me to the fuckin' hospital . . . I didn't say I wanted to die. I just said I'm going to die!"

I squeezed her arm and said, "This shit is killing me. I'm probably gonna be dead long before you, babe. Shit!"

Chapter Twelve

SHAME ON YOU, UNIVERSITY HOSPITAL

In the ER, the nurses probably thought we were a couple of drug addicts, all red-faced and puffy-eyed from crying so much. Maybe that's the reason why we were left sitting in the waiting room from 4:30 P.M. until 3:30 A.M. Un-fuckin-real! They finally had us in a room on some random floor the next morning. Marie's roommate was an incredibly obese woman who could clear a room by the smell of what was coming out of her. As blunt and as rude as that sounds, there is no other way to describe it. I had to exit the room a couple of times to stop myself from getting sick because of the stench, leaving Marie to fend for herself. I probably made a nuisance of myself asking for a different room, but I did not care. It was such bullshit that we had to go back to the hospital.

After a long, lovely night in the stink-bomb room, we finally made it to the kidney floor. Dart was my relief at ten A.M. so I could take a much-needed shower and a well-deserved nap. I was back at Marie's room by three o'clock that afternoon. There was no telling what line of crap someone would say, and I needed to be there to hear it. I stayed that night with her and the following morning. The most grating part was being forced into another hospital stay because we needed the insurance company to pay for the visit to the shithole. It made no sense. I was ready to bust her out of University Hospital, the sixth best in the country. It's a really good thing we weren't in the seventh.

Marie had agreed to treatments again as long as they were administered at home, like last time. So at ten A.M. on her third morning back at the hospital, we were told we could leave, pending a final signature from "the powers that be." It was like being kidnapped and not let go after the ransom was paid. Blood had been shed, we'd surrendered, we had been told we were free, and yet we were held captive five more hours waiting for that final signature.

When I put Marie in the truck, I realized how very tiny she was. I was hoping someone had told Genevieve we were coming home. Marie needed a frittata and some adad-do water, stat! Genevieve split her time between her son Carmine's house in the country two hours away and Dart's house, right next to us. When Marie was in the hospital or recouping at home, Genevieve's motherly instincts kicked into overdrive. She usually wouldn't leave to go back to Carmine's until we were heading back to Mexico or Marie was off the treatments.

By the time Marie and I arrived home, Genevieve had made a white sauce lasagna I just love, as well as the most delicious meatball soup I had ever had, in case the lasagna was too heavy. I carried Marie upstairs. Dart had already changed the sheets, picked up her meds, and had everything exactly how Marie taught her years ago when Dart took care of Andrew. The frozen antibiotics had been delivered that morning and Dart had one thawed in the fridge already. Marie was in charge of how the meds were administered. She considered the doctors more like advisers. She knew what she could and could not handle anymore. I promised her if she said no to any more treatments, I would join the Marie Team and just let whatever was going to happen, happen. All that she would want were pain pills. I promised if she survived the next few weeks, I would get her back to Xcalak.

She was settled in her own bed and I hooked her up to the torture crap that would kill her if it didn't cure her. When she said to shut it off, I shut it off. She was in control, but Marie's hair, her favorite feature, was falling out by the handful, and there was no controlling that. Dart took her to a hairstylist the next day to see what could be done. When she came home, my first impression was how different she looked. I had never seen Marie with short hair before. Her illness had taken everything away from her, including her hair. I knew from the look on her face that she had been crying. Marie loved her long hair and now it was gone. When she asked my opinion, I searched my brain for the most appropriate answer I could think to give. I thought it flattered her appearance because her hair was so curly that what was left curled tighter to her head and covered the bald spots, but I couldn't say that. Think, Gene. Think.

I came up with, "Oh my God, baby! You look like a sexy twenty-year-old." Then I gave her a big wet kiss and hugged her with my whole body and whispered so extra ears couldn't hear, "Wanna go lie down with me and get busy, my little hotty?"

I think it worked. Marie always loved compliments and she loved to be called sexy. Her fitness and physical appearance were of paramount importance to her. Her goal was to always be fit and sexy. As far as I'm concerned, she succeeded.

Dart and I continued to administer the antibiotics if and when Marie wanted them. I had seen Dart carry her up and down the steps. I was glad she felt physically able to, because I had been thinking about the van, which was currently parked at the hotel and had already cost us about $500 in parking fees. Not to mention the three cats that had been locked in a house for six weeks. Marie and I, with Dart's consent, decided I would fly back to Cancún, bail out the van, drive back to Xcalak, and join the cats. Hopefully in two to three weeks' time, Marie could fly down and join me. That was the plan.

I found a very cheap flight back to Cancún the following week. I made a shopping list during my flight back. I bought a month's supply of groceries, a pricier cat food (Little Friskies instead of the usual cheap Special Kitty), and lots of canned tuna for the cats. I was prepared to suck up to them. Jo Cat was the most perturbed, but she came around within a few days. They never ate Special Kitty again, deservedly so.

If the plan went off without a hitch, I would be making a trip back to Cancún in a couple of weeks to retrieve Marie. As long as David, the Spaniard, had working internet, I could Skype. David is a guy in Xcalak who installed a tower in his front yard. He received a signal from Chetumal and charged 600 pesos a month for service. Some days the service was pretty crappy, but it was better than nothing.

I gave Marie a new pep talk every day. I told her I needed her with me and hated being in Mexico without her, and besides, I wasn't going to make that trip we had planned for May without her. I remember her response was, "I totally fuckin' heard you say that. You just said yes. I'll try to make that happen, Genie Boy."

I think Marie was on a mission to make that deal with Laura no matter what, because in two weeks' time, I was picking her up at the airport. I made my way to customs where she was passed off to me and traveling in her very own wheelchair, a recent gift from her brother. I noticed her hair was growing already. She looked so good to me. I kissed her long and hard and told her she looked sexier than ever. We stayed the night in Hotel Chocolate, an auto hotel south of Playa del Carmen. We ordered room service and I made love to my wife for the first time in months. She was like a china doll, so fragile. We had missed each other. There was desire to be intimate and sometimes that was enough for me. I was, for the first time ever, afraid I was going to hurt her, so we stopped. Strange feeling, but fear goes a long way. However, there is something super sexy about those auto hotels.

On our way back to Xcalak, we shopped in Tulum and picked up Chinese to go. We ate in the van, where Marie was the most comfortable, and were at the house by six. When we pulled in the driveway, Marie asked me, "Gene, did you think I would make it back here?"

"I had my doubts at times, but I was praying and hoping and thinking nasty thoughts about you, and I willed you back to me. I made a deal with the devil. I sold my soul for you, baby." I leaned over for a kiss. "I figure you owe me at least a handjob." And we both laughed our asses off. The first good laugh in months. I would not have been opposed to a handjob, though.

I carried Marie up the steps and into the house. I started a movie for her, an oldie but a goody, *Overboard* with Goldie Hawn and Kurt Russell. She was all cozy in bed, so I unloaded the groceries, her red backpack, and our overnight bag. She was loved on all night by the cats. They may have missed her more than I did. It was so nice to have her back here with me, and to honestly answer the question she had asked me—no, I had not thought she would ever make it back to Mexico, but I was not going to tell her that.

Marie had a good first night, and other than being tired and weak, she said she was feeling muy bien. I made her promise one thing: no more hiding any symptoms from me.

"As long as you remember to keep your word to me," she said. "If I say no more treatments . . ."

I knew what she was reminding me of. I promised to support her if and when that time came. Marie rested for the first two days. She tired more easily, that was apparent. We took a shower together and were able to make love that afternoon. It was a good, good day. By the following morning she was laying out with her iPod, playing all our favorite songs. Like so many times before, I looked through the window while she tanned. She was laid back in her black bikini, which was now too big on her little frame. Hanging around the house, she wore layers of clothing and was often covered with a blanket. I stood back and truly saw how tiny she was. Her arms and legs were very thin. Her collarbone and hip bones seemed to protrude from her body. It was my mission to try to get some weight back on her. She was my Marie, and she had been through hell and back. It was not right for her to endure the torture of the past couple of months. I wanted her to live with me forever. If I had caved when she was begging me to bring her home to die, she would not be here with me. At that moment, I thought she was through it all. There was no way God would let her suffer through any more surgeries or treatments. I wanted to believe her guardian angels were on the job, and she had carried her cross, and the worst was over.

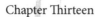

Chapter Thirteen

DART AND LARRY VISIT

When Dart arrived home from bringing Marie to the airport, she said to her husband, "Marie has been asking us for years to come to Xcalak for a visit. We have to go and we have to go now. She won't live through another crisis." At first Larry protested, then he started looking for prices on flights. In two weeks' time, we drove to Cancún, picked them up from the airport, and stayed for two days before making our way south to Xcalak. Marie and I wanted to make the trip as enjoyable as possible, especially for Dart. What that woman had done for us through the years was immeasurable.

Dart had practically lived at our house when we brought Andrew home from the hospital. It was because of her that we were able to keep him at home and alive for as long as we did. She went through training to become a nurse's aide to better care for Andrew and was the first in line to see if she was a match for donating a kidney to Marie. She was a perfect match, a rare one-in-a-million chance, and she lived right next door to us. Her response was "It was just meant to be." She was asked at the hospital why she felt the need to donate her kidney. Her response was "It's a woman's instinct to give life, and that is what I did."

There are very few people I highly respect in my life. Dart is at the top of my list. There are many times when Marie and I went through hell and Dart walked right alongside us without ever being asked. She was at our house every day working with Andrew. She cleaned, brought food, took care of Raquel, went to doctor appointments, and did laundry. There wasn't a chore Dart would not tackle. She is so much more than my sister-in-law. She has been my sister, my savior at times, maybe even like a mother, and always my friend. This was our opportunity to say thank you for all she had done for us over the years. Other than their airfare, their trip was on us.

The travelers were tired after their long day, so we headed to our hotel rooms after dinner. We agreed to meet in the hotel restaurant for breakfast. Marie and I loved the breakfast at this hotel. We brought her wheelchair for sightseeing and shopping at the outdoor market. It was convenient for me when she agreed to use the chair. I had no desire to carry her all of the time, but it makes me smile to myself thinking back on the times I did.

We had made a reservation on the Captain Hook Dinner Cruise. Friends in Xcalak told us we had to take Dart and Larry there. We picked up our tickets at the will call window and were told we would be cruising on the white boat. Marie wanted to sit up top in a corner farthest away from the stage because she did not want to be chosen for audience participation. Not long after we were seated, the actors came out and were met with great applause. The theme of the show was the *Titanic*. There was audience participation, both volunteer and otherwise.

Before we knew it, there was a little person swinging on a rope who flew directly above our table and landed on an X that was taped on the floor right next to Marie. He started tugging on her to stand up. She was trying to tell him she was not the best candidate for the job, but he wasn't having it, and she finally conceded to join him. As she stood up, she looked at the three of us and said, "Oh, shit!" It was pretty funny since she'd handpicked that table way in the back.

The man who pulled her into the skit told her she was going to be Rose in the *Titanic*, and he was Jack. She was to lean out into the imaginary bow of the boat, just like in the movie, while he held her from behind. Marie was afraid she would fall. This guy was literally a very small person, so I positioned myself on the floor and held on to her legs. That poor guy had no idea she was legally blind and somewhat handicapped and was not able to feel the lower parts of her legs very well. It was fairly humorous for the rest of us. When it was over we had a good laugh, including Marie, and she was given a Captain Hook Dinner Cruise T-shirt for being such a good sport.

The boat cruised around in the waters for a while before docking side by side with a red boat. Men dressed as pirates swung on ropes back and forth between the boats to battle. It was great fun and extremely entertaining, a memory we relived many times.

We made it back to Xcalak early the following evening, and Marie showed Dart and Larry around the house and to the spare bedroom. I unloaded the van of our overnight bag and the groceries we had bought in Tulum. It was old home week for the cats, who knew Dart and Larry well. I wasn't sure which one of them had a bigger soft spot for the cats.

Marie and I made arrangements to bring Larry and Dart for a scenic boat ride the following day with our boat captain and tour guide buddy, Moi. Larry was apprehensive about the turtle grass we had to walk through to push the panga out into the water, but when he saw that clear blue water and how deep he could see, he didn't seem to mind. Moi took us down the seaside to the Río Bacalar Chico, and as he was turning into the river, he spotted dolphins. He slowed the boat and the dolphins swam up to us. Marie was so excited. She reached out and touched the nose of one before they swam away.

Marie told Dart and Larry about an experience we had with dolphins while diving years before. We were at La Posetta and the dolphins came swimming up during our ascent. We were hovering fifteen or twenty feet below the surface when they swam around us a couple of times. Underneath one of them was a baby dolphin. It was one of the coolest experiences we had together while diving.

After the dolphins left us, Moi brought us to the Río Bacalar Chico to search for manatees. We weren't quite as lucky there, but I think three dolphins trump one manatee.

We came through the Zaragoza Canal and cruised up to La Poza, the premier dive site in the Xcalak National Marine Park. It is a one-of-a-kind geographical formation on the Great Mayan Reef. The trench runs along the reef wall, starting narrow and ten feet deep at the north end and running about five hundred meters as it widens and grows to a depth of over one hundred feet; it ends at La Copa Del Mundo (World Cup), an eighty-foot-tall pinnacle covered in every color and species of coral imaginable. The top sits fifteen feet below the surface of the water. It truly is one of the best dives to be found in the Caribbean. I took Dart snorkeling at La Poza where we saw schools of tarpon, dog snappers, and horse-eye jacks, along with midnight-blue and rainbow parrotfish, eagle rays, and, of course, coral. Very healthy, beautiful elkhorn coral colonies line the top of the wall. It was a cherished time I spent with Dart one-on-one. It was the best snorkel day I'd had in many years, and I was so glad to have experienced it with her. She is the one person that would never question why Marie and I continued to come down to Mexico even through Marie's health crises. It was our addiction.

While Larry and Dart were in town, we visited Leaky Palapa a couple of times. They were surprised and impressed by the food at our little restaurant in Xcalak. Dart became very fond of the Grand Marnier margarita. We splurged while they were in town, wanting to make sure their visit was memorable and fun.

It was unseasonably warm for the month of April. Although we had a small window unit air conditioner, we had never installed it. Marie was often cold and I was accustomed to the heat. For her, we had space heaters and electric blankets, sometimes year-round. The only time Marie was not covered up was when she was tanning. But Larry was not a fan of the warmer weather with no AC. He was not about to put a bag of ice under each armpit and behind his neck, a sure cure for being hot. So we left a day early and headed back to Cancún, making a few stops along the way. We lunched in Playa del Carmen at a restaurant called Pesca Diaria, which means "daily catch." That's exactly what they serve. Whatever they catch is what you eat. We ate on the deck overlooking the beach, and I pointed out the free diver coming out of the water with a hogfish at the end of a spear. We walked down Fifth Avenue through the market area with Marie in her wheelchair. We looked at all the pottery and Dart fell in love with the Talavera pots. She wanted to buy a few pieces, and since we were driving back to St. Louis in a few weeks' time, we could bring them home with us. Marie told her we would stop at San Luis Potosi, where the pottery is actually made, and pay five dollars per piece as opposed to thirty. I photographed the ones Dart liked, and that is where the beautiful pots with banana and hibiscus plants placed around their built-in pool came from.

After shopping, we continued to Cancún and stayed once again at Kin Mayab. Larry spotted our taco stand, and after buying an assortment of tacos, we sat around the hotel pool, eating and reliving our visit together. Dart and Larry both told Marie she looked much better than she had just a few weeks ago when she was home. It was that magic tan, I swear.

After breakfast the following morning, Marie just wanted to sleep while Dart and Larry lay around the hotel pool. Later that afternoon, we went to dinner at El Cejas, then walked through Market 28. Dart bought T-shirts for the grandkids, and unbeknownst to her, Larry bought a necklace she was admiring and surprised her with it at Christmas that year. Marie spotted a booth that sold temporary tattoos and insisted on commemorating our visit with a tattoo. She was paging through the picture book and came across one that appealed to her. She asked the man operating the booth what it represented. He said it was Mayan for lifelong health and tranquility. "That's the one for me," she said, and she had it placed on the small of her back. She leaned over the table while the guy transferred the tattoo to her lower back. She looked at us and said, "I wish this would last a few weeks so I can show my doctors that I got a tattoo in Mexico. I'm sure it would go over well."

Dart and Larry were anxious to get home, but Marie and I were a little sad their week with us had come to an end. Marie promised Dart she would make it through the remainder of our trip as planned, and that we would be home in about three weeks. It all depended on whether or not we were stopped at the border for smuggling cocaine into the States, but of course, no one knew that part of the plan.

Chapter Fourteen

OUR FIRST FELONY

During our trip back to the house in Xcalak, we started to plan for our Great Smuggling Escapade.

"Just so we are both on the same page," Marie began while hitting her one-hitter, "we are driving back home in three weeks, and we are bringing a kilo to Laura. Are we both saying yes?"

I definitely smelled a hint of sarcasm.

"Yes, we are saying yes. No bullshit. I don't want to be stupid about this, but I think if we both are completely confident, then we're gonna do it. I just want to be without-a-doubt certain we have crossed all the t's and are as careful as we can be."

"Are you wearing your dramatic pants, Gene? That was a little dramatic."

Maybe it was, but it was my freedom we were playing with. "Marie, it's my life we're talkin' about here."

"We will plan to the very number of ice cubes in the cooler." She was the queen of sarcasm.

"So I'm not the only one with a pair of dramatic pants. You know what I mean. Maybe it's overplanning, but I would rather overplan than underplan. And 'fuck you' is the phrase I'm trying to articulate." That last statement earned me a smack across the chest. I attempted to grimace in pain. "Hey, be nice. I'm your means of transportation. Without me, there's no deal."

"Baby, please. I could replace you in a week. I just keep you around to make you look good. And for sex."

God, I loved that lady. She knew what buttons to push. She knew how to hit me without hurting me and hurt me without hitting me. I loved her like I never knew someone could love another. I knew what we had for each other was special. I remember Jerry telling me years ago, "Gene, you two are the ones to beat. Your love is unending." He was right. I would do anything for that girl, and I was about to.

"OK. Thank you for mortally wounding me, you sexy bitch. Now back to the subject at hand."

"You have your finger on the red button to abort any time you want. I'm fully aware. But Gene, have we ever been caught bringing anything across the border—with the exception of the sliced lunchmeat incident?"

Several years ago when driving home from Mexico, Marie, Raquel, and I were stopped and the van was searched. When the Border Patrol agent found the lunchmeat, he held it above his head and marched around the van like he'd made a major bust. Very odd.

"I know all of that. It's just a little unnerving to think next time we might get searched is when we're moving a kilo of coke. I mean, getting over that ham thing took some time. Going to jail may just be a little worse than that travesty. I'm nervous just talking about it. Let's make a list of what we're gonna bring back with us in the van. That'll be a distraction . . ."

I was being both sarcastic and serious. Marie took out the notebook she kept in the pocket on her door and started writing. When we finished, I told her to look down that list and see if something was big enough to conceal the coke. I could tell by the eye roll that she was annoyed.

"Listen, Marie. Am I keeping you from something here?" I gestured to the highway and the land around us. "I mean, am I wasting your time? You have somewhere to go, or maybe you have about two and a half hours to kill before we're back! No bullshit."

Fighting back a little laughter, she replied, "I'm not laughing at you. I'm sorry. We do need to let Becky know when we plan to head back home. The guy probably needs a little time to get that kind of cash together."

"No, I don't think he does. He probably has that in petty cash."

"Well, I hope he does. My point is, we have to let them know our DOA."

"Interesting acronym, sweetheart. Very funny."

I wasn't amused. Typically, DOA means "dead on arrival."

Marie put her hand to her mouth. "I promise I meant date of arrival. I swear on a Bible," she said with her hand to the air.

Then it hit me. "You know what? That kilo is about the size of a Bible. Why don't we just make it look like a book, and we put it up there?" I gestured to the dropdown cabinets above us. "We have books in there all the time."

"That is a brilliant idea! How do we make it look like a book?"

I thought for a few minutes then said, "I'll take the paper cover off a hardback and put it around the coke."

"Oh my God! We've got a plan!" She was practically yelling with excitement. In all the scenarios I had tried to come up with in the past year, that was the best one yet. The coke would look like a book in the event our vehicle was X-rayed. As long as we had books of various sizes stacked together, I couldn't think of a reason why it wouldn't work.

"Gene, there is nothing stopping us from leaving earlier."

She was right. We were planning on leaving mid-May. Now that we had a plan and a designated spot in the van for the coke, I saw no harm in leaving earlier.

We decided to leave May second and hopefully arrive at Becky's around the sixth. I was impressed with the way Marie had recovered. Her energy level had increased and she had a pretty good appetite, though she was still very petite and skinny. She had undergone her worst medical emergency yet and improved more than she ever had before in such a short amount of time. I think it was adrenaline. She was excited and had an adventure to live for. Her body was bronze, and she joked that if she was going to jail, she was going with a tan.

After retrieving one of the kilos from the cistern, I wrapped it tightly with four layers of the Glad Press'n Seal we used to wrap Marie's hand when she showered. I used a couple rolls of white medical tape and covered the entire surface of the kilo. I found a hardback book similar in size, removed the slipcover, and wrapped it around the kilo. With a little trim it was a perfect fit. Our newest book was titled *The Greek Myths*, or so the cover read, so the nickname of our treasure became *Athena*. I selected a variety of books from our collection and stacked them in the dropdown cabinet on the driver's side, spines facing out. If the cabinet was searched, it just looked like a bunch of stacked books. Reading material was not an unusual item to have in one's vehicle for a long car ride.

Marie was bubbling with excitement and enthusiasm. She was like a dog with a bone. She had her adventure, and she was not letting go of it. She was fearless; I was not.

When we left Xcalak, we decided to drive as far as we could and only stop at auto hotels where we could keep the van behind locked doors. We were traveling with the cats. Marie made sure we had all the necessary paperwork when we traveled, including our visas, the cats' papers, and our passports. She wanted to go back to the border by way of the Bay of Campeche. It was a nice drive along the ocean, and there were fewer checkpoints and no X-ray machines—none we knew of, anyway. The day we left Xcalak, we drove twelve hours to Villahermosa. We arrived at the auto hotel at eight P.M. I pulled the van into our private garage, which led to our hotel room. After closing the garage door, I stuck a long screwdriver in the track for added security. We left at four the following morning.

We ate on the road, stopping for food and potty breaks, and were waved through eight checkpoints. That was not unusual. We looked like a couple of gringo tourists. We drove as far as Córdoba, where we stayed at another auto hotel, again with the additional safety of the screwdriver. We had a full night's rest and hit the road about seven A.M.

We drove up the mountains to Puebla to catch the Arco Norte, the same route we had taken before. At the checkpoint, I was asked to get out, which made me sweat. When I opened the driver's door, the soldier looked at Marie. I opened the side doors and he saw the cats, the litter box, and Marie's wheelchair. He asked me, "¿Dónde fuiste?" and "¿Dónde vas?" (Where have you been? Where are you going?) I told him we had been to Córdoba and were on our way to Querétaro. That answer was satisfactory to him and we were back on the road. As I pulled away, I looked at Marie as she blew out a big sigh of relief. It was not unusual to be stopped at that checkpoint, but it was highly unusual to be stopped and in possession of a kilo of coke.

The next day we visited the pot farm (that was Marie's name for it), where we shopped for Dart's pottery. I was comparing the pots to those in the pictures Dart had taken and settled for some that were so similar she would never know the difference. We bought six of them, and after strategically placing them throughout the van, we continued our journey and drove to Saltillo, staying again at The Oasis. I felt the anxiety building in me.

While we were in the shower that night, Marie asked me what my brain was getting busy about. I told her that tomorrow was the day we had been planning and thinking about it for a long, long time.

"Well, Genie Boy, I guess we both need distraction." And she started distracting me. It was a great night, and surprisingly, I slept pretty well. After room service in the morning, I loaded Marie and the cats back in the van and hit the road around eight A.M.

We headed north to Nuevo Laredo and followed the Rio Grande to Columbia and the border. The closer we got, the more anxious I became.

Marie asked me, "Genie Boy, ¿tienes los huevos? Do you have the balls? I think you do. We have been at this very place so many times before."

"Marie, I haven't had custody of my balls for a long time, but I'd rather you have custody of them than a big Mexican who wants me to be his bitch."

So there we were at the border crossing, where just six months prior hundreds of cars were lined up going into the States to Christmas shop. That day there was just a handful. If we were lucky enough to get through the crossing, I saw no reason to not bring the remaining nine kilos back home during the two-week grace period before Christmas.

As I drove to the crossing, I had to keep drying my palms on my pants. My body felt tingly, like little needles were pricking my skin. I pulled the van forward, put it in park, and removed my sunglasses. I knew the importance of being calm.

"Are you two United States citizens?" the Border Patrol agent asked with his hat pulled low over his eyes.

"Yes, sir," I responded as I handed him our passports.

"Where have you been and what have you been doing in Mexico?"

"My wife and I have been spending the winter down by Cancún."

"Where are you headed?"

"Back home to St. Louis, Missouri."

I had my hands resting on the steering wheel, not wanting to move them in case there was sweat left behind.

"Do you have anybody else in the van?"

"No, sir."

"Do you mind if I take a look in the back?"

"Not at all. There's three cats back there."

He opened the back doors, and as he took a look inside, I reached for a napkin I had in the pocket of my side door. I glanced at Marie and casually wiped my hands and dried the steering wheel without him knowing. Then he opened the side door, took a quick look, and shut it. He walked back around to the front of the van, handed me our passports, and said, "Welcome back to the United States. Have a safe trip home."

We were around the corner and both feeling ecstatic. I said, "We did it. One more stop to go."

"Gene, I am so excited I could wet my pants. I can't believe we're doing this!"

I told her I was happy, too, and kissed her on what was left of her hand. We celebrated at Denny's with country-fried steak and eggs. We toasted with our coffee and hot tea to making it that far and having only one stop to go. All through breakfast it felt like my heart beat a little more rapidly than usual. I took deep breaths to try to slow it down, but as soon as we started driving again, my heart rate increased.

We had approximately thirty miles to drive from the Denny's parking lot to the border zone checkpoint on Interstate 35. With every passing mile I became more anxious. I felt like I was subconsciously holding my breath. I just kept telling myself, "You've been through this checkpoint dozens of times over the years. This is no different. Just relax and breathe. For God's sake, breathe." We pulled up at the last checkpoint and I stopped the van. An officer approached.

"Are you US citizens?"

"Yes, sir, we are," I answered. This time I was holding a napkin to sop up my sweaty hands and I was careful not to touch the steering wheel.

"Is there anyone else in the van besides you two?" The whole time he was asking the questions, another officer was walking a drug dog around the van.

"There's three cats in the back."

"Where are you headed?"

"Home to St. Louis."

"OK. Safe travels."

As I pulled ahead and away from the border zone, Marie started squealing, "We did it! We really did it!" She was kicking her legs and waving her arms. She undid her seatbelt, threw her arms around my neck, and kissed me hard on the mouth while I was trying to look at the road and drive inconspicuously. I did not make it this far just to get pulled over for reckless driving.

Marie settled back into her own seat and I helped her with her seatbelt. She reached for the phone and started dialing Becky. "Becky! We'll be there in two and a half hours."

"Are you through both checks?" I heard Becky's distant voice over the phone.

"You bet your ass we are! See you in a bit," said Marie, and she ended her call. "See, Gene? We should have just brought all of it with us this time."

"Hey, Marie, can we just stay in the moment for a while before you go pissing on our parade, Miss Joy Kill!"

"I'm sorry. But I *knew* it would be fine. I told you."

We drove straight to Becky's store. There were big embraces and lots of smiles. Becky gave us her garage door opener and we left.

Marie was quite tired. She had not slept since we left the auto hotel that morning. I opened the garage door and pulled inside. I opened the side of the van and put the litter box, cat food, and water on the floor. I helped Marie out and she wrapped her arms around my neck and her legs around my waist. We kissed each other.

"We fucking did it, Gene."

"Yes, ma'am. We did! Let's get you upstairs." I opened the door to the house and carried her all the way up the stairs to the spare bedroom with those legs wrapped around me. I told her I would be up in a few. I went back out to the van and grabbed the overnight bag, red backpack, and one hardback book entitled *The Greek Myths*. I stopped in the kitchen to get a knife, brought the entire load upstairs, and cut open the kilo on a bedside table next to Marie. We had brought a few glass vials saved from Marie's hot oil hair treatments. Each vial probably held two grams. I filled three—two for Laura, and one in case we decided to have a little celebration. It had been a year and a half since we found the cocaine and partied with it. I put *Athena* back with the other books in the van and lay down with Marie. We fell asleep and woke up when Becky ran up the stairs and jumped in bed with us.

"Oh my God, you guys. You're really here and you actually brought the coke?" I showed her the vials. She said, "Holy shit! Let's open some wine and do a line!" And she jogged down the steps in her bare feet to the kitchen. I carried Marie downstairs. "What do you guys want for dinner? I can order us some Chinese."

"I don't care what we have for dinner. I have dessert." I took out a vial from my pocket. I sat Marie at a barstool and accidentally kicked one of Becky's heels across the floor.

"Sorry, Gene. Sometimes I just kick off my shoes when I walk in the door. Not used to anyone tripping over them except me."

"It's OK. Reminds me of home."

"Cute. Not true. But cute," Marie chimed in.

She was right. Our house was always kept clean and we never had anything lying on the floor. When you live with a person who is legally blind and very unsteady, it is monumentally important to not have any obstacles to trip on.

I opened a bottle of wine while Becky dug out a Chinese restaurant menu. I poured three glasses of wine.

Becky sat down on the stool next to Marie. "Let me see your hand, girl." She took Marie's hand, gently turning it while shaking her head. "That was so crazy. I cannot believe you had ten surgeries in three weeks' time. You are a miracle woman, I swear." She gave Marie a huge squeeze.

"I know. It's awful, and the worst part of all is my modeling career is over," Marie said jokingly.

"You're still gorgeous. Always have been." She kissed Marie on the cheek and squeezed her again. "I'll call in our order around six. Until then, who wants to do a line?"

At one point in her life, Becky had partied every day. Unfortunately, it was to mentally escape her abusive husband. When she finally got away from him, she quit her daily use of coke. I was concerned she wouldn't be able to, but she proved me wrong. She had not done coke for several years and I was not worried about her sobriety for wanting to do a couple of lines with us.

Becky dumped a little pile of coke on the table and retrieved a credit card from her purse. She made five short lines. I pulled a 500-peso note from my pocket and handed it to her. She rolled it into a tight cylinder while she listened to Marie's tales from the road, especially the highlights when we went through the checkpoints. She did two lines herself, I did two, and Marie did one. Becky said, "I can't remember the last time I did this."

I felt so relieved. I was happy to be at Becky's and that Marie and I were able to have this adventure together. I pointed at Marie and said, "I told you I wasn't doin' this without you."

"Hey, did you guys bring one kilo or both of them? Where did you put it in the van?" Like Marie, Becky often asked multiple questions at once. Unlike Marie, she waited for someone else to answer.

"We only brought one. Come out here and I'll show you." I brought Becky out to the van, told her to get inside and look in the cabinet above.

She stepped inside and stooped to look in the cabinet. "Books?"

"Not all of them are books. Pick up that top one."

As she did, her mouth gaped open. She stepped out of the van and said, "Oh my gosh! I have never held a kilo of coke before." She removed the paper cover, examining the medical tape around the coke. "You are so clever. OK, now put it back. Holding it makes me nervous." I put the paper cover back around it and placed it with the other books. "You guys are so smart," she called to her girlfriend waiting in the kitchen. "Whose idea was that to turn it into a book?"

Marie pointed in my direction and explained to her why we now referred to the coke as Athena. While we waited for Laura's arrival, we walked down memory lane to the time we went on a night dive with a group from the dive shop. There were eight of us diving that night. The water was a smooth midnight blue and as flat as a sheet of glass. The moon was full and bright, and when we looked over the side of the boat directly down into the water, we could see the surface of the white sandy floor reflected back at us from forty feet below. There was a twilight glow from below the surface of the water. We all turned on our flashlights and started to descend. One of the first things we saw was an octopus quickening its pace across the sandy bottom. The marine life we saw that night was abundant. During the night, a parrot fish produces a bubblelike cocoon around itself and sleeps. We saw four of them tucked in crevices here and there. We spotted a second octopus racing across the reef, changing color and shape faster than our eyes could comprehend. It looked like a turning kaleidoscope as its translucent body sped over the multicolored reef. We only saw it for a minute, but it left a lasting impression on all of us nonetheless.

What most stuck out in our minds from that dive was the view as we ascended. All eight of us were close in proximity, which is of utmost importance for night dives. We formed a circle and ascended slowly. There was no moving our eyes from the moon. It was mesmerizing. It was bright and full, the water calm and crystal clear. When we reached fifteen feet, I grasped for Marie's and Becky's hands, and we hovered for our three-minute safety stop. It felt like the moonlight had infiltrated the water and was holding us in its light. We hovered in the water, hearing only the sound of our breathing, our hands joining us together like one living unit. It was the most spiritual experience of my life.

Before long, it was six fifteen. Becky called in the Chinese order for delivery. Marie and I were very calm; it was Becky who was anxious. Marie told her this was nothing. "It's crossing the border zone with a dog sniffing the outside of the van and Athena in the cabinet above that will give one reason to sweat."

Laura arrived at six thirty. She came in with a bottle of red and a bottle of white. "I didn't know what was for dinner so I played it safe and picked up one of each. Welcome back. How was the drive?" She had a big hug for us both.

We told her the drive was fine. We had been more hurried in our travel this trip, so we had not stopped to visit some of our favorite places. Laura asked Marie how she felt, noting that she looked very tiny, though Laura was envious of her tan.

"Chinese is on the way, and even though it may not be correct, I'll drink red with mine," Becky said, and walked over to the table and shook the vial at Laura. "We did a little in your absence. If you want to set us up again, I want to go change quickly. Gene, will you watch for the food at the front door?"

"Is that how you're getting me to pay for dinner?" I yelled to her as she walked up the steps.

"Yep, and I can't believe you just fell for that, dumbass."

I opened the front door ten minutes later to a young man holding a box with the most delicious aromas wafting from it. I handed him fifty dollars, including tip, and met Becky back in the kitchen. Laura had set up six lines. Marie passed, but the rest of us did a couple. Becky grabbed some plates and forks while I set the food out buffet-style. I put some garlic chicken, sweet and sour pork, and a couple of crab Rangoon on a plate and set it in front of Marie with a glass of water. Laura patted me on the back. I knew what that pat meant. It was a pat for hang in there, or you're such a great guy for taking good care of her, and sometimes it was a pity pat. I took no offense to it. I told both Becky and Laura that Marie may have suffered the biggest loss with these last surgeries, but this was the quickest she had ever recovered. Marie felt good. She was weak and tired, but good.

Laura did not stay long after dinner. I gave her two of the vials I had filled earlier. She was leaving to have a quick meeting with her friend, our potential buyer. She invited us to come by the store the next day for lunch. There was a Mexican food bus parked near their store on Fridays and the food was good. We accepted the invitation and she was gone. This drug-selling stuff was getting easier all the time.

"My guess is if she invited you to come to the store, she's expecting he'll approve. If it was anybody but you guys and Laura, I never would have gotten involved . . . but it is you guys, so I'm excited this has happened for you. I have some strange friends," Becky said as she started putting the leftovers in the fridge. "She'll probably call me at the store in the morning. This is so exciting!" she said in a singsong kind of way.

"I'm relieved this is almost over. It's very exciting, but being able to make a big deposit and pay off a credit card will be very . . . rewarding," Marie said.

"What about the other kilo?" Becky asked.

Marie and I looked at each other. "Next time," vowed Marie. "We may be rearranging our travel plans in December."

"Hey, care to share some of your weed?" Becky inquired.

I ran up the steps to our bedroom and grabbed the pill bottle containing our pot and rolling papers, then returned to the kitchen table. The pot was very compressed. I had to pull it apart little by little to separate the buds. As I did so, Becky asked, "Why is it so purple?" While I rolled the joint, Marie explained to her how we got it from our buddy Moi.

"I've never seen purple weed before." Becky picked some up and examined it closely. "Interesting . . ."

We passed it around until the joint was gone. "I haven't done coke in so long. I wish Gary was here right now. I'd give him a little introduction to party-time Becky."

She grinned to herself, but I saw it.

"He is sincerely nice. He's into car racing, nothing professional. Just a hobby. He's invited me to watch him race his '68 Corvette in Wisconsin this August. I haven't made up my mind yet. Very nice man. More importantly, we're taking it very slowly. I've been to his house for dinner. He's a great cook—a little heavy-handed on the garlic, but I like him."

"So cool, Becky. You deserve a good guy. Now when do you get a break from the store?" Marie asked.

"We mentioned to one of our favorite renters that we were going to hire someone and she's interested in the job. So we just need to bite the bullet and decide when we want to bring her onboard. I'm ready anytime. I'm thinking Laura and I could alternate having one day off one week, then two days off the following week."

"Oh, that sounds perfect," Marie said. "I'm so happy for you."

"So am I, you guys. For the store to be doing so well . . . I have no words. I really don't." She raised her glass. "To my store. To my friends. To good health. I love you guys." And we all clinked glasses and went to bed shortly after.

I lay awake for a little while in the morning until I heard Becky walk down the stairs. I crawled out of bed, not waking Marie, and joined her in the kitchen.

"I slept like shit last night," Becky announced. "How did you sleep?"

"I almost always sleep like shit, Becky. If Marie has a good night, I still sleep like crap." I watched her make herself a cup of coffee with her Keurig coffee maker. "OK, show me how to use this thing. I didn't want to break it last time we were here."

"Oh, I didn't even think to show you." And she gave me a quick tutorial.

"How much does one of these things cost?"

"I think you can get them on sale for about a hundred."

"Are you kidding me? A hundred dollars for a coffee pot. No fuckin' way!" I was shocked.

"It's a hundred dollars for a super cool coffee pot. Besides, you're about to bank twenty thousand dollars, my friend."

"It is so surreal, I swear. It was strangely easy to drive through the checkpoints. Scary as hell, but easy. I think Marie being in the condition she's in kind of throws off the scent. You know what I mean? When they took that drug dog around the van, it was definitely a 'holy shit' moment. It almost felt like I was watching a movie. It just didn't seem real."

"You guys are so brave."

"It's crazy. Marie kept telling me this is how it would go. She was right."

"You know I have to tell her you just admitted she was right, don't ya? It's totally girl code."

"I know all about your girl code. Who do you think types all of her text messages for her?" I winked. "Think about that . . ." I took a drink. I'll be damned if that wasn't some good coffee.

"Marie has you type her messages? Even the ones to me?" She put her coffee cup down rather abruptly and put her hand to her chest as if she was mortally appalled.

"Becky, she has me type her messages to everybody! I have to read them to her, too. She's legally blind. Hello?"

"Oh my gosh! That's right!" We both bust out laughing.

"I can't believe what you girls text about. Is nothing sacred anymore?"

"Well, Gene, I'm a little bit upset with your wife for that. You just may have to buy my dinner tonight to make it up to me," she claimed as she grabbed for her purse.

"I bought your dinner last night, as I recall."

"I know you did. But I'm very upset," she teased as she went out the front door. "See you in a few hours."

If she could, Becky would finagle a free meal out of us just for sport. She was most accomplished at it. If all went well, Marie and I would be driving home with $18,000 tomorrow, that is, if Marie talked Becky into taking a couple grand of our earnings. I hoped she would agree to it, because Marie can be rather loud and obstinate when trying to get her way.

I looked through the display of coffee flavors next to the Keurig coffee pot. I made myself another cup and found Morning Tea for Marie. I filled both mugs, headed up the steps, and found Marie awake in bed. She was amused by whatever she could hear of Becky's and my dialogue. I kissed her on the forehead and told her I was so happy that I still amused her after all these years. I sat back in a chair adjacent from the bed and handed Marie her tea.

"So how many antique stores are we stoppin' at on the way home, besides Becky's?" I was feeling rather confident that we would be leaving with a sizable amount of cash and that Marie would want to make some stops on the way home.

"Well, I guess that depends on if I find something at her shop. A treasure in an antique store can be a hard find."

I could not begin to calculate the number of hours I have spent walking through antique stores we came across, and I was willing to hold that against her to better suit my cause. "Do you know how many antique stores you've dragged me through in the last thirty years?"

"Like you didn't want to go yourself, Gene!"

"Maybe so, but I'm all about having a quick look-see, then leaving. It's a difference of about two hours per store. And how many stores have we visited together through the years? Two hundred, maybe more?"

"That's probably true. What's your point?"

She knew me well, that girl. I told her we would stop at as many antique stores as she wanted as long as I could buy a Keurig coffee maker for a hundred dollars. She jokingly suggested I switch to tea, but of course she did not care.

"As long as we're negotiating," I added, "I also want celebratory sex."

"Yes, but we can't have celebratory sex until we have something to celebrate, so you better start praying Laura's little boy toy liked that coke."

"Are you allergic to being optimistic?"

"Gene, I've been totally optimistic. I wasn't the one who needed to be convinced we would make it across the border without any problems. I never said he wouldn't like it, so just plan on stopping at antique stores on the way home."

"And a Keurig coffee pot and celebratory sex."

"Yes. All that."

"And a handjob."

"OK. Since we're negotiating, five antique stores."

"No handjob, then."

"Uh huh. Who do you think taught you how to barter?" she said, quite happy with herself. "Boy, please."

"I still get my coffee pot. Do me a favor and don't tell Becky about it. I want to tell her myself."

"Whatever. We're meeting at the antique store to have lunch at noon? We weren't only invited if he liked the coke, right? That's not what I understood her to mean."

"Marie, yes, we're going there for lunch and we can just put the treasure in the red backpack."

"OK. I think that sounds good. Can I talk you into a shower?"

"With you, fine lady? I'm already there."

No one has taken more showers with their spouse than I have. Marie and I had it down to an art form. I was wrapping her hand in Press'n Seal wrap when her cell phone rang. I heard Becky's voice on the other end and the look on Marie's face said it all. I was getting a new coffee pot.

It was a special occasion and Marie wanted to be dolled up. We showered together. I blow-dried her hair and put makeup on her. We were at the antique store by noon and saw the Mexican food bus Laura had bragged about. I thought the number of people waiting in line was good advertisement, and I was hungry. I didn't know what the protocol was for making this deal, so I was just going to follow Laura's lead. We walked into the store and I told them we saw the food bus and were worried they were going to run out of food. Laura suggested Marie stay in the store with Becky, and she and I would walk down to the bus together. It was a very agreeable plan so far. I gave Marie the red backpack, and Laura and I headed toward the source of the spicy aromas. As Laura and I walked down the hill, I told her I was willing to bet Marie's eyes were burning a hole in the back of our heads as she wondered about the sequence of every single word spoken.

"Yes, you're probably right," Laura agreed. "I'm not taking that bet."

She told me she met with her friend last night and he would, indeed, like to purchase our coke for $20,000. She had the money with her. "I want to do whatever is most comfortable for you. I can bring it over to Becky's tonight or we can meet somewhere else."

"Or we can just do this in the office at the store?" I added. "Marie always has to have the red backpack with her meds in case of an emergency. Today there's a kilo of coke in it."

"Well, that's convenient." Laura wanted me to know it was not common practice for her to make arrangements like this, and she hoped that we didn't think less of her in any way for it or her involvement with the swingers club. I just let her know we were rookies as well and her lifestyle choice was no one's concern but her own. Marie and I were about the most open-minded people there could ever be.

We returned to the store in about thirty minutes with two taco salads, a chicken enchilada, quesadillas, a couple of sides of spicy black beans, and Mexican rice. We all headed to the office except for Becky, who was with a customer. The office was long and narrow, containing a table made from plywood and paint-spattered sawhorses.

Laura retrieved some bottled waters for us from the fridge and pulled a gym bag out of a closet. When she unzipped it, I saw tennis shoes and shorts, and a plastic bag with our money in it. I picked up the red backpack and handed the kilo of coke to her. She put it in her workout bag and back in the closet. Then we ate. That was so easy.

Becky came in, grabbed a bottle of water out of the fridge for herself, and attacked her taco salad. "Are we all friends?" she asked.

"We are all friends. And, Laura, thank you for making this so easy for us," I said.

Laura said, "My pleasure. If I'm not mistaken, there's another kilo. Correct? Do you have plans for that yet?"

"Not yet, but we're hoping to be coming this way again in December. We'll let Becky know our travel plans."

Did I just hear her inquiring about perhaps buying more coke from us? Was she for real? I looked over at Marie. She was smiling ear to ear. This was too easy. I would do this again in a minute without reservation.

Back at Becky's, I helped Marie out of the van. She had ahold of the red backpack and was excited to count the money. She pulled the bundles out of her bag, four in total, and we started to count.

When we finished, she set aside $2,000 for Becky. We were looking at $18,000. We could pay off the credit card, leaving us over $10,000. It was so simple. Even crossing the border was easy. We both had reached a new level of euphoria.

"And you heard her say he would maybe be interested in purchasing a second kilo?" asked Marie.

"Well, I wonder if he would be interested in purchasing the other nine kilos," I added.

"I don't know. Let's go get them! We're on fire, Gene!" She was so excited. She was sitting crossed-legged on the bed and had a stack of bills in her right hand.

"I could drive back and do this again, but I think our best bet would be to wait until Christmas if we want to bring it all back at once."

"I was only half serious. We did it, Gene."

"Yes, ma'am. We did."

It was a rush. Everything had gone so smoothly. I could see how someone could make a living at this. I had no intention of doing that, but it was understandable, to a degree.

Marie fell back on the bed and said, "Do you wanna throw the money back on the bed and have sex on it?"

"Do we have to involve the money?"

"No, we do not. Do you think celebratory sex is gonna be any different from distraction sex?"

"Ask me in a couple of hours."

And that was how we enjoyed the rest of the afternoon. In my opinion, the celebratory sex was better, no comparison.

It was four in the afternoon when Becky arrived home. I was in the kitchen, letting Marie take a rest. We hugged each other for what seemed like minutes. I thanked her and we laughed. I was just so grateful to her and thankful it was over. Becky and I sat on the barstools next to each other in the kitchen. "I can't thank you enough for what you've done for us. I can't even find the words."

"No thanks necessary, Gene. You're my closest friends. There was a time not too long ago when I was a disaster. If it wasn't for the two of you, I wouldn't be where I am."

"Can I join you guys, or is it a private conversation?"

We both looked up to the top of the steps where Marie was standing. I made my way up to her and carried her down. She walked over to Becky and wrapped her arms around her neck and just said, "Thank you, thank you, thank you."

"You're welcome, darlin'."

I asked Becky, "What's a good seafood restaurant in town?"

"That's easy, the Chart House. It's like thirty floors up and it spins, so you have a panoramic view of the city and the river walk. Let's go. You're buyin'." Big shocker there.

The following day Becky had the morning off, so she made us breakfast before we hit the road. We had scrambled eggs, sausage, and sausage gravy with biscuits.

"The only time I cook it seems is when you two come through town. I guess I'm going to have to have Gary over sometime, but I have to learn some vegetarian dishes."

"I don't know, Becky. Your sausage gravy could probably make anyone jump the fence. It's a meat lover's delight."

"Thank you, Gene. You flatter me."

We ate family-style with everything in front of us on the table. I helped Marie with her plate as Becky made herself another cup of coffee. "How far are you guys going today?"

"Probably as far as Tulsa. That's usually our destination. Then tomorrow we only have about a six-hour drive home. End of the road."

"Becky, none of this would have been possible without you, you know that's true," Marie began. "We want to give you two thousand of the twenty thousand."

"No. No way."

"Becky! It's the right thing to do and we want you to have it."
I thought this could get entertaining. I had a plate full of food in
front of me and no dog in the fight; my wife was, but not my dog.

"Marie, no. I'm not taking it."

"Becky, let's be real here. You know you could use it and we
want you to have it. Why are you being so stubborn about this?"

"*You* calling *me* stubborn is funny! That's like the pot calling
the kettle black, girl. I'm not changing my mind or my answer, so
if I were you, I'd just save your energy."

"Are you being serious with me?" Marie asked her. She
couldn't believe Becky was refusing the money. I, on the other
hand, had made that very prediction.

"That's your money, not mine. I just put you with the right
person."

"Exactly. If you hadn't done that—"

"No means no."

"Becky, buy yourself something you've always wanted.
I don't care what you do with it, just take it. I think you're being
unreasonable."

"Marie, you're borderline getting on my nerves. I don't want
the money. If you try to leave it here, I will mail it back to you.
I couldn't be more serious. Thank you. But in all sincerity, I do
not want it. If I was to try to put a dollar amount for all you two
have done for me over the years, it would far exceed that amount.
Please, I'm just happy I could help you for a change."

Show was over and Becky won. We left right after breakfast.
Becky insisted she had the cleanup since we had a long drive ahead
of us. We promised to call when we reached our destination later
in the day. Soon the cats were in the van with a fresh litter box and
the pillows were propped up under Marie's legs. Becky commented
that Marie looked very cozy and accused me again of spoiling her.
She also asked if we had Andrew with us, to which Marie held up

her much-loved Mayan bag. Becky smiled. I handed her back the garage door opener.

"I love you guys."

"We love you, too, Becky," I said, and gave her one more squeeze. "We'll talk soon." We backed out of the driveway and were on our way home.

Chapter Fifteen

GOING HOME

I was the first to speak after leaving Becky's driveway. "Well, that's that, baby. What do ya wanna do now?" I squeezed on her thigh. "What's next on our bucket list?"

"We bring the rest of the treasure back. That's what," she said, and shot a grin my way. "We actually did it—twenty thousand dollars! This past week has been so exciting. I'm kind of sad it's over. Are you?"

"No, ma'am." I looked at her like she was crazy. "I'm glad it's over and I'm still a free man. That's what I'm thinking. I'm going to store it away as a happy memory."

She started to cover her legs with a blanket and searched for another. I reached behind my seat, grabbed the Andrew blanket, and handed it to her. As she covered her arms and snuggled it around her neck, she began to gloat. "I told you from the very start we would have no issues crossing with the treasure. I told you."

I believe "I told you so" was Marie's favorite thing to say. "You were right, as usual."

"Say it again," she said with a giggle in her voice as she leaned the seat back and put herself in a position that was certain to put her to sleep within minutes.

We drove as far as Denton, Texas, and stopped for lunch. Marie and I sat across from each other in a booth at the Applebee's on

Interstate 35. "Do you want to try to find an antique mall soon?" I asked her, a little surprised she hadn't told me to keep a lookout for signs.

"No. I'd like to just get home. I'm a little worn out." It wasn't the words that worried me but the tone in which she said them. She held out her hand in defense and said she felt fine, just tired. Then she changed the subject. "Do you remember how you were feeling when we left Xcalak?"

The answer I had in my head was that the last couple of years had been the worst ever for my wife. She was always a woman who loved excitement and spontaneity. The only excitement she had to look forward to most days anymore was laying out and getting a tan. I wanted her to feel happiness again rather than to just exist each day. I wanted to give her something to live for, to let her feel endorphins running through her brain rather than thoughts of doom and despair. I would do anything to make that happen for her. Even though I was apprehensive from time to time, I was so glad we had done this, if not for the money, then just for Marie to be happy and enthusiastic about something. Maybe I could put off moving the rest of the treasure for a few years. That ought to give her motivation to live. But my answer to her was much different.

"I was thinking, 'I hope you don't regret doing this, Gene.' And I also wanted to throw up."

"Seriously?"

"Yeah. Seriously. I mean I like adventure, too, Marie, but if we were financially comfortable with no worries for money in the future, I don't think I would have done this. And, yes, seriously at any time I could have vomited on command. What were you thinking about before we left Xcalak?"

"You know, Gene, we just needed something else to think about for a change. I know it's much bigger, but it's kind of the same as transporting a little weed. The risk factor was greater, granted, but it's the same. Besides, what would they do to me if we were caught?"

"You know it wasn't funny the first five times you said it. It still isn't. And a little pot would just be confiscated at the border and we would go on our way. This kind of cargo, they don't let you go." I took a couple of bites of my food, then continued. "The truth is I'd do anything to make my baby happy. Are you?"

"I'm happy now. It's like a release. I'm not thinking I almost died four months ago."

"Good. I'm glad you don't think about that. I never think about that. Not once has it crossed my mind. I'm happy, too. I've gotten lucky a lot lately and I'd like to keep that on a roll if that's OK with you."

"Yeah, I guess that's OK. I'm looking forward to seeing a zero balance on that credit card statement again."

"I'm lookin' forward to seeing Raquel. When I look back at her childhood and how she was raised compared to other kids, I feel guilty. She was passed around so much while she was growing up. I almost feel like I have to make it up to her somehow."

"Gene, Raquel could have had a childhood like you and gotten her ass kicked for eighteen years, or she could have grown up like Jerry, without a dad. But she didn't. We made sure she was surrounded with loving, caring people. She's been through a lot, but she has never been without love. And that's what it's all about. I love you for doing this with me. Yes, it was crazy, and if it wasn't for me, you wouldn't have done this. Anybody who gets you next should be thanking me."

"Why does it have to be because of you that I do nice things? Can't it just be because I'm an awesome guy?" I protested.

"Given your upbringing, uh no. It is most definitely because of me. I never said I wasn't a better person because of you?"

"I can't tell if we're arguing or making up. I'll tell you what, I'll give you twenty grand for sex." And we laughed long and hard. It was like reality hit us both. We had $20,000 in cash in a backpack next to me in the booth. We weren't laughing because it was funny. We were laughing because we were overjoyed.

We arrived in Tulsa and stopped at Subway for a footlong Italian BMT. I never knew what that stood for and I still don't. We sought out our favorite parking area at Walmart, home for the night. It was pretty funny, considering that we had $20,000 in cash and we were sleeping in our van in a Walmart parking lot. It was just what we'd always done. We ate our sandwich and lay across the bed in the back of the van. Marie wasn't feeling the best and asked for her one-hitter. I gave her a massage from head to toe, front and back. I was an expert at reading Marie's mind. I knew her better than she knew herself sometimes, and she knew me the same. When I massaged her, I felt so intimate with her that I often thought the line where I ended and Marie began was a blur.

We woke in the early morning hours and, after breakfast at Denny's, drove straight through to St. Louis. Marie stayed on the phone with Dart and Raquel and anyone else she could get in touch with. God bless car chargers. Everyone knew our projected ETA within minutes if they kept up with the frequent updates. We were both in a good mood when we arrived home. I'm certain it had everything to do with our successful escapade. I carried Marie in and set the cats free. I did not even mind unloading the van. I was looking forward to a homecooked meal by Genevieve, since she was in town.

It was good to see Raquel after so many weeks. I couldn't help but notice the house was pretty clean. Dart clean. Why would Aunt Dart have to come over and clean the house? It was silly to think our twenty-three-year-old daughter and her friend, a houseguest, couldn't keep the place clean. I had no proof Dart did indeed clean the house, nor did I care. I decided to enjoy the lemon-scented freshness that lingered through the house while it lasted.

We had a lot of visitors the first few days back home. Dart confided she was amazed Marie was able to survive last winter, let alone make it back to Xcalak. All of us were surprised, maybe even

Marie herself. I truly think the only reason she survived was to go on that adventure with me. I'm glad she did, but five months ago I did not think she would still be here.

Chapter Sixteen

MARIE'S BABY TOE

There were doctor appointments with Marie's Dream Team in the first week of June and we were optimistic about her physical condition. She'd had a healthy few months and looked beautifully bronzed. The only time she wanted the doctors to see her was when she had a tan. They would stroke her ego and compliment her on how great she looked. Dr. Luden was the first doctor we saw that summer. Like us, he thought the hand had healed very well. He examined all her remaining fingers on both hands—five in total—and thought they looked fine. He looked at her feet and toes and was pleased with how they looked as well. One doctor visit down and two to go.

Next on our list was Dr. Frank, the kidney doctor. He informed her that according to the recent blood test, her creatinine level was increasing. A healthy woman's creatinine level should be between 0.6 and 1.1—Marie's was 3.8. She told me it wasn't anything to be concerned about and I wanted to believe her. But Dr. Frank had more news. "There's a good possibility there's blood in your urine, and Marie, this should be the time we start thinking about dialysis."

"I'm not doing it."

"I know that would be a difficult decision to make right now, but we should talk about it."

"No, it's not a difficult decision, because there is nothing to decide. You know as well as I do that with the neuropathy I'll never come off of dialysis."

I couldn't say a word because I was now on Team Marie and I had agreed to support her.

"I understand. Then you call me if you need me." He complimented her killer tan and we left. Two doctors down, one positive and one negative.

Dr. Darwin, the infectious disease doctor, thought Marie's hand had healed up nicely, although he never did determine what caused the infection. He had taken samples and grown cultures, but nothing conclusive was found. However, he told her that the tan looked great and that she should check in with him in a couple of months.

With our visits to the Dream Team behind us, thoughts went to the money. We put $10,000 in the safe in our bedroom closet. We made several deposits in the next few months totaling $9,000 in our checking account. It started to burn a hole in our pocket. Marie paid off our major credit card as well as Raquel's Kohl's card. When she was up to it, we went to Sam's and filled the house and freezer with food. We also found my Keurig coffee pot there. I took that thing out of the box as soon as I was home and made myself a cup of coffee. I noticed that instead of just two cup sizes to choose from, like Becky's, this model had a third. That merited a phone call to Becky.

Marie shopped for her great-nieces and great-nephews, taking great pleasure in doing so. It gave her a lot of joy to help out those that she was close to. I didn't care as long as we left the $10,000 in the safe. And I wasn't at all opposed to buying a bigger TV so Marie could see it better. I mean, if it was easier for her to watch TV, which was often all that she could do, who was I to oppose? So we went to Best Buy and bought a sixty-inch TV, and it lived in our bedroom, where it belonged. The nice thing about being home and Marie feeling well was there was another July 4 party at the Buschmanns'. As always, the food was amazing, and great fun was had by all. We were able to catch up with old friends, but what made the visit so special was the amount of leftovers Mrs. Buschmann sent home with us.

It was midsummer, and Marie and I were sitting on the deck outside our bedroom. We were discussing one of Marie's favorite TV shows that she was catching up on. When she discovered we could download an entire season of *Sex and the City*, she watched one right after the other until she was all caught up. It was her thing. I was rubbing her feet as she was telling me about some character I knew little about when I felt a rough spot under my finger on the pinky of her left foot. I looked closer. There was a leathery look to a small spot on the top of her little toe. We both knew what that would mean. Marie called the orthopedic doctor and he agreed to see us in a couple of days. During the next forty-eight hours, I noticed the spot grew slightly bigger and darker in appearance. Dr. Luden confirmed what we already knew. An outpatient surgery was scheduled for the following day, her toe was lopped off, same foot as before. A port was put in her neck shortly after surgery. We knew the same old torture would soon begin. The big question was for how long.

I brought Marie home after surgery and she rested comfortably in bed. That very evening a carrier knocked at the door with the same old familiar box. We received a week's supply. I put six frozen bags in the freezer and one in the crisper drawer in the fridge to thaw. I went upstairs where I found Raquel in the bedroom with Marie.

"I'm not taking that shit again, Gene. We've talked about it. I'm done."

It was Raquel that made the argument. "Mom, I cannot stand to see you so sick from taking those meds. But if you don't, isn't there a greater chance of infection? It may not cure whatever caused you to lose your toe, but it may help keep it from spreading." Usually Raquel was rather quiet, but she was on a roll. "You had almost a dozen surgeries and lost the majority of your hand and didn't die. Are you saying you're gonna choose to possibly die because of a baby toe?" Right out of the mouth of babes. I never said a word. I just sat back and watched and waited to see Marie's reaction.

After that lecture, Marie had to compose herself to come back with her rebuttal. She said she had no intention of starting that day. Raquel's response was, "Don't. Wait until tomorrow or the day after that. But don't ever say that you're gonna let a little toe be the cause of your death." She stood up and kissed her mom on the forehead and asked her if she wanted anything. Before she walked out the bedroom she turned around and said, "I think little toes are kind of weird looking, and they are supposedly the most underused digits we have. In hundreds of years, we won't be born with them anymore. You're just ahead of the game, Mom."

Interesting argument.

Dart came over with a container of freshly made adad-do water and brought it upstairs. Marie was asleep and I was resting my eyes next to her. I jumped up and pulled the door closed behind me when I exited the room to talk with Dart. She had seen the carrier dropping off the drugs earlier.

"Is she getting a treatment tonight?"

"No, and I haven't heard from a nurse either so Marie said she'll start tomorrow." I filled her in on the lecture Raquel had just given Marie. Dart said she was sorry she missed that.

Genevieve had been staying with Dart and Larry for the past couple of weeks, busy making shopping lists and cooking for us all. That night Genevieve and Dart carried over eggplant Parmesan with Italian shredded meat and hamburger buns. It was heaven to me. I made a little plate for Marie and we ate on the table on our deck. It was delicious.

"You know I'm just gonna be puking this up tomorrow. What a waste of good food."

Marie's cell phone rang and I saw Becky's name come across the screen. I cleared our plates and left Marie alone to have a conversation with Becky. She had not told her of the latest with her toe and I knew that might be a lengthy conversation. I walked down to the lower deck and just listened to her talking from the deck above me. I had not taken any time to think about what this could mean. I know this time it was a little toe, but what if this was the same as her hand earlier in the year? What if this was the first of many surgeries and she would inevitably lose her foot? There was no way of knowing what was going to happen. It was the most frustrating thing. One day everything would look fine and that night there could be a discoloration or swelling. I didn't know what was going to happen anymore. I had worn so many brave faces and laughed fake laughs that I could not tell what was real. I didn't know how I felt. I didn't know how to support Marie and how to help myself at the same time. I was worn out and wearing down. Playing the day by day game, which started to feel a little bit like Russian roulette with my wife's body parts, was getting old. No one knew what was coming at us. Her Dream Team of doctors couldn't tell us. All I knew was I had to keep trudging forward with her, putting on my fake brave face.

That night I could not fall asleep, so I borrowed Marie's hitter and headed to the deck. I stood at the railing, revisiting the thoughts I had earlier in the day. What if Marie eventually had to go into a nursing home? She'd made me promise to never let that happen. I would do everything I could to care for her at home. Maybe we should get her a hospital bed for downstairs like we had for Andrew. The very thought of that made me sick to my stomach and I leaned over the railing and started throwing up.

I didn't know what was happening to me. I could think clearly before, but my thoughts were foggy now. I knew Marie wanted me on her team. When she wanted to end the treatments I would support her decision, but Raquel clearly had an opinion that should be heard, and there was Dart and Genevieve and Marie's nieces—so many people to consider. I was tired of making the phone calls and filling in friends about the latest surgeries. It just was not a normal life.

Treatments began the following evening. Marie had me stop the treatment at halfway. I was relieved she agreed to the treatments at all. I complimented Raquel on her speech and told her I hoped she had one or two in reserve just in case her mother needed another pep talk or butt-chewing. She promised to do what she could.

Marie was sick through her treatments just as before. She never had more than half of a treatment, but she was just as sick as ever. I don't know if she could have survived full treatments anymore. Toward the end of the first week, her hair started falling out again. And at the beginning of the second week, I found myself throwing up on a daily basis. Sleeping through the night was a fantasy of mine. I would sit by myself at night on the deck just outside the bedroom door so I could hear if Marie needed me. I had many conversations with God on the deck that summer. I asked a lot of questions and never once received a clear answer that I recall. It was hard to tell who was dropping weight faster, Marie or me. I never wanted to know her weight. It scared the hell out of me.

One very memorable and lonely night out on the back deck, I felt so alone and scared, I called Becky. I didn't even look at the time. She answered somewhat in a panic. I told her immediately everything was fine and reminded her of the offer to call at any time.

"You can, and I'm glad you did. What's wrong?" she asked.

"What's wrong? Well, it may be a little easier to list what's right. It wouldn't take as long. Becky, I don't know how much more either one of us can take." The tears just started rolling. I felt bad for putting my friend in the position of trying to console me. "I think I may be falling apart. I'm sleeping like shit, I'm physically sick . . ."

"What do you mean you're physically sick?" she asked, and I could hear the concern in her voice.

"I think it's ulcers again. I had the same thing years ago when Andrew was alive. It's all stress-related. I'm losing a lot of weight. I can't keep food in me. I'm sorry I called so late . . ."

"Please don't be. I saw how much is involved in caring for her just in the few days you were here. And now she's lost another toe? I can't imagine she can walk very well at all. You have to be worn out, Gene. I mean, you carry her, bathe her, feed her. There's a lot of pressure on you. You are one of the bravest and best men that I know. Anyone else and Marie would be in a nursing home."

"No. Never in a nursing home. She made me promise."

"Who else do you know would have cared for his wife like you have? No one that I know. I wish you could just take a break. It has to be exhausting."

"Becky, I cannot even tell you how tired I am. We were just at your house two months ago. It feels like years to me. If she loses a foot, she won't even be able to walk with help. I'll have to carry her twenty-four seven. I don't know the last time I did anything that didn't involve her. Oh, God, did that sound as selfish on your end of the phone as it did on mine?"

"Not at all."

"And I don't trust her to ever tell me how bad she feels. So you have to be straight-up with me. If she confides in you about feeling bad, you've got to tell me. She has me backed into a corner to let her decide when enough is really enough. I just want a heads-up. How am I supposed to know when she hides stuff from me? If it was up to her, she wouldn't have done anything about the hand, and she'd be dead. Moving that coke is what gave her incentive to keep going. She was alive again for a few months."

"She would have hated herself if she had missed that. Number one, I give you permission to have selfish thoughts and even time for just you. We have extra help now at the store, and I can come up for a couple of days and give you a little Gene time. I know Laura would understand. And number two, what do you mean when she says enough is enough? Do you mean like nothing else . . . treatments, dialysis, nothing?"

"Yes. All of that. And she made me promise not to let her die in the hospital with tubes coming out of her. She wants to be at home. I see her suffer through these treatments and surgeries and I want her suffering to end, but I want her to pull back out of it like she always does and keep living. It's tearing me apart."

"Do you mean to tell me she wants to die with dignity and still be able to form complete sentences?"

"I'm picking up on just a hint of sarcasm there, Becky. Really? I call you, crying in your ear in the middle of the night, and that's what you do to me? Gene-bashing? That's hurtful." I was teasing her and trying to cheer myself up a bit.

"Gene-bashing? No, never. I'm your biggest fan. I think when there is nothing more that can be done, you both will know. I can't imagine how you feel. I'm not even gonna give it a try. That's a lot of pressure on you, my friend."

"You don't want to know."

"Do you feel better?"

"I do. Go back to bed."

"Call you tomorrow. Love you, Gene."

"Love you, too, Becky. Thanks."

And she was gone. I thought about what she had said. I wasn't asking for praise; I just needed an outside ear to listen for a minute. Lesson to be learned here—if you tell someone to call anytime, they just might.

I could not seem to shake the not-so-pleasant thoughts that had a hold on me. I was sick daily and developed an ulcerated esophagus due to stress. The advice I'd received from a doctor years before was to somehow lessen my stress. Brilliant advice! What was so amusing was that he knew Andrew was on life support at home and that Marie was on dialysis and in need of a kidney transplant. Either one of those scenarios on their own was enough to cause great stress, but both at the same time . . .

Genevieve was turning ninety soon and there was a party in the works, so we concentrated on that during those four weeks of treatment. Marie did what she could from her bed at home. She helped with the guest list, venue choice, and menu selection from our favorite caterer, Mrs. Buschmann. Marie wanted to have the party after the treatment was over. She needed to recoup, and so did I. I felt like shit but kept my mouth shut about it. What my wife was going through was hell on earth. Dart tried to push me to go see a doctor and get back on some meds, as if we needed more in our house. We had graduated from keeping Marie's medications on a side table to storing them on a card table. It was obscene. And that didn't include the meds she took intravenously. I did not trust doctors; rightfully so, after what happened with my son. Surely something on that table could help clear up my ulcers.

But Dart and my wife convinced me I would not be able to take care of Marie if I was in poor health. I was defeated. I was surrounded by pushy but smart women. Marie told me to start taking some of her Prevacid along with a couple of over-the-counter meds. In a couple of weeks, I did physically feel better. The ulcers were improving, but the stress and the anxiety and the sleeplessness never ended. It seemed like our house was filled with doom and gloom. Doctors, treatments, hospitals, sickness . . . At least when we were in Mexico, we left all of them behind.

We made it through the four weeks and were ready for Genevieve's party. It was nice to slow dance again with my wife, and I will hold the memory of her dancing with her mother that night forever in my heart. There were mixed emotions for us. We were able to see many relatives, which truly was nice. On the other hand, they were able to see Marie. She was very vain and did not want to be seen in the condition she was in. In her opinion she was pale, which she hated, and was missing her fingers, toes, hair, and her dignity. I imagine it was tricky to wear a fake smile through that, but Marie did her due diligence and kept a smile on her face all the way through. And she definitely wasn't faking her happiness when she watched her ninety-year-old mother jitterbug with her ninety-three-year-old uncle.

A few days after the party, Marie had appointments with her Dream Team. Their responses were, "Your toe looks good. Make an appointment for six weeks," "Go get that tan," and an oldie but a goody, "We have no idea what this infection is. We've run dozens and dozens of cultures, blah blah blah . . ."

The surgeon told Marie, as he always did, that he could write a script for physical therapy, to which she responded, "Now what do I tell you every time you say that?"

"You say, 'Fuck that shit,'" he said with a smile.

Chapter Seventeen

THE TWO RAIDS

There we were at home. Marie was better, but she was sleeping fourteen to sixteen hours a day. I still felt like I was falling apart. It had been two and a half years of the same routine, and I needed a break. I wanted to leave. Becky had offered to come up for a few days. Nope. I needed more than a few days. We didn't have doctor appointments for six weeks and I knew Marie would understand if I left for a week. She probably would be fine, but I wouldn't. I sat next to her in bed and waited for her to wake up. When she did, I simply asked her, "You wanna go to Mexico with me?"

"Yes," was all she said. If she was going to sleep sixteen hours a day, she might as well do it in a lounge chair as I watch the Caribe while nursing on a rum and coke. I needed a change of scenery. I just wanted to look at the water, watch it move, and go very brain-dead. And she needed the power of her magic tan. Our house in St. Louis had a dark-cloud feeling about it, like the grim reaper was hiding in the bushes. I hated being there passionately. In Mexico we had relaxation, no phones buzzing, and a lot less puking. So I booked two nonstop one-way tickets to Cancún and made arrangements to rent a car for the duration of our visit, however long we decided to stay.

It didn't take long for Marie to start laying out and for me to relax. As soon as someone saw Miss Marie laying out in her chair, they yelled up to her. We did not do big grocery shopping on the way down. We decided to just buy fresh vegetables and whatever staples we needed at Flora's little store in town.

We had been there for nine days when Dart Skyped. It was midafternoon, and I answered to a very frantic Dart. "Larry called me at work and told me the police had raided your house and they had arrested that friend of Raquel's, Nicole, that's staying there. Another girl and a guy Larry didn't recognize were arrested, too. And a police officer came outside carrying a baby!"

"What? What? What!" is all that came out of my mouth.

Marie called from the bedroom, "What's wrong? What's going on?" She came into the kitchen, where I was Skyping with Dart. "What did you say?" Marie yelled.

"I just pulled up at home. I'll call you in a few minutes" is all we heard, and the phone went dead.

"Did she hang up? What did she say?"

I repeated the conversation word for word. The coke deal we made five months ago did go through our minds. Talk about sweating bullets.

Dart called within an hour, although it felt much longer. "OK. I called Raquel at work before I called you guys earlier. We pulled up at home at the same time. The DEA took her inside your house and wouldn't let me in. Someone from the sheriff's office told me that drugs were sent to the house, and I told them my sister always gets drugs sent here. It's a large amount of pot, though. They've been surveilling your house from the vacant house next to me. I knew something was going on over there."

"Dart. Where is Raquel now?" Marie shouted.

"She's been arrested. They just took her away in the back of a police car."

Simultaneously we said, "What the fuck!"

"I called Elisa and I told her what happened. She's going to the police station and will call when she knows something. That's all I know."

"Oh, come on! You have got to be kiddin'!"

I wasn't ready to go back to St. Louis, especially to more chaos. She promised to let us know ASAP. So we waited. Elisa, Dart's daughter, called and said she got nowhere at the police station. She was not allowed to see Raquel and all she knew was Raquel was being questioned and then had to be booked. It would be a while, so they told Elisa to just go back home.

"Larry told Dart that Nicole, another girl, and a guy that he didn't recognize were arrested. And there was a baby."

I was trying to fit the pieces. "It's Casie! And Raquel said she doesn't like Casie's boyfriend. She heard he was into dealing dope. They have a baby. It's Casie. I bet you anything. Unbelievable." Marie was livid.

Dart called us at ten that night and said she'd heard from Raquel and she was on her way to pick her up. Raquel would call us when she got home. About an hour later, Raquel called. She and Nicole were both home. Raquel said Casie and her boyfriend had a box of weed delivered to the house, knowing that we were out of town and that Raquel and Nicole work during the day. The DEA was either watching the package that was delivered or they were watching Casie and her boyfriend.

"I knew it!" Marie interrupted her. "I knew it was her!"

"Yep. They released us because Casie admitted to everything, and right now we are walking around the house and it is trashed."

Marie said, "Raquel. Did you know anything about it?" I said, "What do you mean, trashed?"

"No, I didn't know anything about it, Mom. The police searched the house. Cabinets are opened, and all the stuff is on the kitchen floor. Drawers are emptied onto beds . . . they took your bong."

"I cannot believe this!" Marie exclaimed.

"When they were talking to me at home, a policeman came downstairs carrying the bong and the tray you use to keep the pot on. I told them it was yours and about the surgeries and the treatments that made you so sick."

"Are you OK, Raquel?" We both were wondering.

"Yeah, we are both OK, but I'm gonna kill Casie if I ever see her again. I told them at the police station to keep her away from me because I wanted to punch her in the face."

"What about the animals?" I asked.

"Oh! Well, the dogs are traitors! I swear while I was being questioned in the living room, Pete and Max were sucking up to the cops, trying to get affection. The cats were all hiding, I guess. I know someone better be paying me to put this house back together, I can tell you that right now!"

She was laughing a little. Like we didn't know Aunt Dart kept the house clean while we were gone. I was OK with that because it let Aunt Dart get a better idea about who and what was going on in the house.

The whole story was just wild and unbelievable. That night in bed we lay there trying to fall asleep, and one of us would say something like, "Can you believe that happened? What if we had been there—would we have been arrested, too? Was this the first time she did that? Did the DEA seriously surveil our house?" More unanswered questions.

It was about six in the morning when we heard the helicopter approaching. We were used to hearing helicopters searching the coasts for contraband that dropped off boats being chased by the marinos. We often heard the helicopters from a distance, but we had never known one to land so close to the house. I was the first to wake to the sound of the helicopter, not paying much attention to it. The sound of it approaching grew louder and louder, waking Marie, who started yelling, "What the hell is going on?" The noise was deafening as the helicopter slowly descended from the sky, blowing dirt and debris everywhere and sounding as if it was landing on the house. I started running around, shutting all the windows because sand and dust were blowing in everywhere. Screens might keep out the bugs, but when a helicopter the size of a small building lands within fifty feet of your house, no way will screens keep out the sand and dirt that thing was blowing around.

Marie could not see what was going on, so as I ran through the house, I tried to yell back to her a play-by-play of what was happening. The helicopter landed in the yard of the naval base right next to our house. We were both freaking out. I watched from the bedroom window as a dozen marinos exited the helicopter, surrounding it along with our house. Within a minute or two of landing, a high-ranking officer exited and went inside a building on the base. I couldn't believe what I was seeing. I wondered if this had anything to do with our coke dealings with Laura—or did it have anything to do with the bust at our house back home? Then I thought maybe somehow they knew about the nine kilos in the cistern, but I had no idea how that was possible. No one other than Marie and me knew where it was. But why else would a bunch of soldiers be surrounding us if they didn't know something? I always slept naked in Mexico, so I decided to put some clothes on. If I was about to be arrested I wanted to be wearing shorts. I ran to see what was happening in the front of the house and saw the palapa roof at the girls' restaurant across the street flapping wildly. I half expected it to blow away. Marie was still in the bedroom trying to watch the helicopter. I ran back to see for myself and tell her about the marinos around the front of the house.

"Gene! Do you think this has anything to do with the coke in the bodega?"

"I have no idea." And yes, I sounded panicked.

"Holy shit! What are we gonna do?"

I didn't know what to tell her, and before I could come up with an answer, I saw the side of the helicopter open and the steps drop out of it. The officer left the building and climbed the steps, followed by the soldiers. In two minutes' time, they were gone. We were in shock. If there was a good time to have a heart attack, it was now. Within a minute, our front door swung open and Linda and Marla ran inside. Marla was in the lead and said, "What was that about? I thought the front of the restaurant was going to blow off!"

From their place, they couldn't see the officer go inside the building, so we filled them in from our viewpoint. We all just looked at each other, taking turns saying a different version of "Can you believe that just happened?"

We decided to survey the outside. Marie and Linda stayed on the deck as Marla and I took a walk around. There were many neighbors checking for damage. We could still hear the helicopter in the distance. Other than some papers lying around here and there, no damage was found. Everything was covered in sand and dirt, and some branches were lying on the ground by the almond trees, but no roofs were missing, and the palapa survived.

We all went inside our house and I made a pot of coffee and brewed some tea for Marie. We told Marla and Linda about the call from Dart the night before. The girls couldn't believe Raquel was arrested, especially within hours of our house in Mexico being surrounded by the military. They were very fond of Raquel, who had worked for them at their restaurant. Masseuse by day, waitress by night. Marla and Linda wanted to inspect the palapa. As they walked back, I went out to the deck and yelled at them, "Who cares if it leaks? It's called Leaky Palapa," which made them laugh. Then I told them to let me know if they needed help with anything.

I started opening up the windows after the girls left. "Can you believe that just happened?"

"Gene, I thought that was about the coke deal or the bust at our house."

"So did I. Or about the buried treasure."

Marie wanted to go back to bed for a while. I agreed. We could smell the rain in the air and we snuggled in. She laid her head on my chest and the rain started hitting the leaves of the tree outside our window. I stared at the ceiling and played with her curls and said, "I truly cannot believe that just happened." We slept a little longer, but I woke when the computer beeped with a Skype alert.

I closed the bedroom door behind me and left Marie sleeping. It was Raquel on the phone. She told me she had contacted the police station again just to make sure she and Nicole were not going to be charged with anything. She was in disbelief that Casie would do that to us, especially since we'd let her live with us for about a year. Raquel was pretty hurt, I could tell.

"Casie had been coming by more regularly the last few months and asking about your travel plans," she told me. "I just thought she was being friendly, but she just wanted to know when the coast was clear to have the weed delivered." Raquel didn't know if this was the first time she had done it. She told me Aunt Dart was going to help her clean the house today because Nicole had to work.

"Well, you're not the only one that'll be cleaning house today. You are not gonna believe what happened to us this morning." And I told her about our little invasion, the sand blowing in, and the marinos surrounding the house.

"Are you joking with me, Dad?"

"No!" I said, laughing. "I'm dead serious. The girls came running over as soon as the helicopter flew off. I swear."

"That is so weird. So we were both raided, and we both have to clean house."

"I think everyone within a kilometer of this place has to clean house. I'm sitting on a stool in the kitchen and the one next to me is covered in sand. No joke."

We talked for a few more minutes. I told Raquel it sounded like Casie was in a tough place in her life and had made some bad decisions. If she had to do jailtime, I wondered who would keep her baby. Raquel would be able to find out more from mutual acquaintances. We decided to have a race to see who could have their place cleaned the fastest. I told her I loved her, and I started washing down the countertops.

The only time I stopped cleaning that day was when I made meals for the two of us or tended to Marie. I stripped beds and cleaned lamps and light bulbs. Dirt was everywhere. The surface of everything had a coating of dust and sand. Never have your windows open when a helicopter lands next to your house. Lesson learned.

That night as Marie and I lay in bed watching a movie, we were laughing about the events at our house back home and that morning in Xcalak. I told her it was more crazy shit for us to put in our book. The only loss was Marie's bong. We were more accustomed to mistakes like shaving off the top of Marie's toe and misdiagnosing our son. It's a good story to tell if all you have to do is clean the house at the end of it.

After the visit from the helicopter, things calmed down. Marie sucked up as much sunshine as she could. Six women from town, members of the Seventh-day Adventist Church, came to our house and asked if they could pray over Miss Marie. They surrounded the kitchen chair Marie was sitting in and rubbed her down with holy oil while praying in a manner I have never heard before. It was something to see and it must have worked, because two days later Marie tried to sex me out. Thank you, church ladies.

I received a call from my sister Patti out of the blue. We had not talked for a few years. She wanted to know why I never would go see Mom, and my response was, "We go visit them once a year between Thanksgiving and Christmas. I have nothing to say to our dad, Patti." We were back and forth a bit. Marie was cheering me on to finally let her have it. We were cordial to my family if we were around them, but when we left, Marie would tell me how insensitive they were. She was right. Patti wanted me to come to Thanksgiving because the whole family was going to get together this year. I had no desire to see my dad, a pitiful man that brutalized me for years. He never cared about my family, and I didn't care about him.

"Patti, did you grow up in the same house as me? I know you were never hit, but he beat on me for years, and you know it because you saw it! And coming down onto the baseball field when I was a kid and getting into a fight with my coach during a game because he was drunk! Smacking me in the head just for walking past him in the house. Any of this ringing a bell with you? Why does this family want to pretend that shit never happened? It may not have happened to you, but it sure as hell happened to me and you damn well know it!"

"Maybe it did. But he never broke a bone."

Nuh-uh! No way did she say that. No way.

"Fuck you! Fuck you, Patti! I was defending myself from him, you insensitive bitch. I was a kid! You are so fuckin' out of line. I know through that Facebook crap you know all about Marie's surgeries. Did you ever once call to see how she was doing? Do you think our parents did? Don't you dare judge me!"

I lost it. I lost it all over her ass. She started crying, and I managed a quick exit off the phone. Marie was cheering me on for finally standing up for myself after all these years. She was having a very proud moment until I decided to let her have it, too. I had been holding back my feelings for so long, and now it was her turn.

I told her I was so sick of having to deal with crap and there was no joy in my life. I said, "Can't you just wake up and say good morning before you start with the 'I needs' and 'I wants'? Can't you just say to me that you love me or hold me while I'm holding you? I will take care of you like I always have, but do you have any idea how I feel? I'm a slave to you, Marie, and I do it without complaint.

It sounds so simple, but it would mean a lot to me if you could just show some appreciation. How about a fuckin' thank-you once in a while? I wait on you all day, every day, and you never say thank you. How would you like it if you were me? Huh? If you had to feed me, bathe me, do all the cleaning, and everything that is involved in taking care of someone, and you're never ever told that you are appreciated or loved? I may not be a slave, but I feel like one! Have you looked at me lately, Marie? I'm taking your meds because of ulcers, and I'm throwing up daily, and I can't sleep. That's why I had to leave St. Louis. I needed a break. I hate my life there. Trust me, there is no one out there saying, 'Man. I wish I was Gene Hudson. He has quite the life!'"

Before she could respond, I was out the door and down the steps. If Leaky Palapa had been open, I would have sat at the bar for a while, but it was closed, so I made my way to Moi's house. He was out on his boat, so I just walked.

What I said to Marie was not untrue. It was unexpected and harsh, angry but honest. It was indeed how I felt and I was justified in saying it. I was entitled to be pissed off at both my sister and Marie. I'd earned the right and I was wearing that badge proudly. Both conversations were a long time coming. Before I knew it, I was sitting at the end of the pier looking at the water. It had a mystical way of calming me down. It was peaceful, and the longer I sat there the guiltier I felt.

What did I have to feel bad about? Why did I feel the need to apologize, not to my sister, but definitely to my wife? Because I loved her and it was not about being right or wrong. I had my health, aside from the ulcers, and Marie's was slipping away. It's easy being married during the good times, but how one handles the bad times is what a marriage and love is all about.

I got up and walked back to the house and tried to come up with the words to apologize. When I came through the door, she was sitting on the couch in the same position as when I left. I went straight to her and just held her and told her I was sorry. I knew she had been crying. We were holding each other so tightly, and before I could say anything else she said, "No. I'm sorry. You're absolutely right and I am sorry," which made me squeeze her even harder.

"Thank you for saying that, Marie."

"No. Thank you, Gene."

I pulled her away and held her at a distance so I could look at her face and said, "See. Was that so hard to say?" I was trying to make light of the heavy atmosphere I felt responsible for creating. I seriously wondered what happened to my plan to rest and recoup.

We left Xcalak exactly one month later. We both liked the rental car well enough, but we loved the comfort of our van. We had a leisurely trip back to Cancún, where we had sushi for dinner. When we made it back to our room at Kin Mayab, Marie sent me back out for some mango ice cream. We were early to bed and early to the airport for our morning flight back home. Dart picked us up from the airport and we all went out to lunch. When we were home and Marie was comfortable in bed, Dart sat next to her and retold the story of the DEA raiding our house. She said the day after the raid, the roofers working on a house just outside of the cul-de-sac told her and Larry they saw the whole thing. They had a good view. We also relived our helicopter story with Dart. She just shook her head and laughed, saying, "Only you guys." We never sought crap out, but it certainly had a way of finding us.

Chapter Eighteen

I LET HER AGONIZE IN MY ARMS

We spent a lot of time in bed our first couple of days back home. The second morning, I was lying in bed massaging her when I found another spot on the pinky on her right hand. What was it about our house! I mean, did she have some kind of target on her back? As soon as I found the spot, I just held her hand in mine and looked at it. How could something so small cause so much turmoil in our lives? That minuscule spot had the potential to cause weeks of agony and suffering, to say the least. Was that spot going to cost Marie one finger or two? It was so unbelievable. I was instantly sick to my stomach. I hated our house and everything bad that happened in it. Two days ago, we had come back from Mexico, where we went to escape this kind of crap. We had arrived back home and dove headfirst into a pool of shit. How was I gonna tell this lady she was going to lose another finger? She would be devastated.

She never found the spots. I always did. She was down to three fingers and two thumbs, so she couldn't inspect her own body. She was practically blind, and the neuropathy in her hands and feet left her with little sensation. I was tired of finding those spots. Not only did I get to find them, but I was the one to break the news to her. This would crush her.

Keeping it to myself for a couple of days at least made me feel like I was doing something for her. Peace—the best gift anybody could give her. I decided to shoulder the burden alone for a while, and maybe that minuscule spot would miraculously disappear— or that spot could be the very thing that killed her. That tiny, little, diminutive spot. How was I gonna tell her?

Over the next couple of days, I may have massaged her hands an extra time or two more than usual. I had to examine the spot to see if it was growing. If it did grow or change, it would have to come off. The first twenty-four hours, I did not notice a change, and the next morning, there was still no change that I could see. Forty-eight hours—all clear. It could be nothing. By the third morning, it may have looked a little different, but I wasn't sure.

Day four—I knew I had to find a way to break the news to Marie. At least I'd been able to give her four more days of peace. I tried all day to find the words and finally decided to tell her while giving her a hand massage. As soon as I mentioned the spot on her pinky, she fell backward, stiffened her body, clenched her fist, and just gave the loudest cry I had ever heard her make. She wailed and sobbed and said she just couldn't take any more. All I could do was hold her and tell her I was sorry. I held on to that woman for a couple of hours. She was inconsolable, and I let her agonize in my arms.

Maybe I shouldn't have told her yet. I was so tired of finding ways to break the news to her. I knew she said she was done, but she had said that before. I didn't think I could do this again. My guts were being eaten from the inside out. I felt like I was dying, which at the time did not feel like such a bad diagnosis. I didn't want to live like this anymore.

After a couple of hours of crying in my arms, Marie called Dart. We had a routine. Marie would tell her sister, who would call her brother, Carmine, who would drive Genevieve to town to stay with Dart. Genevieve would start making a grocery list and cooking— sometimes before arriving in town. All players knew their roles. It was well rehearsed by now. Marie called the surgeon, who was able to see us the next morning. He said the finger needed to be taken off, but only to the middle knuckle. He wanted to do the surgery the following day before there was opportunity for any infection to spread, but he felt there was no need for Marie to stay in the hospital. He wanted to share the recent finding with infectious disease doctor. Marie explained that we had an appointment with him in two days' time, so she would handle it. We had our schedule. Surgery was a go.

Genevieve made it back to town before we arrived home from the doctor and brought with her a peaches and cream cake. It was on our kitchen table when we walked in the door. That was and still is my absolute favorite dessert that Genevieve makes. Marie wanted to lie down so I carried her upstairs. She just needed to sleep for a while, so she asked me not to let anyone come upstairs if they dropped by. Copy that. I stayed upstairs with her and lightly rubbed on her until she went to sleep. It didn't take long.

I heard the front door open and then slam shut. Genevieve was the only one who came into our house and slammed the door behind her. She's been slamming my front door for over twenty years. I stopped her on the landing coming up the step. She had a container of adad-do water in her hands, but I turned her back around and told her Marie had just fallen asleep and was wiped out. I told her what the plan was for the morning, and she filled me in on the menu for lunch and dinner tomorrow and asked if I saw the peaches and cream cake. I responded with, "Did I see it! I was coming down for a piece as soon as Marie went to sleep." Genevieve appreciated compliments on her cooking. She was and, thank goodness, still is cooking for us and making me peaches and cream cake.

Marie's surgery was scheduled for eight A.M., and by noon we were heading home. She was physically OK, but she was depressed. The house smelled of Genevieve's famous baked minestrone soup. If anything could alleviate the darkness and sadness in that house, it would be the aroma of that soup. Marie felt like eating something when we came home from the hospital and Genevieve delighted in feeding us. It made her feel like she was helping. Although Marie spent the remainder of the day in bed, she was doing well. We watched a couple of her favorite movies. I think the reason she was so fond of watching her favorites was that she couldn't see the TV well anymore and she could just listen with her eyes closed. She would watch the movies in her head, she would say.

She woke up the following morning to her mother coming through the bedroom door with some hot tea and me following close behind carrying a tray with a frittata, toast, and oatmeal. I helped Marie to the bathroom. She was weaker since the last time Genevieve had seen her, but her mother was pretty good at putting on a happy face for her. Marie knew she was doing that, too. She remembered her mother faking a happy face for Cathy. She did eat a little of the frittata, very little, and I ate the oatmeal. I wasn't in the mood to eat that day, thinking about the treatments starting again. The surgeries were always easier than the drugs.

We saw Dr. Darwin the following day and were scheduled to have Marie's C-line put in her neck two floors down from his office at the same-day surgery center. When we scheduled the appointment, we were told we would have an hour-long wait at the most, which was fairly standard. However, the day of the appointment we were told it was closer to a four-hour wait. Marie's response: "Bullshit. We're out of here." We drove to one of our favorite restaurants, Rigazzi's. After lunch, we went home. We were postponing the inevitable, but so what? She was in no hurry to be uncontrollably ill and I could wait to see that, too.

As the days went by, Marie's finger continued to heal nicely. Thank God. We had been a little harassed by Dr. Darwin's office, Nurse Kill Joy, and then the doctor himself called to make arrangements to get her C-line put into her neck. Marie finally caved on December 2. This time, we kept the appointment. I recognized the carrier when the drugs were delivered that night. When I signed for the boxes, the delivery guy just looked at me very sympathetically. He said, "See you soon." Yeah, too soon. I put six bags in the freezer and one in the crisper drawer.

A nurse came by the following day to start the log and give Marie a treatment. Sometimes we were on our own to start the treatments, which was fine with us, but not this time. I was in and out of the room while the nurse was there. I was changing laundry and taking time to fold it as it came out of the dryer since there was another set of eyes on Marie. When I came back, I told the nurse I would give Marie the rest of the treatment later, but she wanted to stay until it was finished. Marie did not protest, and although I could have put up an argument, I did not. That was a decision I would soon come to regret. A little while after the nurse left, Genevieve and Dart came over with adad-do water to help with the nausea that was soon to come. They also brought over pasta with red beans and Italian wedding soup. No one was going hungry while Genevieve was on duty. Genevieve asked the usual question: "How did it go?" Marie was hitting on her one-hitter. I didn't know how to answer that question just yet.

Since Marie was comfortable downstairs on the couch, that's where she stayed. I slept on the loveseat. Around two A.M., I woke up to the sounds of her throwing up. She had her head hanging off the couch. I ran for a washcloth, mouthwash, a syringe, and bottled water. I tried to sit her up, but she kept falling over. I washed the vomit from her face and squirted mouthwash in her mouth with the syringe. I got her cleaned up and she started throwing up again. This wasn't terribly unusual for Marie if her blood sugar levels were way off. On several occasions in the past, I had brought her back from the brink of being unable to speak or move due to uncontrollable projectile vomiting. We had been here before.

We were on the floor and away from all the vomit by the couch. I kept trying to get her to talk or to focus on me. She couldn't make eye contact. She wasn't alert. I wanted to get her to the bathroom, but her body wouldn't work. If I attempted to lift her up, she would just start dry-heaving. I tried everything just to comfort her. Her mouth would move, but only sounds would come out, no words. I thought she was having a very bad reaction to the treatment and that her sugar was low.

Four hours later, Marie had finally calmed down and was resting on the floor. I was asleep on the loveseat with my hand on her waist, which was how her niece, Elisa, found us the following morning, unbeknownst to me. She saw Marie on the floor as well as the mess from her throwing up and ran over to get her mom. Dart arrived and woke me. I gave her a condensed version of the events from two A.M. on. I had a blanket over Marie on the floor. When I uncovered her to pick her up, I noticed all the vomit on her clothes. It was such an awful memory to have in my head. Still is. I picked her up and set her on the couch, but her body was limp. She was awake, but she couldn't speak. Dart helped me get Marie cleaned up and into bed. She mopped up the mess on the living room floor and I called Marie's kidney doctor. We had an appointment that day and I wanted to tell them about her condition and to reschedule. They did not want to reschedule because there was nothing they could do for her. I asked if we could put her on dialysis, knowing that was going against her wishes, but I was told it was too late. I didn't know what to think or what to do.

Raquel came home from her job at the casino and went straight to bed after having worked back-to-back shifts. After a few hours, she woke up, and Dart and I told her what happened and that her mom was in bad shape. It was as if those two knew what was happening. Marie was dying, but to me, she was going to pull out of it. She always did. So to get some answers, I decided to bring her to University Hospital in St. Peters, ten minutes away. I loaded her up in the van, but before we left the house, I told her we needed to do this for me. When we arrived at the hospital, they gave her fluids through her C-line and confirmed she'd had a stroke. I didn't know what to expect or what to do. I was told she would probably do better down on the kidney floor at University Hospital downtown. I agreed.

I walked next to Marie's gurney as she was being wheeled out to the ambulance. Although she couldn't speak, her eyes spoke volumes. I told her again I had to know for myself. I needed some definite answers about her condition. I followed the ambulance in my van.

When we arrived at the hospital, she was brought straight up to the kidney floor. Two woman doctors came into her room together. They'd been informed of Marie's impending arrival and had reviewed her medical history. I filled them in on the events of the night before. I had to know exactly what was going on with her. After running some tests, they told me the stroke had been the defining moment; her body just could not withstand any more, and she had approximately three to four weeks to live.

I had to take more than a few minutes to compose myself. I called Dart and passed on what I had learned. She would take care of telling Raquel. Marie was comfortably resting. It was ten P.M., and I decided to go home. Raquel wasn't there. She may have needed a friend, or maybe she was at work. I didn't want to call. I didn't think I would be very good for her at that time. I needed to wrap my mind around what I'd been told.

I went upstairs and rolled a joint, sat out on our upper deck, and just sobbed. I cried on and off for the rest of the night. What was I gonna do? I was still up when the sun came up. I don't remember sleeping, but maybe I did.

I took a quick shower and headed back to the hospital. I entered Marie's room at seven forty-five and found a nurse hanging a bag of that fucking poison on the IV pole. I couldn't believe my eyes.

"Hey! Hey! She's not getting that crap anymore. I'm taking her home."

"I'm sorry, sir. But it's on her chart to—"

"You better unhook that shit from her neck!" I was furious. If that nurse had been a guy, I probably would have tackled him. "I mean it. You shut it off, or I will! That shit did this to her!" She disconnected the bag before I finished my rant.

I guess she tattled on me because almost immediately the two woman doctors came into Marie's room. I wanted to take her home. Before we left, we were visited by a representative from hospice and a nurse came in to tell me arrangements had been made for a hospital bed to be delivered. The doctors informed me of what meds to stop and what to continue giving her. They told me to watch her blood sugar and insulin levels more closely. They were very concerned for me and made sure I didn't have any unanswered questions. I was grateful for the time they spent with me. Those two doctors were the most compassionate and understanding I had ever met, maybe because they were women. They made a very rough and unpleasant situation a little easier. They were thoughtful of me and appreciated the situation and the decisions that were being made. I have thought about them many times, always with gratitude and respect.

Chapter Nineteen

MARIE'S LAST CHRISTMAS

When we arrived back home from University Hospital, Dart and Genevieve were waiting for us. The hospital bed had already arrived and they had it made with the animal-print sheets from Andrew's old bed and, of course, Andrew's blanket. Marie still wasn't able to communicate or eat solid foods. Dart made her fruit smoothies and brought them over every day. We kept fluids in her by way of the C-line in her neck. She could tell me when she had to go to the bathroom, but she would not allow us to put her on the porta-potty that came with the hospital bed. No way. We had to carry her to the bathroom, which was no easy task since often she did not give us much notice. Day by day, she improved. She could somewhat eat solid food again and her communication was much better. She finally told me to "get that porta-potty out of here," and even if she had an accident or we were not able to get her to the bathroom quick enough, she informed us, "I'm not wearing a diaper." If she wanted to get up to "walk around," I would pick her up, stand behind her, hold her from underneath her armpits, and push her legs out from behind with mine. She looked like a marionette on strings, but that was how we walked. If she wanted to sit up, we would prop her up with pillows in the wheelchair.

Becky was able to come in for our Christmas party, which was held again at our house. She was the best medicine for Marie. She was entertaining for everyone as she relived some wild times with her crazy friend, Marie. When she could, Marie added to the stories. The two of them kept us amused throughout the party. Those were the last laughs I heard from Marie. They were infectious and good to hear again.

Marie's hospital bed was front and center in the living room, but she spent the majority of the party in the wheelchair. She was able to sit at the dining room table with us while we ate. Her meal was a smoothie and a pasta ravioli, maybe two. Her food had to be soft or she would choke on it. She had a good day. Family and friends came by throughout the day, just like every year. It was very different for me that particular year. It was different for all of us. It was undeniably, without question Marie's last Christmas.

Marie's brother, Joe, had the job of passing out presents at the Christmas party. I had noticed a big present up against the wall in the back of the tree. I wondered all day whose present it was. I didn't want to be obvious, but I did take a peek earlier in the afternoon, and did not see a name on it. Uncle Joe waited and pulled that present out last. It was a gift for me from Marie. It was the size of a large laundry basket and it contained every flavor of coffee and tea made for the Keurig coffee pot. When I thanked her for my gift, she told me she was trying to brainwash me so every time I had coffee or tea I would think about her. I just told her, "Lady, I haven't thought about any other woman since I first kissed you." I was looking at her face, taking in every laugh line she had, every fleck in her eyes. I didn't want to ever forget the way she looked. If I had to come up with one word to describe that day, the word would probably be bittersweet. Bitter because I knew the end was near and sweet because she had a good day.

The following morning, I drove Becky to the airport. I knew she had been putting on a happy face for Marie. "It's a little tiring wearing a fake smile, isn't it, Beck?"

"I don't know how you do it, Gene. I feel like I'm dying inside. You need a break."

"Becky, when I heard those doctors say she only had a few weeks left, there was no more guessing what to expect. I know this might sound a little selfish, but I felt a relief. Isn't that odd? I can't adequately explain it to you, but not long ago, I felt like I was gonna die, and I wouldn't have cared if I did. But now I know that I have to live to take care of her—and not just because I have to, but I want to. There's no more question mark at the end of the sentence. I know what to expect now. I'm going to make the last of her time as easy and peaceful as I can."

I continued, "Years ago, when her sister Cathy was on dialysis and in need of a kidney, I knew Marie's fate would be the same. I questioned whether I could go through it and possibly lose her at an early age. But I decided I would have to take what I could get because I wasn't gonna live without her. I told myself if I married her, I would support her along the way and be there at the end. We've had thirty-one years together. Her time is almost up and my heart is breaking in a million pieces." By the time I finished speaking, we were both crying.

"Thank you so much, Gene. Now I have to face thousands of people in the airport with mascara running down my face."

She didn't want to leave, but she had made arrangements for another visit in a couple of weeks. If the doctors were right, that would be about how much longer Marie had to live. I promised to call her if there was any drastic change.

Raquel did a good job distancing herself from it all. When she was home, she was attentive to her mom, but she stayed often at her friend Nicole's apartment. I was OK with that. Whatever she needed to do to get through it.

For the next five days it was Marie and me. Dart had smoothies in our freezer for us, but we weren't eating much. Raquel would
check in and stay with her mom so I could take a shower or run to
QuikTrip if Marie wanted a cappuccino. I was always sure to get a
small cup because she would take a sip or two and be done with
it. For the most part, we were alone. I wondered where everybody
had gone. It felt a little bit like desertion, but in retrospect maybe
it was everyone's time to regroup and prepare themselves for what
was coming. I was functioning, trying not to feel sorry for myself. It
is such a busy season to prepare for to begin with, and Marie near-
ing the end made it a bit more of a struggle for everyone else. Our
Christmas was over, but others had their family functions to attend
and prepare for.

On one of the days when Marie and I were alone and lying in
the hospital bed together, I told her she needed to get better so we
could bring the rest of the coke up from Mexico. It could be our biggest adventure. I could do anything when I was with her, but I didn't
know what I was capable of without her. She told me to take all our
stories and write our book. It would be our love story, and it would
last forever if it was written down. I told her our love story would
last forever, and no one had to read a book to feel the love we had for
each other. There were not many marriages I had witnessed in my
lifetime that I thought were built on a foundation of pure love and
devotion. We had our peaks and valleys during our marriage, but we
got through them stronger and more determined.

Our friend Brandon called and told me he wanted to have a
gathering at our house to carol for us. December 22 was the chosen
date. I thought it was a great idea and when I told Marie, she was
excited about it. It gave her something to look forward to. Genevieve,
Raquel, and Dart made treat bags for whatever kids would be there.
Brandon's son, Jesse, was a fireman and brought with him a trailer
his department had turned into a sled for Santa to greet the children.

Jesse was Santa. It was a very cold night; Dart had hot chocolate available in her garage and her grandchildren passed it around to everyone. There was a fire pit in Dart's driveway, a popular place to stand that night. Brandon had a stereo playing music in the back end of his pickup, but it was shut off when I brought Marie outside and the singing began.

She was bundled in many blankets and wore a thick stocking cap. I wheeled her out and Elisa put a portable heater right behind her. I pulled the wheelchair up by the trailer where the carolers were gathered. It was an overwhelming feeling to have people in our lives willing to do this for us. It was so generous and thoughtful and probably the last good memory Marie had. Jerry's sister Leslie had printed out lyrics of Christmas songs, and one by one they sang them to us. There was "Rudolph," "Frosty the Snowman," "Santa Claus Is Coming to Town," and several more.

The last song was "O Holy Night," and it was sung as a solo by JoJo, Terri's fourteen-year-old daughter. Marie sat through most of the songs with her eyes closed. She would open them for a couple of minutes to look around at everyone while they sang, then close them again. She even sang along a little. It was the last joyful event at our house while Marie was alive.

<hr />

Marie was less responsive after the night of the caroling. We stopped giving her any drugs, including her insulin. She wasn't drinking at all or consuming nourishment and I was eating next to nothing right along with her. The only fluid she received was the saline solution I flushed the C-line with. I continued to sleep in the hospital bed with her every night. I held her and she held Andrew's blanket. Her left arm was the only thing she seemed to have any control over. She would stretch that arm up in the air, collapse it over my head, and with whatever strength she had left, hold me close to her.

I told her with whatever words I could find what she meant to me, how she made my life worthwhile, and how much I would miss her. I told her she made me into the person I had become, and she had shown me what love was. I told her to hug and kiss Andrew for me, to tell him that I loved and missed him. I promised to keep my eye on Raquel. I let her know she was my absolute everything and I had no idea what I was going to do without her. I wanted her to stop suffering, but I wanted to keep her with me. She was all that I knew and all I ever wanted to know. She was the best thing that could have ever happened to me and I did not want to lose that. Yet to die was the best thing for her. It was as if we were both dying right there in that bed. I wanted it to be over for both of us. I told her I was the luckiest man to have her as my own for thirty-one years. I called her my wife for twenty-eight years and four and a half months. I told her I didn't know who I was going to be without her, but if there was any goodness in me, it was because of her.

The last conversation Marie and I had was on December 23. We were lying in the hospital bed, my head on her chest, her left arm around my neck. I had my arm wrapped around her tiny frame. "I love you. I'm gonna miss you. What am I gonna do without you?"

"Write our story. You can do it." Her voice was quiet, but I heard her clearly. "I love you." Those were her last words to me.

Chapter Twenty

MARIE GOES TO ANDREW

Dart came over on Christmas Eve to sit with me for a while. Marie hadn't spoken and had barely woken up since the day before. Becky was flying in the following day. Dart had talked to Carmine, who didn't want to drive in until after Christmas, but they were only two hours away, so they could come at any time. The following day, I picked up Becky from the airport while Dart stayed with Marie. Raquel had the opportunity to work for double time and I told her to take it. She had said her goodbyes a few days before when Marie was still alert and responsive, and nothing had gone unsaid between them. I was happy to hear that. I told her I was here if she needed me. Her response to me was one that she gave to me often: "Ditto." There was nothing she could do; her mom wasn't communicating and her work was only fifteen minutes away.

It was peaceful around Marie. We sat and talked around her, told funny stories, and played her favorite songs on her iPod. I slept with her every night with her favorite movies playing on the TV. She was no longer able to control her bowels and I had to put a diaper on her. "I'm sorry, Marie," I told her. "I want to hold you, but I have to keep us both dry." Becky stayed on the couch that night next to the hospital bed. We would sleep for a while, then wake up and relive some happier times, highlighting Marie at her finest. Then we would doze back off. The following morning, I told Dart it was probably time to call Carmine and have him bring Genevieve. They were there by the afternoon. Genevieve went straight over to Marie. She kissed her daughter and laid her head on Marie's shoulder. I put Marie's arm around her mom's neck. I knew if she was at all conscious, she would want to hold her mother. Everyone stayed very close that day, but that night they all went back to Dart's.

When we woke up the morning of the twenty-seventh, Becky was on the couch and I was in bed with Marie. Genevieve had come to the door, and the dogs started barking. It startled Marie. Her breathing became very heavy and labored; it sounded like she was trying to breathe underwater. It was awful and we didn't know how to help her. Becky ran next door to Dart's. When she returned, I was sitting on the couch holding Marie in an upright position on my lap, just rocking her. I was holding her tight just to try to give her some comfort and let her know I was there. I was crying and freaking out.

Dart called the hospice nurse, who said she would get there as soon as she could, but it would be a while. She told Dart how much morphine to give her.

I said to Dart, "I can't do it. I can't give her the morphine." I knew that would mean the very end. Morphine would knock out her respiratory system, but she was suffering. Dart nodded at me and gave Marie several drops under the tongue.

After what seemed like an hour, she did start to calm down, though her lungs sounded like they were completely filled with fluids. I was still holding Marie on the couch when the nurse finally arrived. She told me it was going to be very unpleasant, but she had to gag Marie. She said, "What we have to do may very well kill her, but she is virtually drowning, so we have no choice." The nurse had me put Marie's legs in the air and flip her head upside down. When I did, the nurse stuck her fingers in Marie's mouth and down her throat. It was brutal to be a part of and it was torture to watch. Marie started hacking and the mucus came out. It worked. She calmed down and could breathe again. I held her a little longer before laying her down in the hospital bed. I stepped outside and just collapsed on the deck railing, sobbing into my folded arms. Becky came out after me and began crying on my back with her arms around my waist.

The nurse gave Marie more morphine again under the tongue. We knew it was close. Dart, Becky, Genevieve, Raquel, Carmine and his wife, Mary, and I spent the day together watching Marie slip away from us. I went upstairs to lie down for about an hour. Mary called up the steps to me. As I came down, she said Marie's pulse was very weak and her breaths were slowing down. I crawled back up in bed and held her while everyone else stood around us praying the rosary. I put the Andrew blanket between us as I held her close to me. I told her to go to Andrew because he was waiting for her and I asked Andrew to go to his mom. I tried to mimic her breaths, breathing when she would breathe. It made me feel connected to her. I told her I loved her and I always would. She was my everything and my island girl. I breathed the last breath with her and she was gone. I held her for the last twenty minutes of her life and then for another twenty minutes after. I put her down, went upstairs, and called Jerry. It was eleven P.M.

"Hello. Gene?"

I couldn't speak. I tried to, but only a couple of sounds came out.

"Do you need me there?"

Still nothing came out of my mouth.

"I'm on my way!"

Within fifteen minutes Jerry was walking through my front door. I was by Marie. I looked over and saw my lifelong friend. I walked over to him and, as he would later tell me, collapsed in his arms. He held me, and I held him for a long, long time. When we finally let go of each other, Jerry went over to Marie and kissed her. He hugged everyone there. He was my best friend growing up, the best man at my wedding, the godfather to my son, and now my support during the darkest hours of my life. For the next three-plus hours we would walk away, then come back to her, go cry outside, then come back to the hospital bed. Jerry took a seat next to Genevieve on the couch. She told him that was her second daughter she'd lost, how it wasn't right to bury your children, and how it should have been her instead. Jerry said, "Your daughter was the toughest fighter I know. Muhammad Ali and Joe Frazier battled for forty-five minutes, but Marie battled her whole life. She was a warrior." He has said those words many times since.

Two men came to my house around 2:30 A.M. They asked us all to step into the other room for a few minutes, then told us we could come back and say our final goodbyes if we wished. I don't remember what everyone else did, but I went back to the living room where Marie was now in a black plastic bag that was zipped up to her abdomen. I bent over and kissed her some more and told her I loved her and would miss her. I headed back outside to the deck while they took her out the front. I didn't want to witness them taking her away from me. I have no idea how many tears were shed that day, but they just kept coming. Jerry came out back and held me some more. He asked me if I wanted him to stay, but I was exhausted, and said I would call if I needed him. He said he would take care of calling our friends. I was spent.

Chapter Twenty-One

MARIE'S MEMORIALS

About an hour after Marie was carried out of our house, we all went our separate ways. Carmine, Mary, and Genevieve went with Dart back to her house. Becky went upstairs to a spare bedroom, and Raquel retreated to her room. I took Marie's pillow off the hospital bed and lay across our bed and cried. I held that pillow close to my body and smelled it and told her again how much I loved her and how much she meant to me. I asked how I was supposed to live without her. The last thing I can remember is sobbing into that pillow. I must have passed out at some point, and I woke to a phone call from my mother around eight A.M.

"Gene—"

I interrupted her and said, "She's gone."

I sounded pitiful. Thinking back, it was a tone of great loss and a voice of someone in considerable pain. I do not remember her response or any other communication or even hanging up the phone.

If I can put into words how I felt or how anyone feels when losing someone they love so dearly—a part of you dies, too. It is like being fileted open; everything is exposed, and you feel vulnerable. There is a death inside of you, but somehow you are still alive. You continue to breathe involuntarily, but part of you doesn't want to. I looked back and questioned what could I have done differently and how I could have made it better and easier. When we lost Andrew, we had each other to lean on. We had each other to hold and cry with and talk to when we couldn't sleep. I didn't feel like I had anyone. I felt alone and no one could understand the pain or the loss. Raquel had a significant other to turn to and I was very happy for her. Sometimes there is comfort to be found only in a lover's arms, no matter what it is that is hurting you. And if I could have shouldered Raquel's pain, I would have.

I was in that place between awake and asleep, and I thought I heard our doorbell ring. As I reentered consciousness, I realized someone was indeed at the door. I went downstairs as Raquel was opening it. There was a man wearing a blue shirt and dark pants; he was there to collect the hospital bed and equipment. Raquel's boyfriend, Scott, had pulled up as the guy was finishing his "I'm sorry for your loss" speech. I hugged Raquel and told her I loved her and she went out the door. I stood back as the guy collected the bed, the bed tray, and the portable toilet I had moved to the garage weeks ago because Marie made me get it out of her sight. I signed some invoice and shut the door behind him.

Once he was gone, I walked over to the couch. I fell back on it and realized I had Marie's pillow under my arm. I didn't remember carrying it down the steps or holding it while that guy was in the house. But there it was, under my crisscrossed arms, pressed to my chest. I remembered feeling like I was holding Marie. It felt warm and still held her scent. I stared at the empty space where her hospital bed was a couple of minutes ago. It was where she had died in my arms the night before. And as much as you think time should stand still and everyone in the world must be mourning your powerful loss, they don't feel it. Time keeps on ticking, and life goes on, and you're forced to live it.

It was a short time later that Becky sat down next to me and put her arm around my shoulder. She stared with me at the empty space where the bed had been.

"What am I supposed to do now, Beck? Really, tell me, because I don't know."

"I'm not sure, Gene. I wish I could tell you."

We sat in silence for a while. I put my head on her shoulder. She laid her head on mine. We were quiet for a long time.

It was me that finally spoke. "What would Marie want us to do?"

In a few minutes Becky responded with, "I think she would want us to go have sushi for lunch."

I took a shower and fielded a couple of phone calls that came to the house. One was from Carlos in Xcalak. He and his wife, Alicia, had received an email about Marie passing. He just wanted to tell me Xcalak would be hurting for a long time over losing Miss Marie. I told him I appreciated the call and that he and his family were always very special people to both of us.

At lunch we ordered Marie's favorite—shrimp tempura, tuna, and Mayan roll—and Becky had to have her seaweed salad. We both drank amaretto sours, Marie's favorite drink in the rare event she would have one. We swapped some Marie stories and Becky promised to always be there no matter what time of day or night. I promised the same.

"It doesn't seem real, but at the same time it is too real. I just can't believe she's gone. Do you know what I mean?" I said, still trying to process my thoughts.

"We both know it's been coming for a long time. I'm surprised she survived as long as she did. That only shows me how well you took care of her. She would have died a long time ago if it wasn't for you." Becky's words were sweet and genuine.

"Do you really think so? Because I keep going over in my head if there was anything else I could have done for her."

"There wasn't anything left undone, Gene. You did all you or anyone else could have done for her. You have to put that first and foremost in your head." She looked at me intensely.

"I'm gonna try."

She cocked her head sideways at me and asked, "If I had a message from Marie for you, would you want to hear it now or wait a while longer?"

"Well, thanks for playing the Ask a Stupid Question game. Um, now!" I replied.

"Thought so. When I was here for the Christmas party she wanted me to tell you two things after her passing. She wanted you to know there wasn't anything more you could have done for her to have a fulfilling life. She knew how much you did for her, Gene. She just didn't express it. Everyone knows it. You have to believe it."

"What's the second thing?" I asked, trying hard not to cry.

"She wanted you to know that you can move the rest of the treasure on your own. If something could go wrong, she will stop you somehow."

I must have looked quite dumbfounded, because Becky put her arms up in surrender and said, "I swear. That is what she told me to tell you. I am not making this shit up! I actually have it written down word for word."

I chuckled. "She's gone and she's still gonna tell me what to do."

And then we laughed, and it felt good.

That night while I was lying in bed, I thought about our relationship. I thought about how much we truly loved each other. I was and still am thankful we followed in the path of Marie's family and not mine. I'm glad that during our years together, we were surrounded by the love and care of her family. And when I thought about it, the only other time I felt that love and care was when I was young and at the Buschmanns'.

The following day, I took Becky to the airport, then went to Mrs. Buschmann's to tell her that very thing. I knocked at the door, and Liz, one of Jerry's sisters, answered. She told me how sorry she was about Marie's passing and gave me a big hug. I thanked her and told her I wanted to talk to her mom. I walked through the living room and into the kitchen and hugged Mrs. Buschmann. I broke down and cried before sitting at the table with her. The first thing I told her was that of all the people I knew, compared to what I felt I had experienced, she was the one person in my life who had experienced just as much loss.

I said to her, "Burying three babies, losing your husband so early, and raising six kids on your own—I have no idea how you did it. When we lost Andrew, we had each other. You didn't have anyone, and you had six kids. How did you do that?"

"I did not have to keep my son alive for many years and I did not have to take care of my spouse like you did. And you know as well as I do, you just put your head down and push through it because there are others that need you more than you need yourself."

"I do admire you. You don't know it, but when I was young my father would beat me. I vividly remember him whipping the crap out of me as early as four years old."

"No. We didn't know that, Gene," Mrs. Buschmann said. Liz walked into the kitchen and sat at the table with us. "We didn't know."

"Well maybe you didn't, but that's what happened. And for a long time when I was a kid, I practically lived here and you never turned me away, or told me to go home. It was because of you that I survived my childhood. The only happiness I had was when I was here golf-ball hunting or building a track for sleigh riding . I'm dead serious. The worst time was when you guys would go to Grandpa's lake. Sometimes I would come down to your house and sit on the porch, hoping you would come home early. It was a good day when I would come around the corner and see the station wagon in the driveway. I was never so glad to see that car.

"This house and your influence in my life saved me. And then I met Marie, and her family has felt more like a family to me than mine ever did. And they mean more to me. My family hasn't been around through Andrew's or Marie's illnesses. I used to fill them in on the latest developments, but none of them ever seemed to care or ever came by, so I just quit calling. I haven't really talked with any of them in years. I didn't mean to come over here and bring you down. I just came over here to tell you thank you for all that you have done for me over the years. I sincerely mean that."

"Gene, you are part of our family and you will always be welcome here anytime," Mrs. Buschmann said, and she reached over and squeezed my hand.

That week in the mail I received many "With Sympathy" cards. There was one that stood out in my mind the most. It wasn't a sympathy card at all. In fact, it was a "Wishing You Peace and Joy for the Holiday Season" card. The front of it featured a pony kicking it up in the snow. The handwritten note on the inside of the card read:

There are so many things that we will always
Question about our lives, why things happen
And when they do, and in this earthly world
We will probably never know the answers.
But I wholeheartedly believe when we leave
This world and go to our heavenly home,
We will be greeted by loved ones with open arms.
For me it will be my three sisters who passed
Away at their birth, and my father.
For you it will be Andrew and Marie, happy and
    healthy, walking and talking and embracing you.
God bless you.

Terri Buschmann

Back in October, Raquel spotted a van advertising the name and number of a crematory. Dart gave her stamp of approval after a visit to the facility with Raquel. Marie was fine with that decision, and the three of them spent an afternoon picking out songs for the impending memorial, all unbeknownst to me. I was so proud of Raquel for taking the initiative, but at the same time, I felt left out. It was a selfish thought on my part and I knew it, but when it came to Marie, I was very protective with her and decisions regarding her.

The memorial service was held at Sts. Joachim and Ann church. I talked with people as they came through the doors of the vestibule. I remember my sister Patti's first words to me: "You shaved your mustache off!"

"About ten years ago."

What a weird thing to say to me at my wife's memorial service, and I tried to shake off the thought that my family was strange. Then I spotted Mrs. Buschmann along with three of her kids—Randy, Liz, and Terri. I hugged all of them, Terri being the last.

I told her the card she wrote was so touching, and although I had a hard time reading it, I'd read it many times since. She said she truly believed our loved ones would be there waiting for us. She said, "Where Marie is, there is no more hurt or pain or disappointment. There is only joy, and we are the ones left to figure out how to go on in life without them."

I do believe that Andrew, Cathy, and Marie's dad, Pete, were there for Marie when she passed away.

When the music started, Raquel and I proceeded down the church aisle. I carried Marie's ashes in a cherrywood box with a picture of her on the front of it. Raquel carried a picture of her mother smiling next to Andrew. As Raquel and I were walking down the aisle, I realized that Genevieve and the entire Certa family were in the first two rows on the left side of the church. The first pew on the right held my mother and my sister Cindy. A couple of rows back sat my sister Patti, and many rows back was my sister Mindy and her husband. After placing the ashes and photo on the table up front that also held a vase with two dozen red roses (an annual anniversary gift from me to Marie), Raquel and I sat with the Certa family. They are the only family my daughter ever really knew and the only family who ever cared for my wife, our children, and me. I knew my mom's relatives had a problem with people of color and I imagined Mom may have not been thrilled to see Raquel with her black boyfriend. Sometime during the service my mother came over and sat next to me.

I was standing off by myself during the reception that immediately followed the service, feeling overwhelmed and humbled, when someone came up from behind and put their hand around my arm. I immediately turned my head, fully expecting to see Marie because that was how she would hold on to me when we walked. It was Terri. She asked me if I was all right and if I had eaten, and then we went through the food line and ate together.

It was a nice service—I think that's what one is supposed to say—and after the luncheon, I went home. I had made a promise to phone a couple of friends in Mexico and Becky, who was distraught for missing the service. A few hours later, Jerry called and asked how I was and if I was in need of company. I'd held it together pretty well through the day, and yeah, company would be great. So Jerry came over and we talked and did shots of Don Julio Añejo, the best tequila. For every shot we did, we made a toast to Marie or told a story about her. I told a story of the first time Marie became raging mad at me, and it was Jerry's fault. She was six months pregnant with Raquel when Jerry and I went to our fifteen-year grade-school reunion. Marie passed on the invite. Jerry talked me into going out to an old classmate's house after the event was over. I wanted to go home, but he insisted and we drove together. I got home at 3:30 in the morning and she was hot. I had not called to tell her where I was or who I was with, and before I knew it, there was a kitchen chair coming my way. Of course, Jerry and I had a good laugh over it, but at the time no one was laughing. We spent the afternoon and evening together, and by the end of the night, we had toasted a whole bottle of tequila to Marie. We spoke of old times, reliving many memories that day. He told me Marie and I were "the couple," one of the happiest he had ever known, and no one could have lived the hand I was dealt any better than his best friend, to which we cried and hugged again.

———•••••———

It had only been a few days since the memorial service. I needed an escape from my home life, and Dart needed a break from me, so I started hanging out at Mrs. Buschmann's catering kitchen. I did their dishes while Terri and her mom worked. I would occasionally hang out at Terri's and watch a movie or just talk. We were quickly becoming good friends.

Marla was driving from Canada down to Xcalak with her new van and wanted to know if I wanted to make the trip with her. Our friends in Mexico wanted to have a memorial service for Marie so I was heading south anyway. We split the driving, something I wasn't at all used to, and stopped in San Antonio to visit Becky. The two girls knew each other from Becky's visits to Xcalak. We had dinner at a steakhouse and hit the road again, making it to Xcalak in four days' time. As soon as I was back at my house, I set the cherrywood box containing Marie's ashes on a corner table in our living room along with a picture of Andrew and a few candles. I made a trip to the bodega to check on our treasure. If anything was missing from the girls' pile of crap, I could not tell, so I locked it back up after I turned on the pump and opened up the house. Friends were stopping by continuously to pay their respects. It was a difficult week.

Marie's memorial service was held at Leaky Palapa. It was quite a casual affair; I wore shorts and flip-flops. The service started with our good friend Jack Bellman as the master of ceremonies, who thanked everyone for coming and proceeded to give quite a love-ly speech about my wife. He told the story of when Marie talked him into buying a couple of motors for the dive shop; now, he was Carlos's investor. He spoke of Marie's intelligence and her strength and determination. He said there was no braver soul than that of Xcalak's very own Miss Marie. He introduced a few members from the Seventh-day Adventist Church, the very same women that came and rubbed oils on Marie. They called me forward and rubbed me down with oil as well.

After my blessing by the members of the church, people in the crowd took turns coming forward to give speeches about Marie. Carlos's speech stands out the most in my mind. He said he couldn't believe how this angel had come from out of the jungle and ran his business so well and with such professionalism. He was just starting out and she had stepped in, organized, and restructured what had already been done. He went on to say how she was at times like a mother, scolding him when he deserved it. He spoke of her bravery and how her life was a true example of love and perseverance. He closed by saying that he was a better man for having known her. These words were from a man that I knew respected and truly loved my wife.

Afterward, Linda and Marla put out hors d'oeuvres, and we all were able to salvage some happy memories about Marie bandaging up a neighbor child or stitching up a local dog. Yes, there were many tears, but there was much laughter that day as well.

I spent five weeks in Mexico. I managed to do quite a lot of diving. It was a relaxing trip, even though I was sad that Marie was not with me, a new norm I was trying to get used to. There were life-altering decisions that I had to make and I didn't want to make them on my own. Marie and I had a plan to purchase the house in Xcalak and work for ourselves renting out the two units we were going to build in the bodega. That could still happen, but I would be doing it on my own. A decision about the coke still had to be made. Per Becky's message to me, I already knew what Marie's plan for me was. The only thing that Becky left out was writing the book. If and when that happened, I was hoping to have the view of the Caribe in front of me for inspiration.

During my time alone, I sat on the deck and played our music and watched the water. I wanted to take my time deciding what to do with the house in Xcalak, the one in St. Louis, and the coke. I knew if I made a hasty decision, it could come back to bite me in the ass.

Every once in a while there was a visit from someone at the dive shop asking if I wanted to help out with some dive groups. Sure I did. It felt good to think about something else, and it's always a good day if you can go diving. There had been additions at the dive shop: a covered outdoor patio as well as a new dining area upstairs. Carlos had purchased the humongous house next door. The main floor was for his family when they were in town, and a few rooms below were to rent out to tourists. Carlos offered me a job overseeing the dive shop and the rental units, and proposed the idea of buying Mark's house together. That sounded promising, but I needed to think about it.

Jack, the MC at Marie's memorial, was driving back home to Wisconsin and wanted a travel companion, so I accepted his invitation. We spent three days on the road, taking turns driving. From the time we left Xcalak until the time we pulled in my driveway, his car sat idle approximately eight hours.

I arrived home the second week of March. The first thing I noticed was the Christmas tree still standing in the family room. The second thing was the picture of the ultrasound Raquel handed me. She was pregnant. I was instantly filled with joy, of course, but there was a sense of sadness, also.

Marie would have loved to be a grandma and had spoken of it many times through the years, especially as her siblings had grandbabies. I was going to have to love the baby enough for both of us, and I was secretly hoping for a little girl, a little Marie reincarnated.

Chapter Twenty-Two

PUTTING THE PIECES BACK TOGETHER

I needed to take a trip to Texas to visit Mark and discuss the house in Mexico. I wanted to have the conversation face-to-face. My sister Mindy had told me my ole man was not doing well and that mom was getting her assets all in line in case something happened to her. Mom shared with Mindy the approximate amount that each of us would receive in the event of her passing. I decided to visit her on my way to Texas. I saw my dad, and of course he didn't bother to say anything about the recent events in my life. There wasn't a "Hey, Gene. How's it goin'?" or "Sorry about your wife," nor did I expect there to be. He'd never said anything to me when Andrew died and hadn't bothered to attend his memorial service, either. We just acknowledged each other's existence like we always did.

I told Mom about my possible plans to buy the house in Mexico and our idea to build the rental units. I just laid it out there that we had been able to live on Marie's disability for quite some time, but now that it was gone, I had to make some changes. If I could have some of the inheritance now, I could buy that house as Marie and I had planned, and move on with my life.

She told me she had to think about it, and if she did agree to it, $25,000 would be the most I would receive, but not until the following year. She wanted to sell my dad's vehicles—five cars and a truck. I offered to come back with a buddy who was a knowledgeable car guy to help get her a decent price.

I also told her that Raquel was pregnant. She didn't have much to say about that. We had lunch together and I hit the road.

Next stop: Beaumont, Texas. I spent a couple of days with Mark and his wife. We spoke in great detail about the plans for the bodega. He agreed that the idea was a good one, and he shot me a price of $150,000. The visit seemed to go well, although it was a little difficult to see my friend not looking very well. Mark's heart condition had kept him from Marie's memorial services back home and in Mexico. I understood completely. He looked more worn out since my last visit with him. I was used to seeing people who were ill, but like Terri has said to me, just because you're used to something doesn't mean you've got to like it. How true that is.

Becky made it known to me that no way was I allowed to be within driving distance and not stop for a visit, so from Mark's I drove to Becky's. It was strange being on the road alone. I drove the six hours from Beaumont to San Antonio and pulled up at Becky's around six that night. She had two steaks resting on a platter in the kitchen. I wasn't sure what else was on the menu, but I saw some peaches in a bowl on the counter, which instantly put a smile on my face. We embraced for quite a while. She said it was always good to see me, although she would have to get used to not seeing the little Italian with me. She walked to the counter and held up a bottle of red. I just nodded.

She and Laura had hired two employees and she was thrilled with how well the store was doing. She seemed very pleased with her relationship with Gary and I was happy for her. Marie would have been ecstatic.

There were a couple of baked potatoes wrapped in foil on the grill and Becky laid the steaks down next to them. I carried our wineglasses outside and she asked the inevitable question. There were dozens of ways to ask it, but they all had the same meaning. How was I holding up without Marie?

I usually didn't know how to answer that question. My most typical answer was I was doing fine. With Becky, I knew I could go into a little more depth. I told her some days were better than others. If I didn't feel like getting out of bed, I did it anyway. I was grateful that Marie's suffering had come to an end, but I missed her so badly it felt like physical pain. Sitting idle left me alone with my thoughts, and they weren't always the best of companions for me. So I did my best to stay busy.

She agreed that I was holding up well and maybe had even gained a little of my weight back. If I hung out in Texas with her, I would surely put more weight on with her cooking.

I told her about my visits with Mark and my mom and also about the conversation I'd had with Carlos regarding the possible partnership in the purchase of the house. With what he was able to invest and my mom's money, all I had to do was sell the coke through Moi in Mexico and financially, I would be fine. Our home in St. Louis has four bedrooms, plenty of room for a baby, Raquel, and Scott, who had moved in recently, and me. I could split my time between home and Mexico. And then I added, "I wouldn't have to think about bringing that coke across the border anymore. It's a constant nag at my gut."

Her words were simple. "You can live in Mexico for a while and work at the dive shop and give the household expenses in St. Louis to Raquel and her boyfriend for a few months. Then you go dive and surround yourself with that awe-inspiring underwater world, and take your time deciding what to do. Both houses will still be there in a few months. And if you want to bring the coke across the border, I know there is still interest there."

"You know for certain there's interest? How much interest?"

"There is one hundred percent interest in your treasure. Laura wanted me to tell you that her friend would be interested in buying whatever you had."

"Now if I'm hearing you correctly, you're telling me that Laura's boyfriend wants the rest of the coke. Is that what you're telling me?" Becky had just put a sizable bite of steak in her mouth so she just politely nodded her head yes, to which I responded, "Holy shit!"

Taking a second to swallow, Becky said, "Holy shit, indeed. The question is, did he come to that decision on his own or with Marie's help? I think it was the latter of the two. Just a guess."

"And you were going to tell me when?" I think I was in shock.

"When you brought it up. I'm not the one taking the risk. It's you. I'm Switzerland here, and I will support you, whichever way you feel is best."

"Well, you know what Marie would tell me to do."

She interrupted my speech. "Marie could be a daredevil, fly-by-the-seat-of-her-pants, thrill-seeking freak at times, and I mean that with all my heart as much as I love and miss that girl. As she would say, 'Well, what are they gonna do to me?' It's not about what she would do. It's about what you're gonna do. You decide what's right for you. I'd trust your decision every day of the week and twice on Sundays . . ."

I appreciated her kind words and suggested she stop before she botched the scene from *A Few Good Men* where Kevin Pollak's character gives that same speech to Tom Cruise's character. She busted out laughing, hand to mouth, and almost spit out her wine.

She said, "Oh, you caught on to that."

"Yeah, it was one of Marie's favorite movies. I watched it a thousand times with her. I can repeat the whole thing. But I don't, because that would be plagiarism."

"Oh, are you accusing me of plagiarism? Be nice to me, or who will you call if you get arrested for smuggling drugs across the border? I'd think a little bit more clearly before accusing your ole friend of plagiarism," she said with a wink, tipping her wineglass.

"I wouldn't call you. You don't have any money."

"That is true. But my boyfriend does, and he would loan it to us if he knew it was to help your sorry butt. You're my best friend." There was a complete change in her facial expression, and she looked down at her plate. After a moment, she raised her head with tears in her eyes. "Things happen almost every day and I think to myself how much Marie would have liked that piece of furniture or laugh at the stories Laura tells me about the swingers club. She would have laughed so many more times." She wiped her tears with her napkin. "You know, sometimes I forget for a second she is really gone. I've gotten as far as starting to text her before I remember she's gone. Does that ever happen to you?"

"No. Because I never texted Marie, Becky. I was always with her."

"Holy crap!" she said with a laugh. "I know that. Well, it happens to me, and then I either laugh about it or I cry."

"I'm all cried out today. I spent my daily quota this morning when I woke up again without her. And do not think that just because you're crying it gets you out of making me grilled peaches."

The next morning, I was the first to the kitchen and made myself a cup of coffee. I was definitely still brainwashed. I could smell coffee and think of Marie. God, how I missed that girl.

"Morning. Wanna make me a cup since you're just standing there? What are you deep in thought about?" Becky asked.

"I was thinking about the last Christmas gift from Marie," I said as I made a cup of coffee for her.

"That was a pretty cool gift. I remembered when she came up with it." I handed her a cup of coffee and she continued. "I don't think I helped you work through anything, but Gene, no one can tell you if you should live in Mexico or in St. Louis. I hope in some way I helped shed some light, my friend."

"Beck, you told me I am pretty much guaranteed to have a buyer for the rest of the coke! I kind of chewed on that little piece of information all night. Hell yeah, that shines a little light on things. What I'm thinking right now is if my mother doesn't give me an advance on my inheritance, and if all players cannot agree on the amount for the house in Xcalak, then I'm coming back home and bringing the coke with me. Hopefully, I'll know sooner than later. We'll see."

I suggested breakfast at a nearby Denny's, where Becky and I said our goodbyes. Afterward, I headed home, and she headed to her store.

I had been home from Texas for about a week when I received a call from my sister Patti, who said our dad was pretty bad off, hospice was involved, and Mom could use a break. It sounded as if she was hinting I help take care of my ole man because I didn't work and now had the time since my wife was dead.

"No fucking way. I can't stand that guy, and I do not care if he lives or dies. Do you understand that? His death will not mean anything to me."

Her best argument was "Gene, he's your dad."

"I'm not doing it, Patti. You go if he's so important to you."

"I have to work—"

"Do you?!" I interrupted before she could finish. I couldn't believe the gall of this woman. She was an idiot. "Then you take a family leave."

I'm not sure how the conversation went after that, but I got off the phone and dialed Terri. "Are you busy? I was wondering if you had time for a visit."

"Sure. Come over."

I talked to Terri about the situation with the house in Mexico, but mostly about the latest with my dad. She had no idea how ignorant my family was. She and I were standing outside on her deck, watching her dogs wrestling in the backyard. Mattie, the Saint Bernard, was always the victor; Odie, the mastiff, would admit defeat. I brought up my dad's impending funeral and told her I had no desire to go. I didn't like the guy; he had made my life hell for years.

"Where has my family been as far as helping me with anything . . . Andrew and Marie? You know, they never even brought over a meal for us."

Terri said, "I don't know what that was like for you, but growing up there were two people I was afraid of. One was my friend Jackie's dad, and the other was yours."

"The whole idea that someone will stand up on an altar and say nice things about this wonderful human being . . . makes me sick to my stomach just thinking about it," I ranted.

"I guess you have to ask yourself if you will have more regrets if you go or if you don't. You're not expecting me to tell you what to do, are you?" she asked.

"No. It would be easier, though. If Marie was still alive, she would say we were going, and that would be that."

"Did you just figure out what you're going to do, Gene?"

My dad passed away within a few days and Raquel went with me to his funeral. We sat in the front row with my mom, my sisters, and their spouses. I listened to the priest speak about how my father was an upstanding man who loved the Lord and was always generous with his time for his neighbors and friends. I wanted to puke sitting in that pew and thinking about how hypocritical a man my dad was. He would drink every day and beat on me. Growing up, I was afraid of just walking past him. I had that cowering-dog syndrome. I would freeze in my tracks. I learned at an early age how to tell if my dad was already drunk when he got home from work. I would watch him get out of his car from my bedroom window, being cautious not to let him see me. If he slammed the car door, the back door, or if he was stumbling while he walked, I knew he was drunk and that I needed to start hiding. The best place to hide was the basement, but I had to wait for him to shut himself in the bathroom to make a break for the basement steps. If he happened to go downstairs, I could hide in the closet or in the storage space under the steps. When I was a little older, I would watch out the front window for him to pull in the driveway, returning from the bar after work. As he would come in the back door, I would leave through the front and head to the Buschmanns'. I would get hit if I was stupid enough to be caught at home.

But my father was a churchgoing man. He would go to church every Sunday and to confession, which would wash away his sins. A real Catholic, that guy. It sickened me to think about it. In his mind, as long as he went to church and confession, he was guilt free.

After the service Raquel and I stayed for the church luncheon and visited relatives, many of whom I did not recognize or care to reacquaint myself with. I felt like a hypocrite. I could not think of one good reason to be there. Raquel was pregnant out of wedlock with a black man's baby. These relatives, including my parents, were racist and had no qualms about using the N-word regardless of their setting. It astounded me, and when we'd both had our fill of their small-mindedness, we left.

I hung out with Terri, trying to figure out how to put the pieces of my life back together. Mrs. Buschmann was recovering from a terrible fall where she broke her hip, fractured a bone in her knee, and tore her rotator cuff at the age of seventy-eight. This was a woman who worked fifty to sixty hours a week—seventy to eighty during the busier months. While she recovered, Terri was handling the catering business. I did her dishes as she worked. She was running herself a little ragged. I was planning a return trip to Mexico and invited her to join me when her mom was back on her feet.

I hung out at Terri's house when she wasn't working. We would talk for hours and sometimes well into the night. We talked about everything in our lives. I shared things I had only shared with my wife. She was becoming my confidant. Over the past several years I'd had more women around me than men, and after Marie passed away, I felt more emotional. I felt like I didn't have to hide those emotions with women. With Terri I just spilled it all out. She listened to my "what should I do with my life" dilemma. She knew about everything except for the coke.

I was planning on leaving in a couple of weeks for Mexico, but I was waiting for Mark to locate all the files necessary to buy the house in Xcalak. I wanted to drive to Mark's house in Beaumont and pick up all the documents personally, but he couldn't locate the original paperwork. Handling real estate in Mexico is not at all like it is in the States. I was in limbo and my life was on pause.

I wanted to get out of St. Louis, so I decided to just leave for Mexico. I told Terri to watch for airfares and come diving with me. She really looked like she could use a break and her daughter, JoJo, was going to visit her dad in Wyoming for a few weeks. No excuses.

I flew back to Cancún with only two backpacks, and neither one of them had papers from Mark. It was disappointing. It truly was like someone had their finger pressed down on the pause button of my life. I heard advice from people telling me I needed to get on with the next stage of my life. In my head my response was, "I'm trying. I have a plan, but all the players aren't playing fair." But I usually just said, "I'm working on it." Marie was so right when she said she felt like a piñata, or like her life was a videogame and someone else had their hands on the controls. I wanted the feeling of a great accomplishment in my life. I wanted to put my hands on something tangible and say I made it happen. I needed something good and positive. When we were home and Marie was recovering from a surgery, as long as someone was there to keep an eye on her, I would go outside and work on the house. It was therapeutic, and maybe in my mind, if my house had more curb appeal, then maybe it would be pleasant to be there. I needed a boost. I wanted something to look forward to. Xcalak was where I wanted to be, but without Marie I found myself with a lot of time on my hands, which made me miss her more deeply. I had no idea what my role was anymore. I was Marie's husband and caretaker until she passed away, and now I was just Gene Hudson, a man with no direction.

I threw myself into working on the house. I raked all the weeds out of the sand-filled yard and decided to cut down a few almond trees, bringing a little beach-appeal to mi casa in Xcalak. I busied myself going through the twenty totes Marie and I had accumulated. In one of the totes, I found a large package of photos, some I had not seen in years or had forgotten about altogether. There were photos from barbecues on the beach with friends from the village, and gatherings at Leaky Palapa. Marie had the biggest smile on her face in every photo she was in. That was how she would have wanted to be remembered, so with Carlos's permission, I borrowed his scanner at the dive shop and made copies of some photos to share with friends and blew up several for myself to adorn the walls at the house. She may not have been with me physically, but seeing her smiling back at me in those pictures gave me a sense of her presence and peace.

Chapter Twenty-Three

TERRI VISITS MEXICO

I worked intensely on the house, both inside and out, and even managed to hang out with a friend now and then. I realized that not only was it a unique experience to be flying solo, but it was also a new experience for our friends to see me without Marie. She was loved and missed by everyone. We were all handling the change pretty well, although I had my moments of loneliness. I was asked to work at the dive shop periodically and accepted the opportunity every chance I got.

While watching a movie one evening, I received a call from Terri asking if the invitation was still open for her to visit. I was ecstatic. Her work was slowing down, and her mom was back on her feet. "I need to get the hell out of here!" were her exact words.

Before I knew it, I was driving to Cancún to pick her up. I was excited for company and I could not wait to bring her scuba diving. The look on her face at the airport told me she was happy to be there. Her flight was good and she spoke about people she met in line through customs. I swear she could talk to anyone and have a more meaningful conversation with a stranger than some people could have with their own family. We stayed at the Kin Mayab hotel for one night and I showed her around Cancún. I took her to an open restaurant under a huge palapa with mariachi bands walking through it, within walking distance from the hotel. It was the best day I'd had in a long time.

The next morning we set off for Xcalak, talking nonstop until we arrived at Sam's in Tulum to shop. I knew I was in for a treat when she pulled out a grocery list. I don't know what I liked most about Terri: her company or her food. I was looking forward to both.

We made it to Xcalak around six that evening and immediately noticed that someone had kicked in my locked bedroom door. The drawers had been gone through, but other than the two ounces of pot in the fridge, nothing was missing that I could see. Terri found a split screen in the kitchen window. I immediately knew it was Moi's brother, Jorge, since he had dropped by two nights before. I don't know if he knew about our share of the coke, but he did know we were with Moi when the coke was found. Four years before, he was into crack cocaine and was stealing to support his habit before his family kicked him out. Marie and I had locked him up in our house for a couple of weeks while he detoxed.

The last conversation I'd had with him left me with the feeling he was using again. His substance of choice varied. He preferred cocaine, and witnessing his struggles with the drug played havoc in my head. I knew that what I was in possession of could cause someone to relapse or worse. Those thoughts were never far from the surface, but I shook them off. It was not the time to question my morals. I wasn't going to let the break-in or anything else put a damper on Terri's visit. Other than the split screen and the messed-up door trim, there was no harm done.

My first mission was to set Terri up for diving. I introduced her to Paco, an instructor at the dive shop. After a couple of short lessons with him, we were boarding a boat and heading for the site where she would dive for the first time in her life. Her excitement was contagious.

I watched from below as she made her descent. Within a minute or two she was on the sandy bottom doing exceptionally well, and I kicked ahead of them. I wanted her to see everything, so I searched for unusual coral and unique fish, like the indigo hamlet we saw within minutes of our dive. When I spotted something unusual, I would point it out to Paco, who would show Terri. Thirty minutes into our dive, I noticed Paco was picking up rocks and putting them into the pockets of her BCD (buoyancy control device) to weigh her down. He must not have brought down enough weights, but this was easily rectified. The rocks worked and she was none the wiser as she continued to glide through the waters.

After an hour, we made our way back to the boat. Terri could not contain her excitement over her dive. As Paco took the rocks out of the pockets of her BCD, I noticed something pinkish and somewhat transparent moving across the seat of the boat next to Terri, and I picked it up. It was a baby octopus that had crawled out of a hole in one of the rocks. It was the second one I had ever seen in thirty years of diving. Very cool. I held it in my hand so we could all get a closer look. Its head was the size of a fingerprint. It was a truly exceptional find and I was quick to set it free in the water.

Back at the house, Terri started to make her rendition of guacamole and I told her how we made ours. So we wound up with a combination of the two. She had not stopped talking about her dive since she came out of the water.

"I swear, Gene, that is the most incredible experience, other than having my two babies, I have ever had. I was forty feet underwater for an hour today!" She paused and shook her head in disbelief. "I am so glad I'm here, but I wish I would have come when Marie had asked me to."

I lifted my glass and said, "Well, you're here now, so here's to you finally coming to visit." And we clinked glasses. I was enjoying her company, her energy, and her food.

Our topic of discussion that night bounced around quite a lot, but seemed to settle on her work. "I was so exhausted and burned out."

"Marie and I made a rule, long before we had kids, that we would not talk about work on vacations. And we didn't, or we tried not to." I shared my frustrations about Mark's lackadaisical effort to gather his documents for the house. "According to my potential investor, there may be a chance of getting the house for a lesser price in a year or two."

"That's a good thing. Right?"

"A lower price would be great, but what do I do for a year or two? A decision has to be made. Do I stay here or do I go home?"

"I can see why you love it here. That water is beautiful, and today I saw an eagle ray!" And she went off on a tangent about her dive again.

During Terri's eight-day visit, we enjoyed four scuba dives, two snorkeling and fishing trips, and one long boat ride, during which Terri saw her first manatee. She could not have gotten a better view as a manatee floated against the boat. We ended most nights with a game of Farkle—first to five thousand was the winner—and then a movie. They were eight of the best, stress-free days I'd had in years. My only regret was that Terri was unable to experience our beloved Leaky Palapa, as Marla and Linda were back home for a long visit to Canada.

We spent the last night of Terri's trip in Cancún, eating at Marie's favorite sushi restaurant then visiting the market to buy souvenirs. It was hard to see her leave the following day, but after I brought her to the airport, I wanted to get back to my house ASAP to see if I had any intruders. Terri and I had "accidentally" run into Jorge at his parents' little shop a few days before. I may have laid it on a little thick when I said to him, "I cannot believe someone could slap me in the face after Miss Marie had practically glued or bandaged every kid in the village, including yours, Jorge." I was hoping the speech would discourage any future break-ins.

I decided to visit Moi that evening and tell him about my suspicions of his brother breaking into my house. He assured me the only ones that knew of the split of the treasure were Marie, him, and myself. I stretched the truth just a bit and told Moi the remainder of the treasure had gone back to the States with us in May of the previous year. I even shared details about how I disguised the kilos to look like books. I don't know if he believed me or not, but by the end of our conversation, he was congratulating me.

I had a hard time falling asleep the next couple of nights alone in my house. I lay in bed thinking of the endless conversations Terri and I had, and one stuck out in my mind. Since her son was living with her again, she was able to see her granddaughter every week. Every week sounded pretty good. After a couple of sleepless nights, I finally concluded that I missed my family.

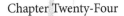

Chapter Twenty-Four

BABY RAPHAEL IS BORN

I was genuinely bored the last couple of weeks in Mexico while waiting for the pieces to fall in place to buy the house. I flew back home for the birth of my grandson, and one week past his due date, baby Raphael was born. He was a full-term, healthy baby boy with lots of curly black hair. To me, he looked just like Marie's baby pictures, especially his eyes and tiny nose. I was very excited for Raquel. I did not have experience with full-term babies. My kids were born twelve weeks early, but this little man was alert and strong. After just a few short weeks, he could follow the sound of my voice by turning his head, and he was so strong he could hold his head up when he was just a month old.

Terri teased me profusely when I talked about him. She would mock me and say, "Isn't he just the cutest baby in the whole world?!" Yes. Yes, he was.

I waited a week after Raphael's birth then drove to visit my mom, bringing the birth announcement with me. I started bragging about how cute and alert he was. When I showed her the picture, I said, "Doesn't he look like Marie?"

I will never forget her response. Her voice was raised with discontent and displeasure and she said, "No, he does not!" She threw the picture, which slid across the counter and onto the floor. I picked it up and could tell she was completely disinterested, so I changed the subject and asked if she'd put any more thought into giving me the money. Once again, her response was hateful and mean. "Nope. You're not getting it. If you want to buy that house down in Mexico, you need to kick Raquel and her boyfriend out of your house and sell it. Use that money."

OK, that was harsh and not what I was hoping for, but at least I had my answer. I changed the subject again and asked about the cars and if she'd had any luck selling them. She had decided to give her truck to my sister Patti and her husband, and had I known he was without a job for two months? Wow, that must have been hard for him to not have a job for two whole months. His wife had worked at the same government job for the past thirty years and he worked regularly, as far as I was aware. I could see why that entitled them to a truck valuing $15,000. Then she told me how she gave one of the cars away to my dad's cousin's kid, Keith. It was a 1961 Thunderbird that belonged to my ole man's cousin, and my dad had bought it off him long before Keith was ever born. She told me what "hard lives" they'd always had. I wondered what she thought my life had been like for the past twenty-five years. But how would she have known, having kept her distance.

So, Patti got a truck because her husband was unemployed for two months and my dad's cousin's kid got a car for no reason at all. If it wasn't meant to be a slap in the face, someone should have told me, because it sure as shit felt like it. When I got in my van and drove away from my mom's house, I reminded myself that my family had never been there for us in the past. None of them had shown up to help with Andrew's needs or to babysit Raquel. I literally laughed out loud at myself for believing she would help me now. Her response to the picture of my grandson disgusted me, but I was not surprised. I had been better off without the negative attitudes, and the farther I drove away from their house, the more convinced I felt to leave my family in the past. I needed to make a plan to bring the coke up from Mexico. I called Becky that night and told her the same.

Chapter Twenty-Five

LEAVING XCALAK

I visited a used bookstore not far from my house and took my time looking for hardback books whose subject matter was of interest to me. More important than the topic of each book was the size. I purchased nine books that day, ranging in price from one to three dollars. I also went to the grocery store and bought four rolls of Press'n Seal wrap, then stopped at a hardware store for double-sided tape. When I arrived home, I headed to the basement and started digging through the boxes of medical supplies we still had. We had syringes, suction catheters, oxygen tubing, cases of gloves—all kinds of crap that we would not need again, God willing, but Marie had insisted we keep. I had not taken the time to go through it since her passing, but when I found the case of white paper medical tape, I congratulated myself on my procrastination.

It was late in the evening on November 6, and I was holding my grandson while talking with Raquel. I reminded her that the cats and I were leaving for Mexico early the next morning with a plan to be home by Christmas. I told her to take good care of my grandson, gave her and Raphael kisses, and went to bed early.

I left at about three the following morning and drove until I reached Becky's house. I pulled right inside her garage, closed the door behind me, and set the cats free in their home for the night. Waiting for me inside were Becky and freshly grilled peaches and a glass of wine, which I accepted.

"How was your drive?"

"It was fine. We gotta talk about the coke."

"Gene, I really think if crossing the border is as busy as you said it is, you're gonna be fine. And according to Laura, he wants all that you have. But if you don't want to do it, then don't. I told you I'd support you either way." She took a bite of her ice cream and asked, "What's the problem here? Why do you have that look on your face?"

"Beck, you don't know how much I have, do ya?"

"I don't. But if I was a betting person"—she paused to eat a bite of ice cream—"I would say another kilo or two?"

"Nine."

"Holy shit, Gene!" She put her spoon down and rattled off a series of questions. "Are you serious? Holy shit! How much did you guys find? Where did you hide it? Who all knows?"

"Only one other person knows those answers and she passed away. Don't take that personally, but I'd rather not say."

"I won't—I'm just surprised she could keep that a secret from me. No wonder she was so obstinate about selling it. Gene, that's a lot of money."

I tilted my head and looked at her. "I know, Becky. It's kinda high risk."

"I just didn't see that one comin'. I might be in shock." She swallowed a mouthful of wine. I rather expected that reaction.

"What's the possibility of Laura asking her friend how much he wants? The price is still twenty grand per kilo and it's all coming back with me regardless of his answer."

———————

The next morning, I found a note on the counter in the bathroom: IF I FIND OUT ANYTHING FROM LAURA TODAY, I'LL

CALL. EITHER I WILL BE PICKING UP TACO BELL, OR YOU'RE BUYING DINNER AT THE CHART HOUSE.

—B

It was almost nine A.M. when I made a cup of coffee and headed to the back patio. I thought about the times I had massaged Marie's feet and hands while she sat in the chair opposite me. I just looked at that empty chair and said out loud, "I wish you were here for this one. You'd love it. I miss you." I finished my first cup of coffee on the patio and my second in Becky's garage visiting the cats. I was scooping a litter box when my cell phone rang. It was Becky.

"Good morning. How's the junk business?"

"Ha. Just for that nasty comment I'm going to order an expensive meal, and maybe even dessert."

"How many does he want?"

"All of it! I'm not shitting you!" She was laughing. "I had a feeling he would."

"Oh my fucking God!"

"Gene, you still have to make it back across the border. I'd think twice about saying the F-bomb in front of the Lord's name. I'll make a reservation for seven. And do not expect me to be seen with you if you're in a pair of your beach shorts, T-shirt, or flip-flops!" She squealed that she was so excited.

The first victory of Gene flying solo had the potential to be a very big one. The only foreseeable problem at that very moment was that I did not have a pair of pants with me, so I headed for Kohl's. When Becky arrived home, she found me in a freshly ironed pair of khakis and a black pullover polo.

"You look very handsome."

"Thank you," I said graciously.

"Are those flip-flops, Gene?"

"Yes, but they're brand new flip-flops. I'm not gonna buy a new pair of shoes just to take you to dinner, but I ironed and everything, so we've gotta go." An hour later, we were in Becky's car heading to the Chart House.

"So the amount that we are talking about is one hundred and eighty thousand dollars. Yes?" I asked.

"Sí. Laura said she didn't care if it was one or nine kilos, as long as it fits in her gym bag."

"They'll fit just fine," I said.

Over dinner, I told Becky I would be greatly relieved to be out of the cocaine business and to concentrate on something else, like my grandson. I shared some recent photos of Raphael I had received that morning. "I swear, Becky, this baby is so smart and strong. He almost rolls over already."

She interrupted. "And he looks like Marie. He's the strongest, smartest, cutest baby ever. Gene, you are so in love with him."

There was no denying he had my heart.

Becky told me that since losing Marie, she'd had a complete physical, her first colonoscopy, and vowed to have annual mammograms. "Not taking my health for granted."

I stopped for a minute to listen to the song the musicians were playing on the other side of the restaurant—"Lady" by Kenny Rogers. "This is my and Marie's song. I haven't heard it outside of our house since the night of our wedding reception."

She stood and said, "Let's dance."

"Are you for real? Yeah. Let's do that." I led Becky to the dance floor and we danced. I thanked her for being there for Marie and for me when she passed away. She knew things about my wife I did not know. Every time we saw each other, she would tell me one of those "Did I tell you about the time when Marie and I . . ." stories. I loved those stories, and I wanted to hear every one. For me, it was getting easier to talk about Marie without a feeling of despair and emptiness. I missed her, but I was getting used to it.

I was the first one up the following morning and scooted downstairs to the kitchen to see what I could make for breakfast. I was hungover, but happy. After taking inventory, I decided on the precooked sausage links I found in the freezer, diced potatoes with onions and spinach, and a fried egg on top. I woke Becky up to join me. I handed her a cup of coffee and the bottle of Advil. "I wanted to make you breakfast. Let's eat on the patio."

"You are too cheerful. At least fake like you're hungover." She sat on a stool and swallowed some Advil with my OJ and then laid her head on the counter. "How can you not be suffering?"

"I took three Advil. Listen, I might be having a manic moment, but I really feel OK with the decision to move the coke. That sounds so strange to say out loud. So you tell Laura to let her fuck buddy know I'll be back before Christmas."

I brought our coffees to the patio and came back for Becky and our delicious (if I did say so myself) breakfast. Shortly after breakfast I hit the road, promising to call when I made it to Xcalak. I knew Marie was with me. There was no way she was going to miss this.

I made my usual stops in auto hotels on the way back to Xcalak and at Chetumal for a month's worth of food and supplies for both me and the cats. I was back in the village in three days' time. I was so happy to see that driveway, even if it did have a lot of weeds growing in it. I was damn tired, but I was back. I unloaded the cats one by one, a duffle bag of clothes, the food, and the red backpack I still carried with me. I unlocked the bodega and turned on the pump. The girls' stuff had not budged, so I knew the treasure was safe. I locked up the bodega and walked upstairs, put away the perishable groceries, and went to bed.

The next day, I went to see Carlos and told him I had decided to move back to the States for now. If it was a different time I might have stayed, but my heart was in another place—with Raquel and baby Raphael. I thanked him for all that he had done for Marie and me through the years.

He shook his head. "It's me that should be thanking you and Marie." We hugged for a minute, and he wished me the best of luck. He reminded me again that I would always have a job with him if and when I wanted to come back. Before I pulled out of the parking lot, I told him I'd be getting rid of my furniture, washer, dryer, and whatever else I wasn't bringing back to the States and to pass that along to anyone who may be interested.

As soon as the word that I was selling everything hit the coconut telegraph, people started knocking on the door and calling out to me from the driveway. It wasn't only a sale I was having, but a question-and-answer session with my friends from town, which sometimes led to sharing very emotional goodbyes. I gave away a lot of Marie's clothes and a couple of totes filled with baby garments. Marie loved a sale and she loved buying baby clothes. Anybody having a baby or a first birthday, we had a gift for them, in pink or blue. We had several totes filled with supplies we would have needed for the rental units we were going to build—sheets, dishes, pots and pans. I got rid of it all. I gave a few buddies a chunk of purple pot and told them it was from Miss Marie. I started with twenty-five containers before the sale and whittled it down to twelve by the end, making certain to keep the clear ones. I knew Border Patrol agents would be less curious if they could see the contents inside.

The day before leaving Xcalak, I pulled the van into the bodega and locked the door behind me. I tossed my supply of medical tape, Press'n Seal wrap, nine paper book covers, and double-sided tape on my workbench. Once I had removed the girls' stuff from the cistern, I lifted the lid. I knew I was safe behind a locked door, but it still felt very risky and exciting at the same time. I placed a ladder down into the cistern and gave a quick look inside with my flashlight. Still dry. A musty smell hit me on my descent. There it was, hanging on a piece of rebar in the back of that empty hole where I had left it. I lifted the bag out of the cistern and laid it on the workbench. After removing the ladder and replacing that heavy-ass lid, I returned the girls' stuff to its original spot. I carefully inspected each kilo as I lifted it from the duffle bag. I wrapped each one with no less than five layers of the Press'n Seal. Then I wrapped the entire surface with white medical paper tape, overlapping for extra security. The book covers were fitted to each kilo. I trimmed the covers as needed and secured each one to the "book" with double-sided tape. There were nine new books to join the forty we had collected over the years.

I put three kilos in each of the overhang cabinets above the two front captain chairs. We kept books, movies, maps, and keepsakes in the cabinets. I added more books to each cabinet, stacking the treasure in between. I rearranged the miscellaneous items around each stack so the only visible part of the books was the spine. I put the three remaining kilos in one of the two book totes along with some cone-shaped incense, then I stored the tote in the back of the van and piled blankets and clothes on top. The incense would possibly not deter a drug dog, but it made me feel better. The purple pot was hidden among the bathroom and cleaning supplies in a dark green glass jar with a sealed lid. I had twelve totes in all, ten clear, and two blue. In the blue ones, I packed only towels and bedding items. I didn't want anything suspicious in the totes that were not clear, so I kept their contents simple and unassuming. When I was satisfied with my packing job, I took a well-deserved shower and headed to Leaky Palapa for dinner.

Within an hour, I was eating dinner at the bar and talking with Linda. I drank margaritas and visited with friends and locals that were either having dinner or just coming to say their goodbyes and offer well-wishes. When the kitchen slowed down, Marla came out and sat to the right of me at the bar. Shortly afterward, Moi was sitting on my left and drinking a beer. Linda poured four shots of Herradura Añejo tequila, one for each of us. She raised her glass and said, "To our dearest beloved friend, Marie—we love you, we miss you, and we will never forget you. To our dearest friend, Gene—we love you, we'll miss you, come back for a visit soon." We all clinked our glasses and sipped on our amber-colored, aged tequila.

"Thank you, Linda. I'm truly gonna miss you, too, each one of you." I glanced over at Moi. His head was down, and I knew he was close to tears. He reached his hand to my shoulder and squeezed. Saying goodbye to these three was no easy task. They were our best friends in Mexico. I didn't want to say goodbye. I just wanted to say see you soon, but I didn't know when that would be. Moi wished me luck and a safe crossing, giving me a wink and his crooked smile. He hugged me and was gone. That left Linda and Marla to say goodbye to. I told them to take their time moving their belongings out of the bodega. I had emailed Mark and he was fine with them still having a key to the house and storing their possessions there as long as they could come by occasionally to check things out. Next time they drove back to Canada, they would hopefully be able to stay in town for a couple of days and meet my grandson. I hugged the girls goodbye and told them I hoped to see them soon.

As I fell across the bed that night, I was thinking about how grateful I was that the bed belonged to Mark so I didn't have to sell it. Otherwise I might have had to sleep in the van or at Moi's. I didn't have a hard time falling asleep that night, but when the alarm went off at four A.M., it felt like I had just dozed off. I lay there for a few minutes and then adrenaline started to flow. I loaded my cooler, cat supplies, and the remaining 33,000 pesos from the safe—more than enough to see me across the border. Last to be loaded were Grace, Allie, and Jo. I made my way back upstairs and took a quick peek in each room just for a final walkthrough. As I headed to the front to leave, I grabbed the red backpack from the kitchen counter and walked to the door. I pulled it closed behind me rather hastily. I was getting a little misty. I walked to the deck and looked at the Caribe. It was still dark, but I could see the water with the help of the moonlight. I hoped to see this view of the water through those two coconut trees again soon. This place was my getaway. It was base, and you are always safe when you're on base. I didn't want to lose my safe place.

I was anxious to get on the road. The fewer miles between me and San Antonio, Texas, the sooner I could close this chapter of my life. I was scared to death, but I was excited, and I was not alone. I knew Marie was with me. I believed that if I wasn't safe, she was going to let me know somehow, and I would abort the mission.

The first stop on my trip was at the vet to get travel papers for the cats. I was not going to take the chance of getting stopped and searched over fake papers. Besides, they were due for their shots. I took the same route Marie and I traveled when we carried the kilo back with us nineteen months ago. I drove across the Yucatán to the Bay of Campeche. I stopped again in Sabancuy and admired the foods at the various street vendors. I was ravenous. Finally deciding on a bag full of deliciousness, I headed back to the van, snacking on a warm churro and licking my fingers.

I drove up the coastline along the water, looking for that same stretch of deserted beach where Marie and I picnicked a couple of years back. I pulled over when I spotted it. I grabbed my food and a water from my cooler and headed to the beach. I sat on an oversized rock and watched the sunlight dance off that turquoise water as the waves crashed onto the beach. I could never tire of that everchanging view. It was like a living canvas with altering shapes and shades of color. I had to get my feet in it one more time, so I kicked off my flip-flops and headed to the water. I walked along the beach, letting the waves splash up against my lower legs. Water always makes me feel alive, but it was the sound of the waves I was thinking about the most. Why didn't I think to have a recording of the waves playing for Marie in the last couple of days of her life? She would have loved that. Puddles started forming in my eyes as I added that thought to my mental list of "should haves" and "would haves."

Several more strides down the beach, I noticed the sunlight bouncing off something half buried in the sand. The gleaming object disappeared and reappeared as the water crashed onto the shore and then receded. I picked it up; it was a beautiful shell about the size of my hand. I squatted in the water and washed it off so I could get a better look at it. I started walking back in the direction I came, examining my find. I held it out in front of me, letting the sun dance off it both inside and out. The inside of the shell was golden, and when the sun hit it, there were rainbows of every color ever created. At first glance, the outside of the shell was an off-white, but as the sun played with it, the surface transformed into a soft shade of blue. I sat on the big rock and looked at that shell for the longest time. And then I started talking to my wife.

"Did you leave this for me to find, Marie? This would be a good one for your collection. I may be getting more used to you not being with me, but I still hurt like hell for you." The puddles were in my eyes again, and before long, they were tears running down my face. I was still looking at the shell and turning it in my hands while I talked to her. "I know where you are your pain is over and you and Andrew are together, happy and healthy. There is a comfort in believing that, but I want to be with you so badly sometimes it feels like there's a knife in my gut."

"I know you know about our grandbaby. He is so cute and smart, and he looks like you. You would never want to put him down if you were here. I'm going to do my best to love him enough for both of us. I miss you so badly, baby. Thank you for being my wife and teaching me about love." I sat quietly for a couple of minutes and collected myself before walking back into the waves. "Thanks for putting the shell in my path, but I'm going to leave it here so you can show it to someone else. I'll love you forever." I held the shell to my mouth and kissed it, then I gave it a long toss back into the water. "You're my eyes now, Marie. Keep me safe."

———————

That first day, I was waved through every checkpoint, reconfirming my impression that I did not fit the profile of a smuggler. With the exception of the vet visit, I had been driving for fourteen hours, and I was whipped. The cats and I stayed at the Auto Hotel Venecia in Córdoba. After sticking a screwdriver in the track of the garage door for additional security, I ordered room service and slept seven hours. In the morning, I continued my journey up and over the mountains of Veracruz to the Arco Norte—and more important, to the checkpoint directly before them. I just kept our music playing and memories of Marie singing aloud alive in my head.

As I approached the checkpoint, I whispered, "Here we go, baby. Do or die trying. Stay close to me." I knew they would open the van doors and look inside. My heart was pounding so loudly I could hear it in my ears. I played endless scenarios in my head about the dialogue that would take place. I kept taking deep breaths to help me stay calm. I was just a gringo moving back home after the passing of my wife. *Here we go.*

"¿Dónde vas y dónde fuiste?" asked the first soldier.

"I'm coming from Córdoba and heading for Querétaro." I was playing it real cool.

"Is there anyone else in the vehicle?"

"I'm alone, but there's three cats in the back."

"Can I see inside?"

And there it was. The dreaded question that I knew would be asked.

"Yes. Of course."

Why did I just say "of course"? Did that sound too inviting and overconfident? He walked around to the side door of the van and opened it. They never came inside the van before, but this time a soldier stepped up on the running board as his partner stood close behind and watched. The cats were frozen and staring intently. They weren't used to strangers invading their space. The soldier leaned in and picked up a blanket and jacket I had behind the driver's seat. I twisted the napkin I held in my hand for my sweaty palms as he opened the cabinet door above the passenger seat halfway, glanced in, then shut it. Lastly, he popped open the lids on three of the totes. I think I stopped breathing momentarily, until he snapped the lids back down, exited the van, and said to me, "¡Buen viaje! ¡Vaya con Dios!" (Have a good trip! Go with God!)

"Gracias."

I drove away. It was over. That was the stop that had kept me up at night, and it was behind me.

"Thank you, Marie. We're doing it, baby!" I turned up the volume on the radio. My anxiety lessened with every passing song on the iPod. I noticed that the traffic at the checkpoints heading south was bad. Some of the cars were heavily loaded down with tarp-covered boxes tied to the roof, like I had witnessed before. I was counting on it. I stopped for fuel, potty breaks, food, and brief leg-stretching excursions. When I traveled with Marie there was no need to pull over to stretch my legs because the potty queen, a name she rightly deserved, had to stop every two to three hours to use a restroom.

The night before I reached the US border, I arrived in Saltillo at the Auto Hotel Oasis. I pulled in, closed the garage door, put the screwdriver in the track, and set the cats free. I took a shower and then ordered a club sandwich with fries from room service and retrieved a soda from the cooler in the van. I ate and put on a movie. I didn't pay much attention to it. I mostly just lay back on the bed and stared at the ceiling and let my thoughts run around in my head, playing a plethora of different scenarios of the following day. Worst case scenario—if I got caught, I would notify Becky. She would rescue the cats and contact Dart and Raquel. I called room service in the morning and ordered sausage, an omelet with spinach and mushrooms, toast, juice, and coffee. It was going to be a long day.

I reached the US border crossing by eleven A.M., or rather, I reached the line of cars that led to the border. In front of me there were hundreds of cars evenly dispersed across four lines. It was a blessing and a curse. It was a blessing because I just looked like an American moving back home among hundreds of Mexicans trying to go Christmas shopping in the United States. It was a curse because it was agonizing to wait that long. I told Marie she had to help calm me down. I became increasingly restless with every car length I moved forward. There were street sellers walking between the lines of cars selling their goods. They were a nice distraction.

I reached the toll booth and paid my fee to cross. I was inching forward onto the international bridge that straddles the Rio Grande; halfway across I entered US territory. It was do or die. I had not scooped the litter box for the last couple of days as another deterrent for a drug-sniffing dog. It was getting rather stinky. A healthy forty-five minutes later, I crawled off the bridge and slowly approached the booth on American soil. I had to be nonchalant and composed. I told myself over and over again that there was no way Marie would allow this to happen if I wasn't safe. My pulse was more rapid than usual, and I was sick to my stomach, but I had managed to remain calm.

I was three cars back. I had driven through this border crossing many times throughout the years and had experience on my side. An American coming home for the holidays wasn't anyone to be concerned about in the eyes of Border Patrol, or so I kept telling myself. I had arrived at the border at eleven, and it was now two in the afternoon.

"Here we go, Marie. Tengo los huevos. I have the balls." As I pulled forward, I put the van in park and handed the agent my passport. In the pocket on the door I had my ID, Marie's death certificate, and the wellness papers from Dr. Sebastian for the cats. "Where are you coming from and where are you going?" asked the Border Patrol agent, the universal checkpoint questions.

"My trip started in Cancún. Last night I was in Saltillo, and I'm heading home to St. Louis."

"What have you been doing in Mexico?"

"My wife and I ran a dive shop in Xcalak, and she recently passed away. I cleared out our house, and I'm moving back home. I'm just trying to get there before Christmas."

"Are you alone?" he asked me. The questions were all routine.

"Yes, sir."

He asked me if I had any dirt in the van, and by dirt he meant what you literally grow plants in. "No, sir. I don't."

"Do you have any alcohol in your vehicle?"

"I have two old bottles of tequila, never opened." If he wanted the alcohol, he could have it.

"Go ahead. You can go through. Welcome home." And he handed me back my passport.

"Holy shit! We did it, Marie! Who has the huevos? I do!"

All the months of worrying and planning, and I was at the threshold of it all being over, back in the land of the free. There were thirty-five miles between me and the last and final border zone crossing. I was pumped. One crossing to go. Either this was going to be my day, or I was going to jail.

I pulled up under the steel canopy at the last border crossing in thirty minutes flat. On either side of the van was a Border Patrol agent. In a few seconds, I'd be talking to the one by my window, but the guy that concerned me was the one on the right. It was his drug-sniffing dog that made my stomach turn upside down.

"Are you a US citizen?" asked the agent nearest my window.

"Yes, sir." While we made our little communication exchange, the other agent walked the dog around the van.

"Anyone else in the van with you?"

Before I could answer, the dog jumped on the passenger door, his nails hitting the window. I nearly had a heart attack, then I realized Grace was sitting on the passenger seat looking out the window. "No, just my three cats."

"Go on. Safe travels."

I pulled forward and out of sight and yelled out loud, "We did it, Marie. I'm home! I love you so much!" I had our music playing, and I cranked it up. I was two hours from Becky's and I had all the coke with me and the remainder of the purple pot. I was not at all worried about making the exchange with Laura.

It had been over three years since we found the coke and there were times I didn't know if it was a blessing or a curse. It was a blessing to have met Laura and sell it in one huge amount. It would have been too risky to break it up and sell it gram by gram. I could have probably made a million bucks, but that was not my world, and I was elated to be handing the entire treasure over to Laura. From there I didn't know where it was going, and I tried not to go there in my mind.

"It's almost over. I miss you . . . I love you." I said those words aloud to my wife.

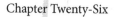

Chapter Twenty-Six

THE DEAL GOES DOWN

Becky had left the side door to the garage unlocked for me. The cats, the treasure, and I were safe behind closed doors. I located the "books" that were dispersed through the van and stacked them on the passenger seat. The key to Becky's house was in the top tray of her toolbox and let I myself inside. I noticed her Christmas tree in her front room. If Becky didn't have an antique store, she could have been an interior decorator. Her house was filled with antiques of all sorts as well as newer pieces. Her tree was tall and very thin, stuffed with dried flower bundles in various colors and sparsely adorned with old-looking ornaments on the branches. At the top of the tree was a punched tin star. I had to see what it looked like with the lights on. I found the cord at the back of the tree and plugged it in. The tree instantly lit up with a multitude of colored twinkling lights. As I stood back admiring the tree, my phone rang. It was Raquel.

"Hey, Dad. Where are you on the road?"

"Hi, babe. I just arrived at Becky's. How's my grandbaby?"

"He's great. I'm calling to find out when you were planning to get home because we need a babysitter for Christmas Eve."

It put a smile on my face to think about holding that little guy in a couple of days. "I can do that."

I told her I would see her soon. I was finishing up my soda

on the back patio when I heard Becky come in. She flew to me and threw her arms around my neck.

"You did it. You really did it! I knew it would go well. I just knew it would be OK. How do you feel?"

"Relieved." I just hugged her for a minute. It was nice to have human contact. "Merry Christmas. I like your tree."

"Well, how soon do you want to do this? Here's why I'm asking. Laura suggested instead of bringing it to the shop, we thought we could just do it here." Before I could say anything, she just held up her hand to me. "Laura will come over in about an hour or so and she has your money in her workout bag. You just take out the cash and put in the . . ." She was searching for the word.

I finished it for her. "Coke."

"Yes. The treasure. I'm fine with it happening here. It's actually my idea. OK with you?"

"If you're sure, Becky."

"I'm sure. Good. Let me call Laura quickly."

I walked back outside just to think for a minute. I thought the exchange would happen tomorrow, but this would be better. I just had to wrap my mind around it. If Marie was here she would tell me to "man up." This was the easy part. I wished she would have been with me. On second thought, she was there.

Becky met me outside and said for dinner she was making her awesomely famous taco nachos. Marie and I loved Becky's taco nachos. The day was just getting better and better. First I made it across the border, then I found out we were doing the deal that night at Becky's, and taco nachos! I was a happy guy.

Becky invented the nachos when she was staying with us for a few weeks in Xcalak. She was actually in the process of leaving her husband and was hiding from him at our place. I remember the day her "taco nachos" were born. I was in the bedroom picking up, and Becky and Marie were laughing in the other room. They had been smoking a little weed, and Becky had a couple of her pineapple-juice rum drinks. I joined them and found Becky in the kitchen and Marie sitting on a stool at the kitchen counter. When the girls had the munchies, Becky would cook. She was browning ground beef and had lined a cookie sheet with aluminum foil, which was covered in tortilla chips. Various ingredients covered the countertop: corn, green onion, cheddar cheese, jalapenos, green pepper, black beans, and spices. I was hoping I would not have to clean up.

If Marie really liked something Becky made, I had to learn how to make it. So I paid attention. Plus, I was intrigued. After they were heated in the oven, Becky put the nachos in the middle of the kitchen table and the three of us gorged ourselves until they were gone. Oh my God! Those were the best nachos I'd ever had. I've made Becky's taco nachos many times over the years.

Laura arrived at Becky's house around 6:30 carrying a duffle bag, which wasn't unusual. Most of the neighbors knew they were partners at the antique store and had seen the girls carry items into Becky's garage in bags as well as off the back of a pickup. Laura was also carrying a bottle of red and a bottle of white.

"I didn't know what went best with nachos, so I brought both." She put the bottles on the counter and put her arms around me. "Gene, I was so sorry about Marie. She was a neat lady. I enjoyed the time I spent with her. You were very lucky to have each other."

And I thought I was going to escape tears today. Maybe not. "Thank you. And thank you for the cards you sent. That was very thoughtful."

Becky asked her how many cards she'd sent.

"She sent me three cards."

"You sent him three cards? I didn't know that!"

"Hey, mind your business. I didn't send them at the same time." Becky pulled two cookie sheets out of the oven, each covered with tortilla chips loaded with goodness. "Becky's been telling me about these taco nachos for days."

"Did she tell you how they were invented? No? Well then, I will enlighten you."

Becky interrupted. "You can enlighten her all you want, just clean up the story if need be. I may not remember all the details."

I did remember the details, and I remembered how much fun those two used to have together. They would lay out together, laugh and cry together—I even remember one night many years back when Becky called Marie to tell her one of their favorite childhood movies was on. Grease. Marie turned to the same channel and they watched the movie together while on the phone, singing the songs and making comments to each other all through the movie. When I told Laura the story of Becky cooking that day at our house in Mexico, I may have embellished a little on the mess she created, but I did not have to exaggerate how much fun they had that day. If they were talking, they were laughing. "And I had to clean the kitchen up by myself.

"You did not, you big liar! I helped," Becky protested, and handed me a plate that I proceeded to load up. We visited and chowed down. I retrieved a book from the van and handed it to Laura, who was still working on some nachos.

"And there's nine of these books?" she asked with amusement as she examined the package. It looked like *Home Remedies and Cures* until she removed the paper cover.

"Yes," I said and handed her a knife. I felt it was more appropriate for her to cut the package open. She thought the books were an inventive disguise. Marie had praised me many times for coming up with that idea. Every once in a while, I did manage to pull one out of the hat.

Laura cut a two-inch slit in the top of the kilo. She lifted a little out and formed a neat little pile on the table. She went into the living room and came back with her wallet. She pulled out a credit card and a twenty-dollar bill. She used her credit card to form the coke into a couple of lines and the twenty she twisted into a thin cylinder. She asked each of us if we cared to join her. I declined, but Becky decided to partake. After Laura finished her line, she handed the twenty to Becky. Laura stood up and once again retreated to the living room. This time she came back with a black duffle bag. "This is the same coke as last time, Gene?"

"That's correct."

"Here is your money, and do not think I will take offense if you want to count it."

Hell yes I wanted to count it, but not at the kitchen table. I dumped the money—thirty-six bundles in all—on my bed and thumbed through them one by one. It was all too surreal.

Laura wanted to get going to meet up with her friend and deliver the treasure. I carried the duffle bag, now containing nine books, to the car for her. She popped the trunk, and I lowered it inside and shut the trunk on that chapter of my life. Becky and I told her goodbye and headed back inside.

I poured myself a glass of ice water and sat on a kitchen stool. Becky sat at the table.

"Well, that's that, Genie Boy."

I hadn't heard that name for a while. I involuntarily grinned.

"What's the smile about?" she asked.

"Marie used to call me Genie Boy."

"I know. And I know why she called you that. And I know it's from Dirty Dancing."

"One of her favorites!"

"How many favorites did she have?" Becky asked.

"Lots. She always had a new favorite, and some of them are in the totes in the van. Becky, thank you so much for making all of this possible for us. For me. Now I don't have to rush out and try to find a job." I felt completely indebted to her.

"I didn't do much, but you are sincerely welcome. What do you think you will do now?"

"I'm not sure. If Mark could ever produce all the paperwork we need and if the price is right, I can buy the house in Xcalak. I'd like to pay off the house in St. Louis and put some work into it and maybe just be Raphael's babysitter for a while."

"Good plan, Grandpa. Hopefully I can come up this spring and see that little man. He is so cute! I check out all the posts of him on Facebook. He's a doll."

"I know. Beck, I could collapse. It's been a long day." We were both in agreement and went upstairs. I opened the door to my room. "Hey, Becky. Come in here for a minute."

She walked over to the bed where the stacks of money were and stared at it for a minute. She picked up one of the stacks and examined it.

"Oh my word, Gene. Outside of a movie I have never seen anything like this before."

I sat on the bed and stacked three bundles of bills in front of her. "We both know this wouldn't have happened if you wouldn't have introduced us to Laura. You have five grand in your hand. There's fifteen more," pointing to the stack in front of her.

"Gene, it was my pleasure to be able to get you guys together with Laura. Marie was my best friend. I just stood back helplessly for so long and watched you both struggle with her illness and Andrew. Being able to help you out means so much to me. I don't want your money."

"Becky, I stayed out of it when Marie was discussing this with you before, but now I'm gonna have to insist we agree on a dollar amount for you. Call it a finder's fee if it makes you feel better."

She was at the bedroom door about to walk out when she turned and walked back to the bed. She grabbed a bundle and said, "There. I'll take this one. We're even. Go to bed."

I just fell back on the bed. What a journey it had been. I didn't mean just the last few days of driving. I meant the last three years and the ten before that. And the ten before that. I thought about what Marie would do if she was on a bed with all this cash. If Marie was happy and healthy, she would insist we both get naked and have sex on all the loose bills. Then she'd give me about a thirty-minute turnaround time and we'd probably do it again. If we were home, Marie would go shopping for the baby and have his picture taken. She would take Elisa shopping with her kids and enjoy a spa day with Raquel and Dart. I pushed the money to the other side of the bed where she would have slept. I grabbed a spare pillow and pulled it close to me. I said out loud, "There it is, baby. I couldn't have done it without you. I love you."

I fell asleep like that and woke up a couple of hours later. I changed into my lounging pants and a T-shirt and brushed my teeth. I walked back into the bedroom while still brushing and looked down at the money. It did not seem real yet. How would I deposit that much cash? A question for another day.

The following morning, I had to find something to carry the cash home in. From the van I grabbed a duffle bag that held a couple of keepsake blankets Marie always wrapped herself in. I left them on the bed in the back for the cats. I put thirty-two bundles in the bag and three in my red backpack. I took a quick shower and packed my stuff. I was in a bit of a hurry to hit the road. I wanted to put at least ten hours behind me and then drive the remainder the following day. I heard a blow-dryer going when I walked down the steps. I moved quickly to the kitchen, retrieved the three bundles from the backpack, and hid them under a bag of romaine in the crisper drawer. I loaded my bags in the van, leaving the side door open for the cats to wander back in. Inside the house, Becky was standing in the kitchen.

"I'm ready to go. I have to be home day after tomorrow to babysit Raphael."

"Your first babysitting job, Grandpa. That's so sweet."

"I know. If you hold his fingers, he pulls himself right up and just wants to stand and bounce. Don't you think that's amazing for a three-month-old?"

"It does sound amazing, Gene, but I have never had babies so I don't know. But I do know you're crazy in love with him, and that's all that counts."

We embraced each other long and hard. "I still cannot believe it's over. I wonder how many times I'll say that to myself on the way home." Still holding her, I gave her an extra hard squeeze and said, "Thank you. Thank you. Thank you. You've done more for me than you can ever imagine."

"You are welcome, my dearest friend. Be safe."

I released her and made sure the number of cats in the van totaled three, then I closed the side door. We said our goodbyes and, as always, I promised to call when I reached my destination.

As I left Becky's that morning and turned onto Interstate 35 North, I was stoked! I was so pumped up I didn't know whether to cry or laugh. If I did cry, they would have been tears of joy. I was exhilarated, overwhelmed with feelings of excitement, and found it hard to stay in my seat. My future had options and promise. Who would have thought a simple boat ride over three years ago would have affected our lives like it had? I know it may sound morally wrong, but I think it was God's plan for us to be with Moi on the boat that day. I wholeheartedly believed it was the excitement of making the first deal with Laura that kept Marie encouraged to live. And even Becky benefited, although she had no idea how much just yet. Finding the treasure was either a gift from God or a test from God that I failed miserably. But my wife and son were in heaven and I was sure they would vouch that I was indeed a good guy. Flawed, yes, but a bad guy, no.

So many thoughts and memories were jumping in and out of my mind. I was still not completely comprehending that the coke was gone and that for the first time in nearly twenty-five years, so were my financial worries. I just wanted to enjoy this emotion of freedom and elation. I had a joy in my heart, exhilaration for having accomplished something perilous. It was me, Gene Hudson, that rolled the dice, and I won. It was a rush of adrenaline and I did not want to lose that feeling. I wanted to encapsulate it in a bottle and take a swig of it from time to time.

After many miles passed down the road and many memories passed through my mind, I began to feel peaceful. I had not used that word to describe my life since my son was born. It felt like my mind was slowing down. This was the first day of the rest of my life and the van was transporting me from the old life to the new.

I received a call from Raquel saying she and Scott had decided to bring the baby to his cousin's Christmas party, so my babysitting job was canceled. So now what was I gonna do for Christmas Eve? I called Terri.

"Merry Christmas . . . are you home yet?"

"Nope. I'm on the highway, but I will be tomorrow. I was actually wondering what you were doing for Christmas Eve. I was supposed to babysit, but there's been a change of plans."

"Well, I am working for a while, but I'll be home by five. Wanna come over?"

"Yes, I would. I have some things to tell you—a story actually."

"A happy story, I hope?"

"That is for you to decide."

After I got off the phone with Terri, I made a call to Becky.

"Hey there, Mr. Moneybags. How's the road trip?"

"All's well. Just reminiscing and listening to music. I'm actually calling to tell you I left you a Christmas present. Check your crisper drawer."

"Gene! I told you I didn't want your money. Besides, you already gave me some." She was a feisty girl.

"Marie and I both wanted you to have it. Go get yourself something you always wanted. Buy an airline ticket to come and see my grandbaby. I don't care what the hell you do with it, just enjoy yourself." I tried to be stern.

"It is so unnecessary, truly. This isn't over yet."

"I'm sure it's not. I'll talk to ya later, Beck."

I usually would have stayed the night in the Walmart parking lot in Tulsa, but I just wanted to get home. A few months ago, when Raphael was born, was the first time in many years I'd had the desire to be at our house in St. Louis. I was usually trying to retreat from it.

It was kind of ironic how I felt like I couldn't get there soon enough. It's funny how life shifts so quickly. I hit the cruise control and just kept rollin' on. I reached inside the red backpack and pulled out the Mayan bag that now held a vial of Marie's ashes as well as Andrew's. I pressed the bag to my lips and kissed it and laid it on top of Andrew's blanket that was folded on Marie's seat. I said, "Let's go home. We've got a grandbaby to love on."

I listened to the iPod the entire trip from Xcalak to St. Louis, never hearing the same song twice. I was a few minutes from home when I told Marie, "OK, baby. You pick the last song. Make it a good one." And she did.

I take whatever I want, and baby I want you . . .

I instantly knew the time and the place. It was November and Marie was living with her sister Cathy in the duplex owned by her parents, directly behind the family home. I drove to the duplex to pick up her up for our first date. In the living room was an entertainment center with a stereo/record player combo and shelves filled with albums. Leaning against a bunch of other albums was the empty cover of *Bad Company*. The album was spinning on the record player, and the song "Can't Get Enough" was playing.

I pointed to the album cover and said, "I have that album."

"That is your album," she responded. Then she pulled out the Styx album *Crystal Ball* from behind the *Bad Company* cover. "This one is yours, too. Anytime I go over to see Cindy, I go through your albums in the basement. I borrow them for a while, then I bring them back."

Anybody else, that might have irritated me. But since it was this adorable young woman, I thought it was kind of romantic and didn't mind a bit. I just smiled and laughed about it. Love that story. I pulled up in front of my house, listened to the end of the song, and shut off the engine.

"Merry Christmas, Marie. We did it!"

My favorite photo of Marie and me.

SPECIAL THANK YOU GOING OUT...

To the family and friends who have read one of the many editions of the book.

To Raquel, Dart, and Jerry for helping put the pieces of this story together with their input and memories.

To Lori for the assist with the cover and the beautiful website.

To Jane for the beautiful painting that adorns the cover.

To Amber, my editor. Your diligence and efficiency are beyond expectation. You are a treasure.

To Meghan and Rhonda with My Two Cents Editing.

To our graphic/book designer, Carolyn Vaughan at cvaughandesigns.com.

To my mother, Joan Buschmann, for teaching me strength, the importance of hard work, and unconditional love. I miss you.

To my children, Travis and JoJo, who are my reason to continue breathing in and out. You are my true loves.

To Gene Hudson who saw something in me I did not see in myself. Thank you for your faith in me and for the journey.

GRATITUDE

I will always appreciate Marie for helping me become the man I am today. She often would tell me, "There's a reason and a purpose for every situation we are in. At the time, we can't see it." I do not know how I made it through the past twenty-five years, but I did. I would never want to relive those years a second time, but I am grateful for having the strength to make it through because it made me the man I am, the man that I am proud to be today. Had I not experienced the trials and tribulations of my abusive childhood, Andrew's life, and Marie's diabetes, I could very easily have become a bitter man lacking compassion and understanding. I truly sympathize with human agonies and can relate to how someone feels during the darkest times of his or her life, whether it's an illness or the death of a loved one or even financial disaster. I've seen it, I've felt it, I've lived it, and I feel for those who have hardship in their lives, especially when the situation is completely out of their control.

To feel gratitude is a new revelation for me. I am appreciative for many aspects of my life these days. Not long ago I could not have named more than two things in my world I was thankful for. Although it seems only a short time ago that Marie was still with us, everything is different. Having financial security is a nice change to become accustomed to. I miss my wife and my son, but I do not miss watching their suffering. I am grateful for my daughter and the relationship we have. I now have three grandsons that hold my heart and it has been nothing but pure joy watching them grow.

Although my biological family has not been a big part of my life, I know how very fortunate I am to continue to be a part of Marie's family. My love for them and theirs for me has not swayed or diminished in the slightest since Marie's passing. Dart continues to be a significant person in my life, and every time I babysit my grandsons Raphael, Leonardo, and Michael Angelo (yes, these are their real names), we have to go visit Aunt Dart and Nana Genevieve, who recently moved in.

I will forever be indebted to Terri for conceding to write this book with me. It has been a growing and learning experience for both of us.

—Gene Hudson

WORDS FROM THE AUTHOR

AFTER THE WRITING IS OVER...

After the writing is over . . .

Never, ever did I dream I would have been a part of writing something so profoundly important in another person's life. When Gene asked me to help him write a book about his and Marie's life, I thought he had way overestimated any literary talents that I had. Once he planted that seed in my head, the idea rooted in my heart, and six months later I asked him, "You still want help writing your story?"

Over the following five years, Gene and I spent endless hours together, and I saw him go through countless emotions. I heard many details of painful events of the past twenty-five harsh years. It was hard to hear; I can only imagine how difficult it was to live through. I probably would never be able to come close to the reality of the suffering and great loss this family has had to endure. During these past two decades, I heard secondhand of the medical difficulties of Andrew and Marie. Compared to what I know now, I didn't know squat. I was never aware of all the care Andrew required. I also was not aware of all the surgeries Marie had to sustain, nor the horrendous treatments she endured.

Along with Gene and Raquel, I believe that each member of Marie's family had a horrible cross to bear. I had the privilege of getting to know some of them while writing this book. Marie and Andrew were terribly unfortunate to be sick or handicapped in the manner in which they were. But they were incredibly blessed to have such a loving, goodhearted, benevolent family surrounding them.

Writing this book has changed me in ways I cannot explain. Gene and I both feel *Livin' the Hand I Was Dealt* is much more than we had imagined it to be. I will forever be grateful for being a part of Marie's last wish. I hope and pray that she approves.

—Terri Buschmann

MEET THE AUTHOR

Terri Buschmann, the mother of two children, was born and raised in St. Ann, Missouri where she learned from an early age the importance of hard work, a supportive family, and good friends. She is an avid gardener who fancies herself a do-it-yourselfer and an accidental author.

Terri owns and operates the family catering business started over 40 years ago by her mother.

CPSIA information can be obtained
at www.ICGtesting.com
Printed in the USA
FSHW010323120620